Spirituality
of the
Beatitudes

Spirituality of the Beatitudes

Matthew's Vision for the Church in an Unjust World

NEW REVISED EDITION

Michael H. Crosby, O.F.M.Cap.

ORBIS BOOKS

Maryknoll, New York 10545

Founded in 1970, Orbis Books endeavors to publish works that enlighten the mind, nourish the spirit, and challenge the conscience. The publishing arm of the Maryknoll Fathers and Brothers, Orbis seeks to explore the global dimensions of the Christian faith and mission, to invite dialogue with diverse cultures and religious traditions, and to serve the cause of reconciliation and peace. The books published reflect the opinions of their authors and are not meant to represent the official position of the Maryknoll Society. To obtain more information about Maryknoll and Orbis Books, please visit our website at www.maryknoll.org.

Imprimi Potest:
Daniel Anholzer, O.F.M.Cap., Minister Provincial
Province of St. Joseph of the Capuchin Order

Nihil Obstat:
Francis Dombrowski, O.F.M.Cap.
November 1, 2004

Published by Orbis Books, Maryknoll, New York, NY 10545-0308

This is a revised edition of *Spirituality of the Beatitudes: Matthew's Challenge for First World Christians,* copyright © 1981 by Orbis Books.

Library of Congress Cataloging in Publication Data

Crosby, Michael, 1940-
     Spirituality of the Beatitudes : Matthew's vision for the church in an
unjust world / Michael H. Crosby.—2nd rev. ed.
        p. cm.
     Includes bibliographical references and index.
        ISBN 1-57075-549-3 (pbk.)
        1. Beatitudes. I. Title.
     BT382.C73 2004
     241.5'3—dc22
                                    2004012207

Contents

Why "Revisit" the Spirituality of the Beatitudes?

Twenty-five years ago Orbis published my *Spirituality of the Beatitudes: Matthew's Challenge to First World Christians*. Since then it has gone through twenty-one printings. Some writers have classified it as a kind of "liberation theology" for people of means.[1] I do not know if they are correct; however, I do know that the book reflects my struggle to be faithful as a disciple of Jesus Christ, given my reality. This "reality" involves my being an able-bodied, educated, white, straight, male, North American, Roman Catholic cleric. Needless to say, all these characteristics that help define my "I am" put me in a position of power in a world and church where power is often used to the advantage of the groups of which I am a beneficiary. Given this context, my perspective can easily reflect the unconscious bias that comes from my position of privilege. Others not so empowered and privileged might consider the Beatitudes quite differently.[2] Nevertheless, despite this bias, many people told me the book helped them in their discipleship.

Upheavals in Our World and Church
Challenge Us to New Approaches

A quarter of a century ago, the lens through which I viewed my world was influenced by the East/West divide between communism and capitalism. Now, with the demise of the Berlin Wall, the trumpeted "triumph of capitalism" has revealed a globalized chasm that increases divisions between the rich "north" and the poor "south." In the United States, we are realizing more fully the insights gained from the research of sociologists Robert Bellah and his colleagues: that individualism is undermining the possibility of authentic community.[3] As this individualism is translated in the U.S. brand of globalization, most people remain silent as our leaders minimize warnings regarding global warming knowing we will not change our "way of life."

In more recent years a new threat of terrorism has emerged, leaving people easily manipulated by politicians who play to their fears and obsessions regarding survival, safety, and security. For people in the United States the phrase "9/11" has been etched into our corporate consciousness. This phrase easily eclipses any remaining memory of what happened on that same date in 1973, when the United States aided and abetted the overthrow of the democratically elected government of Chile because its leaders' efforts to bring about social justice were considered "Marxist." Immunizing ourselves against such memories allows us to forget just how much terror the United States itself has inflicted across the globe. It also makes us unable to fathom "why they hate us."

Our politics and economics have changed dramatically in the past twenty-five years, and perhaps the greatest transformation has taken place electronically. For instance, in the late 1970s, when I wrote *Spirituality of the Beatitudes,* I needed a secretary to keep retyping my many revisions. Now I need no secretary; my own limited ability to use Microsoft Word enables me to revise my writing until it goes to the press. Even the way I sent the book to Orbis has changed. A quarter of a century ago, it took at least a week via the United States Postal Service. Now I don't even need to send disks; I can send the book electronically. Orbis gets it in less than a minute.

The church too has undergone tremendous changes. Twenty-five years ago almost everyone in my graduating class at St. Mary's Springs Academy in Fond du Lac, Wisconsin, participated in Mass; the promises of the Second Vatican Council still made them hopeful about "their" church and eager to share their understanding of an inclusive church with their children. Now, if my informal poll at our forty-fifth reunion in 2003 can be any gauge, the majority of my classmates no longer participate. Some have joined other denominations (often "Bible-believing churches," as they say); others have just stopped going to church; many no longer find meaning in the church's institutional apparatus; while others disagree with its disciplines. Their disagreements range from dissent about "official" declarations against the practice of artificial birth control to the merger of the city's six parishes into one, to anger at the unwillingness of the bishops to sanction their own in the scandals around priestly pedophilia, to the way they thought some bishops implemented the "Decrees of Dallas" (2002): punitively with impunity.

As I consider such events since publishing the first edition of *Spirituality of the Beatitudes,* my life also has changed dramatically because of the influence and confluence of two powerful things: (1) the personal help I received by going into therapy and (2) my growing understanding of the interconnectedness of everything in our ever-expanding universe.

The first thing that helped change my thinking has been therapy. Because I have written about this elsewhere, I need not repeat it here.[4] However, my therapy and the Twelve Steps have helped me understand that healing is necessary not just at the level of the group and collectivity (in our institutions) but within ourselves as well. Indeed, I found that a lot of the things "out there" that I was challenging were really keeping me from addressing their micro-expression in myself. As the song from *Hair* had it: "How can people be so heartless . . . especially people who care about strangers, who care about evil and social injustice . . . ?" The therapy I have had has helped melt a bit of the hardness in my heart—I hope! This has had a powerful impact on my stance in life, including my spirituality.

When I wrote the first edition of the book, I operated from a trilevel analysis of "the world." I stressed the individual, interpersonal, and infrastructural (or "systemic") levels of life. However, I was being challenged to go further even then. One of my co-workers, Sr. Betty Wolcott, was unable to convince me that the world had four levels. Indeed, according to her, the fourth level, the universe itself, was the most important. She made it clear, ever so gently, that, if I did not de-center myself from my anthropocentric mind-set, I would be doing a disservice to God's word, through whom everything in the universe has been made and in whom all is held together. Needless to say, I did not grasp what she was saying; I thought she was weird. Twenty-five years later I have embraced her vision, even if I still cannot articulate it as powerfully as she and even if I have not made the consequent and necessary changes in my lifestyle, as has she.

Now we know that energy lies at the heart of all matter, and that, as far as where we exist, the "world" is merely a microcosm of the power of the universe itself. Consequently, my effort or the struggle of others to control anyone in this universe shows a deep perversity of that power. My own awareness of my futile efforts to control "my world" has helped me unmask the similar drive to control that lies at the heart of the two key institutions that most affect my life—the United States of America and the Roman Catholic Church. This "empire" and this "*ekklēsia*" have become obsessed with power, in one case in relation to increasingly globalized markets, and in the other, in ever-deepening forms of clerical control. Where I once found their drives for power to represent addictive dynamics,[5] I now find them to be more destructive of their respective founders' dreams, whether the vision of our founding fathers or the gospel of Jesus. I have come to believe that the ruling authorities are using power in abusive ways that keep us from living our ideals as citizens and as Catholics.

In the last decade of the twentieth century I tried to address the "sin of the world" in these two powerful institutions. In the process, vis-à-vis my country, I was not only called unpatriotic but treasonous; vis-à-vis my church I was labeled not only disloyal to the Holy Father but heretical. This led me increasingly to return to the Gospels, especially those identified with Matthew and John. As I tried to "read my reality in light of the word," I came to the conclusion that the very same institutional dynamics—of empire and *ekklēsia*—that Jesus critiqued in Matthew and John are writ large in the contemporary world of my nation and my religion.

As I tried to address the abuse of power that too often characterizes the dynamics of the empire and the *ekklēsia*, I came to resonate with the insights of Bruce Malina. Using findings from cultural anthropology, this scripture scholar found the Gospels portraying Jesus as one who offered a new code of conduct in an honor/shame world wherein the organizing dynamics of power, sexual status, and religion were intertwined.[6] This new "code of conduct" was called the "gospel." It was this gospel, not that of imperialism or clericalism, that I had vowed as a Capuchin Franciscan to proclaim in my world. My effort to ground my church again on this gospel led me in 2003 to write *Rethinking Celibacy, Reclaiming the Church.*[7]

As I write this second edition of *Spirituality of the Beatitudes*, I find the two areas that have affected me—the new science and my experience of therapy—coming together around my adaptation of an old Chinese proverb: "Here is everywhere; you just have to find it." In other words, I must find in my spirituality the cosmic unity that our efforts at bringing about personal peace, group harmony, and justice in our institutions seek to realize. This demands that I challenge any and all stumbling blocks that dishonor the reign of God at work in our "world," and, with the power of God's rule in me, that I help extend God's reign to the ends of the universe so that, as in "the beginning," all will be blessed (Gen. 1:26-31).

My Understanding of the Audience
Hearing the Beatitudes Today Has Changed

Now that almost a quarter of a century has passed since the publication of the book, and as the efforts at global hegemony over our political economy are ensured through the strongest military the world has ever seen, the image of "empire" seems stronger than ever. Similarly, as the scribes and Pharisees of Matthew's day seem to have achieved a new form of abusive domination over the entire apparatus of the Roman Church, I find more evidence of the apocalyptic warning of Matthew's Jesus: "because of the increase of lawlessness [*anomia*] the love of many will grow cold" (24:12). Whether considering the imperial and globalizing reign of corporate capitalism or the unilateral and infallible ways of the Petrine church (see Matt. 16:17-19 to the exclusion of the church of Matt. 18:15-20),[8] the Beatitudes found in Matthew's Gospel seem more and more removed from the realm of possibility. Why do I say this? My own experience.

Allowing for the significant numbers of people who have struggled to become "people of the Beatitudes," two powerful experiences color my belief that we have a long way to go before we become a People of the Beatitudes, much less (for us who are Roman Catholics) a church of the Beatitudes and, for us trying to live in alternative communities, to become Disciples of the Beatitudes.

The first comes from my experience of teaching a ten-session course on the Beatitudes, especially at the Summer Institute of Retreats International at Notre Dame University. The second arose from an experience of giving a day-long workshop for Catholic school teachers in the Diocese of Charlotte, North Carolina.

Even before the first edition of the book on the *Beatitudes* was published, Tom Gedeon, S.J., the director of Retreats International, invited me to teach at the Summer Institute he had founded. For almost twenty years I led thousands of people there and elsewhere through the course on the Beatitudes. Invariably I would begin the course promising the participants that I'd give them a complimentary copy of any one of my books if they could recite the eight Beatitudes of Matthew's Gospel. "You don't even need to have them in order, but you can't have the last part of one be linked to the first part of another." Even today, I often do the same when I give talks on the Beatitudes. That the Beatitudes have not even been tried and found wanting, but, even more, are unknown entities became clear when I realized that the average participant (usually someone in professional ministry in the Roman Catholic Church) could not recite them. Only one in forty-two could do so. We simply never learned them, much less struggled with how we could translate the words into deeds.

Consequently, when I was asked to give a workshop on "The Beatitudes and Discipleship" for the Catholic school teachers in the Diocese of Charlotte in February 1998, I came ready to challenge them as to why they were not teaching the Beatitudes of Matthew's Jesus to children at the grade-school, middle-school, and high-school levels.

When I entered the environment for the three sessions, I encountered resistance on the part of a significant number of the teachers. They were concerned that the time frame demanded for their participation was greater than that of the regular day they would have spent at school. Few seemed very interested in the topic. It made me wonder why I had even accepted the invitation. But then I received an insight that has guided me since: many of these teachers were not ready to discuss a topic like "The Beatitudes and Discipleship" because their very idea of being Catholic did not invite them to be open to probe its meaning. Their level of religious formation had locked them into a Catholicism that kept them at the same level of faith development as the students they taught. The Beatitudes represent an adult choice to follow Jesus, with the concurrent demands such discipleship entails; they knew only a child and adolescent kind of religion that made demands on them that encroached on their freedom and, at these in-service sessions, on their time as well.[9]

With that insight I made a grid on the blackboard. I postulated that there are three levels of life we all experience: childhood, adolescence, and adulthood. Each of them has a level of moral development that must be its task. Children learn society's codes, which define how one must act with other people; these are called the Ten Commandments, basic and obligatory dos and don'ts for right living among people throughout the world (especially the last seven of the ten). Adolescence represents that time in life when one moves from the wider social codes defining generic belonging to more specific codes that define membership in a group. For those belonging to the group called "Catholic," I explained, this involves learning its obligatory rituals and ways, its norms and expectations. These first two levels of obligation, which constitute the main concerns of religion(s), ground our discipleship but growth does not end there. I explained that, when it comes to adult development, we move from being defined by the obligations of religion to being defined by the spirituality of discipleship, even though these ideally should never be mutually exclusive.[10] These must be freely embraced. Maybe, I suggested out loud, with little or no challenge, many of us who are Catholic, even among professional ministers, have never really had an adult way of embracing the teachings of Jesus Christ. We seem more aware of the teachings identified with Moses (the Ten Commandments) and the norms and mandates of "the church" (meaning the tradition) than of that other font of our church: the core teachings of Jesus that constitute the heart of the scriptures, in this case, the Beatitudes themselves. These core teachings make it clear that belonging to Jesus demands solidarity with people who are poor and marginated in a way that finds us doing good or being just toward them.

The relationship between the three levels can be described as follows:

The Child Level	The Adolescent Level	The Adult Level
Societal belonging defined by observing the Ten Commandments	Group belonging determined by observing the norms/rituals of the religious institution	Belonging to Jesus' household determined by doing good (being just) toward the poor
The Domain of Religion's Rules Levels of Religious Obligation		The Domain of Spirituality Beatitudes

Exegesis Is Changing to a More Literary, Narrative Approach

As noted in the opening paragraphs, I worked on the first edition of *Spirituality of the Beatitudes* in the late 1970s. My approach to biblical interpretation reflected what I had learned in seminary regarding the formation of the scriptures. The result reflected what is called the "historical-critical" method.

This style of interpretation asks two main questions: What does the text say? and Why did the author write it this way?

Even though I had been steeped in this approach to the scriptures, I found myself increasingly dissatisfied with this Enlightenment-inspired style of scripture study, which stressed the scientific method. This was grounded in the belief that all interpretation is neutral, that the text can be divorced from the stance of its interpreters and that objectivity can be assured simply by using the correct interpretive tools, especially if these can be enhanced by material from the social sciences. This was before I became convinced that, as an able-bodied, educated, white, straight male, in Roman Catholic clerical institutions, I did indeed operate from a bias. This insight was enhanced by study of the social sciences, which helped me better understand the "context" for the text. Furthermore, and most importantly, I became influenced by a certain group of exegetes, such as Walter Wink; these scholars argued that the historical-critical method, in its attempt to imitate the scientific method, can too easily transfer the Gospel's context of a vital faith community into a guild of biblical scholars intent on getting published.[11] The result is science without spirituality.

Gradually it became more important to me to find a way to treat the Word of God (i.e., that Word expressed in Matthew's Beatitudes) less from concern about "what the text meant" in itself and more to study its original author and the original audience to determine "what the text means" today. Consequently, when I decided to write my doctoral dissertation on the word "house" in Matthew's Gospel, I tried to develop an "interactive hermeneutic," a way of having the scriptures come alive in our hearing. This "engagement" method of interpretation would concentrate on the ways the material of Matthew's Gospel, especially the Beatitudes, could become the matter of our lives. I wanted any theology of the Beatitudes to become the "story" of our lives: individually, communally, and collectively for the integrity of creation.

The result was my own brand of "reader-response criticism";[12] however, at that time I felt quite alone in my approach to Matthew. The original ideas for this method that I learned from such pioneers as Wolfgang Iser and Seymour Chatman have since been further nuanced and better developed and applied to Matthew's Gospel by other scripture scholars.[13] Now the emphasis is on understanding the author and the audience as symbiotically connected. One of my favorite authors in this endeavor is Warren Carter. He writes: "In this perspective Matthew's Gospel functions as an identity-forming, action-interpreting narrative for the audience. Given the story's demand for allegiance to Jesus, it is *the* story in which the audience is to find itself. . . . In the light of this story-formed identity, the audience is enabled to answer the question, 'What am I to do?'"[14] For me, the answer to Carter's question is simple: in this new edition of *Spirituality of the Beatitudes* my challenge is to make the words come alive in the individual, interpersonal, and infrastructural levels of

life for the integrity of the world and all creation. Its "story" must be translated at every level of this world. However, given the fact that very many people approach the scriptures from ignorance or inadequate information
regarding the power of God's word to transform the various levels of their
lives and world, the task of interpreting Matthew in this way will not be easy.

It is clear that exegetes have spilled much ink trying to understand the
actual meaning of the Beatitudes in the context of the social world that gave
rise to their inclusion in Matthew's Gospel. Others who stress a more system-
atic approach to theology interpret them from various understandings of
ecclesiology and/or christology. We have seen also that, for people who have
been trained to develop their religious lives from the perspective of observing
regulations, the Beatitudes will be irrelevant to salvation. Given these different scriptural, theological, and religious approaches, why, it might be asked,
do I approach the Beatitudes from the lens of *spirituality*? Basically, since spirituality is the personal witness to a theological stance that makes the theology
our biography and the christology our ecclesiology, I believe the Beatitudes
are meaningless unless their vision grounds the way we live. As Matthew's
Jesus insisted: we can't just hear the words; we must enact them in our lives,
individually, communally, and institutionally (7:24-27).

Spirituality of the Beatitudes
as a Guide for Our Faith Journey

Entire encyclopedias have been written on the topic of spirituality. There
are whole journals devoted to probing its various meanings. When I consider
spirituality I begin by making a distinction between "spirituality" as a structured academic discipline and the discipline that each of us is invited to
develop in order to fulfill the "Great Command" of love (of God, self, and
others [Matt. 22:37-40]). Whether the academic discipline or the life of discipleship, there are inner, outer, and communal dimensions. All authentic spirituality is grounded in the experience of that which is considered spiritual,
transcendent, or godly. At the same time, if this religious or "spiritual experience" is not expressed in some concrete way that manifests the authenticity or
fruits of that experience, it is bogus at the worst and deficient at best. Consequently, spirituality cannot be confined to a merely therapeutic level; it must
be expressed. Furthermore, both the inner and outer dimensions of one's own
personal "spirituality" must be translated in the form of some concrete community. Indeed the communal dimension serves as an appropriate context to
determine the integrity of the experiential and expressive dimensions.

I believe that what "Matthew" wrote was not intended to be a biography
or gospel about Jesus; rather he sought to offer a lived ecclesiology, a spirituality for the members of the various house churches, that would enable them

to pattern their lives faithfully on that of Jesus. From this perspective, Matthew's Gospel was/is meant to be evangelical spirituality. Since the power to put Jesus' teachings into practice would be given to all those who would be baptized, it should be applicable to disciples of every age who desire to pattern their lives on the good news that Jesus proclaimed (28:20).

In the following chapter I will show how the notion of "house" serves as the underlying and primary "metaphor" in Matthew's Gospel. However, Sharon Parks, a developmental psychologist and geographer of our faith journey, has shown that the notion of "house" is a core theme of the spiritual journey and the life of faith itself. First of all, about "metaphor" she writes: "A theory of faith development must necessarily . . . be attentive to the . . . deep, culturally confirmed metaphors—by which meaning is given form and upon which moral-ethical being and becoming depends."[15] She goes on to explain that, given this understanding of the key role of metaphor, the notion of "house" or "homecoming" must be considered the goal of and at the heart of our spiritual journey. Around this image we must allow God's dwelling to abide in us as well as serve as the context and environment in which we indwell our world. She writes:

> the primary task before us, both women and men, is not that of becoming a fulfilled *self* (or a fulfilled nation) but rather to become a faithful *people*, members of a whole human family, dwelling together in our small planet home, guests to each other in "the household of God." If we are to be faithful stewards of our planet, our traditions, and our future, we need to restore the balance between transcendence and immanence in our common discourse, in our economic-political-theological vision, and in our spiritual practice. . . . In other words, we will not find the wholeness we seek until the imagery of home, homesteading, dwelling, and abiding is restored to a place of centrality in the contemporary imagination.[16]

Ever since the late 1980s, when Robert Ellsberg became editor-in-chief at Orbis, he continually has asked me the same question when I submitted my various manuscripts for publication: "Mike, who is your audience?" Until now, I have fudged in my response. I tried to explain that I am addressing two audiences: people who are serious about living out their baptism in those countries that are the most powerful and those scholars who research the Gospels, especially Matthew's. I wanted to be helpful for those wanting a biblical basis to ground their discipleship that would enable them to integrate the inner and outer dimensions in a way that would bring them into greater solidarity with the poor. I also wanted to be accepted by "the academy," the scholars.

"Mike, sooner or later you are going to have to decide," Robert would say gently but firmly.

As I started doing my research for this revision of my earlier book on the spirituality of the Beatitudes, Robert Ellsberg's question stuck in the back of my mind. Then, on New Year's Day, 2004, I was challenged with the issue again. This time the question was raised by Sr. Marce Connolly, a housemate of my friend Sr. Mary Kremer, both of them Sinsinawa Dominicans. "Mike," she said in her probing but unthreatening way, "Whom do you really want to be impacted by this new edition?" As I repeated the mantra about wanting to please both groups, I found my rationale increasingly hollow. I may have written one book that the "academy" seems to accept (i.e., my dissertation, which Orbis published as *House of Disciples: Church, Economics and Justice in Matthew*) but the "public" hardly read it. However, it is just the opposite with my other books: the "public" accepts them but they get little or no mention in the "academy."

This has made me realize that I am more effective trying to translate what I've learned from scholarship into daily living for the broader public. Consequently, in this book, I will "bite the bullet." Except for the first chapter, which offers a new approach to the Beatitudes, I will offer a minimum of notes. I will stress what I have learned from my research but, even more, what I have tried to put into practice from what I have heard and read that Jesus teaches me and my world in those core teachings called "The Beatitudes." If this book is an improvement on what I wrote twenty-five years ago, I will be happy.

A comparison of the two books will make it clear why I have given it a new subtitle: it is not just a revision; it is quite different. The emphasis of *Spirituality of the Beatitudes* in this "revisiting" lies on a more communal approach to spirituality. This is based on the realization that Matthew's Gospel was written not to individuals but to house churches. Given this more communal context, only a few chapters remain similar to the first edition.

If good theology is good spirituality, I hope this "spirituality of the Beatitudes" will also, in the process, be good theology as well. Whether or not scholars affirm what I say herein is no longer as important as how my readers can be discipled to Jesus Christ in a way that will find the scriptures fulfilled in their lives.

I am deeply indebted to Liz Wisniewski for help in getting the book to the publisher. I will be forever grateful to Tom Plakut, the director of our Loaves and Fishes Meal Program here at St. Benedict's in Milwaukee, where I live, for his critique of the first draft. His editing and insights have been invaluable.

Finally, I dedicate this revised edition to those who have told me how the first edition impacted their lives. These have come not only from the First World—my intended audience—but from all over the world. In particular I am thankful for the friendship of Chris Gortat, who was part of a group studying the first edition of this book in a program on the Spiritual Exercises of St. Ignatius at Manresa Retreat Center in Detroit.

CHAPTER ONE

The Relevance of Matthew's Gospel for First World Christians of the Twenty-First Century

Keith Clark, a Capuchin Franciscan from my province, has created what he calls "perversity principles." My favorite one states: "the lower the motive, the better the results." Twenty-five years ago, as I researched Matthew's Beatitudes and their contemporary relevance, I had mixed motives; one of them was quite low. By investigating Matthew's *eight* Beatitudes rather than Luke's *four*, I figured I'd be able to get twice as many outlines for future talks (or book chapters)! As I investigated what led Matthew to write the First Gospel, however, I found my initial pragmatism evolving into an exciting and challenging journey of faith. I discovered that the author of the First Gospel was addressing people who had some key similarities with many of us First World Christians: more prosperous than poor, more urban than rural, and more pluralistic than insular. Similarly, his "good news" or gospel itself was written to address concerns not unlike our own: lack of concern for the poor who are always with us, our tendency to be conflicted within our churches, our reluctance to become involved with social justice issues, and our quickness to dismiss people who disagree with us.

Who was this Matthew? What was his[1] message? How does this Gospel offer us a life-giving biblical spirituality, especially for those of us who have questions about God's presence among us, about living in our own "empire,"[2] and about the (mis)use of authority in church structures and society? Does Matthew's Gospel have anything to say about our responsibility toward those poor, (often) non-white, and marginalized neighbors (domestic and foreign) whom Matthew's Jesus says will always be with us (26:11) and whom we must love as ourselves (22:39)?

Moving to the communal dimension, we can ask: What implications exist for our spirituality as a church when we realize that Matthew's Beatitudes were addressed not so much to individuals as to local households called *ekklēsiai* (16:18; 18:17)? How does our thinking need to be changed when we realize that Matthew's spirituality demands a corporate discipleship with economic, political, and religious consequences? What kind of "house church" do

1

we need to create if we will reflect the vision of God's reign found in the First Gospel? In other words, what if our families and groups as well as our local churches and dioceses were recognizably communities of the Beatitudes?

Matthew wrote his Gospel so that his conflicted community-in-transition could deal with questions not addressed in Mark's story of Jesus. Where could God's presence be found in the community's experience, especially since Jesus did not return in the *parousia* (24:3, 27)? How could the community move from a closed, nationalistic sect[3] to an open, universalistic community with an evangelical message for the wider world? How were authority and leadership to be exercised in and among the house churches that now bore the name "Christian"? How did their involvement in God's reign demand an identification with poor, needy, and marginated peoples?

The Contrast between Matthew's Gospel and Society's Prevailing "Gospel"

After his baptism and temptation in the wilderness, Matthew has Jesus appear announcing the "good news" or gospel (*euaggelion*) of God's reign, also called the "kingdom of heaven" (4:17). In the world of that time, "kingdom" had definite political, economic, and religious overtones. Given that the word for kingdom (*basileia*) is also "empire," Jesus' way of using the phrase, combined with his preaching the "good news" (*euaggelion*) of another kingdom in the midst of the Roman empire was clearly subversive.[4] Since this *basileia* involved a God other than those identified with Rome, Matthew's Jesus was saying that the very religious underpinnings of the political economy needed to be transformed, not just individual and communal lives.

This subversive understanding of "gospel" must be regrasped, especially for people like us who think of it as quite religious in meaning. In fact, the word *euaggelion* appears only one time in all of the Septuagint (2 Sam. 4:10). Consequently the reference to "good news" did not come from Israel's tradition but was "one *expropriated from the Roman Empire*."[5] In that imperial reality, when people heard "good news" it had to do with a new territory being conquered, the birth of an imperial heir or some kind of *dogma* or decree of an existing emperor. In this imperial context, any other *euaggelion* would be perceived as a direct challenge to the system.

For Jesus to "proclaim the good news of the kingdom" (4:23; 9:35), especially in a way that resulted in the spread of *his* honor, rather than Caesar's, was tantamount to treason. The subversive nature of his message is reinforced when Matthew portrays Jesus as showing that discipleship in God's empire involves living certain Beatitudes. This invited another kind of loyalty; it also indicated that Jesus' gospel of God's reign, rather than the empire's, offered a way of life that was "beatitudinal," or worthy of honor. Since Jesus' Beatitudes of God's reign stood in resistance to the abusive dynamics of the kingdom defined by empire, those individuals and households who embraced the new "gospel" could expect trouble for coming under an authority other than Rome's and its religious surrogates among the Jewish leaders. But not for long.

As the decades passed after Jesus' death/resurrection, the "good news" of God's reign preached by Jesus got eclipsed by the "good news" of his death, resurrection, and abiding presence. In the process the original radical elements of the gospel seemed to be toned down. At the same time, an evangelical message that once appealed to many living at the margins began to attract the more prosperous strata of society. Furthermore, a transition was being made from the rural and village culture of Palestine to Greco-Roman urban culture, from the Aramaic to the Greek language, from an ethnically homogeneous constituency that was largely unlearned, relatively poor, and of lower social status to an ethnically heterogeneous one that included people who were more educated, financially secure, and successful. The latter, while attracted to the person of Jesus, struggled with the received message vis-à-vis the poor. It was the task of Matthew to make clear to them that true discipleship demanded neither poverty nor an itinerant lifestyle. Rather it demanded that all the members find a way of relating to the poor in the way they used their resources in imitation of the woman with the alabaster jar, the one whom Jesus held up as the model of true discipleship. Indeed, he solemnly proclaimed: "wherever this *euaggelion* is proclaimed in the whole world, what she has done will be told in remembrance of her" (26:13). Indeed, like the faithful Joseph of Arimathea, disciples of Jesus could be rich—provided that they too were just in the sharing of their resources toward those in need (27:57-60).

Who Was the Audience of Matthew's Gospel?

In writing a book or in any public expression of one's thoughts, one must always keep in mind the composition of one's audience. "Matthew" was no different. When the First Gospel was written, his audience, or the early Christians for whom he wrote, was organized around various households. The *oikos,* or household, constituted for the Christian movement as well as for the wider imperial environment a chief basis, paradigm, and reference point for religious and moral as well as social, political, and economic organization, interaction, and ideology.[6] As such, the house (*oikia* and/or *oikos*) represents the core organizing principle of the gospel—be that "gospel" Matthew's or the empire's.

Because both the "church" and the political kingdom of the empire were structured around the household, the house is essential to any contemporary understanding of Matthew's "world." In fact, because the household represented the basic unit of life in the empire—be it economic and social as well as the life of the local church—the notion of "house" in Matthew's Gospel must be viewed as a self-evident, "primary assumed metaphor"[7] in much the same way that "air" is an assumed primary "metaphor" to human life or "water" is to fish. Without air, human life could not exist; without water, fish would die. Without the house, church and economics simply were unimaginable at the time when Jesus lived and Matthew wrote.

The house (*oikia/oikos*) involved persons and resources. The ordering of each household (*oikonomia*) was determined by various structured and sanctioned relationships that took place among the persons (male/female, parent/child, master/slave) and their available resources (property [such as home, boats, and nets], farms and equipment, monies, and other goods). These dynamics constituted the "house." In the first-century Mediterranean world, households tended to be based on the prevailing system of the empire; thus the majority were patriarchal in their structure. Even those of a more inclusive, voluntary type of association were never really egalitarian in our contemporary understanding; they were always somewhat patriarchal.[8]

Given this background on "house" as the basic unit of the imperial and religious reality, who was Matthew's audience? With the help of the social sciences,[9] an examination of the language of the First Gospel, including the Beatitudes and the Sermon on the Mount, reveals that the audience was a group that considered itself quite unique vis-à-vis the wider society. However, if before his death Jesus limited his message to the "house" of Israel (10:6; 15:24), now his disciples realized that his living Spirit in them demanded that his gospel be addressed to all nations. But because the values of those "nations" would be alien to the gospel, Jesus' followers recognized their need to come together in new forms of alternative households to sustain their faith. In turn, Matthew's Jesus would declare, this faith must be practiced in justice in all its forms if the scriptures were to be fulfilled in us.

Leland J. White notes that the Sermon on the Mount—which begins with Jesus' narration of the Beatitudes—"contains norms that serve to set Matthew's community apart from its environment as the righteous [just ones] from the unrighteous [unjust ones]. . . . Both the norms and the Beatitudes which introduce the sermon strategically respond to this situation by identifying the community of disciples as a quasi-family living under God's protection."[10] His house-based audience considered themselves alienated from the wider society not only in their social structures but especially in their values and worldview.[11] They were trying to embody justice within a world of injustice.

Since Jews and Gentiles constituted the "world" that Jesus' followers were to evangelize, by transforming themselves within their households they would be making the first steps toward societal transformation. "Change the house; change the empire," seemed to be the understanding. This approach to transforming the empire by changing its basic economic and religious unit seems quite evident in the Beelzebub controversy when Jesus declares: "Every kingdom divided against itself is laid waste, and no city or house divided against itself will stand" (12:25). If you change the house, you change the city; transformed cities shake the basis of the empire itself.

How Matthew Structured the First Gospel

An understanding of how Matthew organized the First Gospel helps us understand its key theme. Within the "bookends" of his infancy narrative (1:1-2:23) and passion/death/resurrection narrative (26:2-28:20), Matthew structures the heart of the Gospel around five "books," each with narratives about Jesus (*gesta*) and narratives of Jesus (*verba*). All are arranged as a "chiasm" insofar as we find parallels in the first and last parts, the second and second-last part, and so on. For instance, we find parallels in Matthew's prologue and climax.[12] Both make it clear that Jesus' reign is that of God "with" us (1:23; 28:29). Matthew has Jesus declared "king of the Jews" (2:2; 27:37) in a way that threatens the religious representatives of the empire. This threat results in their willingness to have him destroyed. Their efforts will be futile because he is not just king of the Jews; he is something more: he is God's son (2:15; 27:43, 54).

At the center of the chiasm and, therefore, constituting the core message of the Gospel, we find the passage wherein Jesus articulated the difference between his own disciples (inside "the house") who do the will of his Father and those in the crowd "outside." Matthew writes:

> While he was still speaking to the crowds, his mother and his brothers were standing outside, wanting to speak to him. Someone told him, "Look, your mother and your brothers are standing outside, wanting to speak to you." But to the one who had told him this, Jesus replied, "Who is my mother, and who are my brothers?" And pointing to his disciples, he said: "Here are my mother and my brothers! For whoever does the will of my Father in heaven is my brother and sister and mother." (12:46-50)

In this passage Matthew, following Mark, distinguishes between the blood family "outside" the house and those "inside." However, changing his Markan source (which speaks about those "who sat about him" [Mark 3:34]), he points specifically to those "disciples" (*mathētēs*) in the house as those who do his Father's will (in contrast to Mark's reference to "God's will" [3:35]). This familial connection enables them to be constituted as a new kind of family: his "brother, and sister, and mother." What Jesus earlier asked of his disciples—the breaking of patriarchal familial bonds (4:22; 8:21-22)—the Gospel now makes even clearer. In Jesus' new family of disciples blood means nothing. What counts is being a disciple who does the will of the heavenly Father. This involves "doing good" in a way that ushers in God's reign within the empire. The will of the Father will be further explicated in the teachings of Jesus. It contrasts starkly with the violence of the "father" in Rome.

The structure of Matthew's Gospel makes it clear that Jesus' disciples are those found in the household of the heavenly Father rather than servants in a world defined by empire. As Matthew structures Jesus' deeds and words, the implications for Jesus' disciples living in the world of that era or our own become clear. If they embrace the pattern of his life in the empires of any age, they too can expect what happened to him: the cross—the sign of being publicly rejected by society not only for noncompliance with its norms but for subversion to the system itself (16:24-26; see 16:21; 17:22-23; 20:17-19).

PROLOGUE:	Genealogy, Birth, and Infancy (1:1-2:23)
NARRATIVE:	Baptism, Temptations, Capernaum (2:24-4:25)
DISCOURSE:	Beatitudes and Justice in the House (5:1-7:29)
NARRATIVE:	Authority and Healing (8:1-9:38)
DISCOURSE:	Mission to and from the House (10:1-11:1)
NARRATIVE:	Rejection by This Generation (11:2-12:50)
DISCOURSE:	Parables of God's Reign for Householders (13:1-13:53)
NARRATIVE:	Acknowledgment by Disciples (13:54-17:23)
DISCOURSE:	House Order and Church Discipline (17:24-19:1)
NARRATIVE:	Authority and Invitation (19:2-22:24)
DISCOURSE:	Woes to the House of Israel and a Blessing for Just Deeds (23:1-26:1)
CLIMAX:	Passion, Death, and Resurrection (26:2-28:20)

For the Audience Today,
Who Is the "Matthew" of Matthew's Gospel?

Tradition attributes the "First Gospel" to the Matthew who sat "at the tax booth" and followed Jesus (9:9f.; 10:3). Today few hold the "Matthew-the-tax-collector" view of authorship. While this "Matthew" may have been an original source for the Gospel, the final form as we now have it seems to be the work of a Gentile Christian who was well versed in the Hebrew Scriptures but who made enough mistakes (e.g., translating Zechariah 9:9 to have Jesus come into Jerusalem mounted on a donkey and a colt! [21:2 vs. 21:7]) to suggest that he was not totally conversant with its nuances.

While scholars may squabble about such things, I find something more meaningful in trying to figure out who the "Matthew" of the First Gospel is to be. I find a connection in the Greek words of "Matthew" and "disciple."

Given this historical context, especially for us disciples of our various nations today who are called to put into practice "everything" Jesus has taught (28:20), the Matthew (*Matthaios*) of the First Gospel appears likely to have been a representative for any disciple (*mathētēs*) who has been taught (*mathēteutheis*) and who understands (*synienai*) the implications of what has been taught. This involves putting the teachings of Jesus into practice.[13] In this sense the question immediately before the core passage of the Gospel (12:46-50) stands out: "Have you understood (*synienai*) all this?" Jesus poses this question after completing the third discourse on the parables (13:1-53), which sets the disciples apart from those who see but do not perceive and hear but do not listen since they do not understand (13:13). When they answer "Yes," he says to them: "Therefore every scribe who has been trained (*mathēteutheis*) for the kingdom of heaven is like the master of a household (*oikodespotēs*) who brings out of his treasure what is new (*kaina*) and what is old (*palaia*)" (13:52).[14] While there is both continuity and discontinuity (the old and the new) in Matthew's version of the gospel of Jesus, the "new," by being mentioned first, may indicate a priority.[15] However, even more, "understanding" is not to be something merely in the head, but head knowledge that is formed in the heart and translated in our lives. It is much like parents saying: "Do you understand?" by which they mean: "Put into practice what you have come to know."

From where in the treasure-house did Matthew get his material? The "old" treasures brought from wisdom's storehouse would be found in the way of justice expressed in the "law and the prophets," which Matthew interpreted Jesus as fulfilling (3:15; 5:17; 26:54, 56; see 1:22; 2:15, 17, 23; 4:14; 8:17; 12:17; 13:35; 21:4; 27:9).[16] Matthew's "old" material also came from the treasure of Mark. In fact, Matthew's Gospel contains all but about fifty of Mark's 661 verses. He uses 8,555 of Mark's 11,078 words. A secondary source that the Matthean scribe found in the storehouse has been called the "Q document." Q refers to the words not found in Mark that can be found in Matthew and Luke. It is a supposed collection of sayings (and some stories) of Jesus shared by Matthew and Luke (as in their Beatitudes). The other treasures from the storehouse brought forth as unique by the Matthean scribe/household are called the "M" material—an overall term for the unique traditions used in the First Gospel but not found in either Mark or Q. An example would be the Beatitudes of Matthew that are not contained in Luke.[17]

Another example of the "M" tradition is found in Matthew's threefold use of the unique word *mathēteutheis*. While it refers to "one learned" in the teachers' ways, "one discipled" to a teacher, or those who put into practice the master's teachings, here it refers to any "householder." Later it will identify Joseph of Arimathea (27:57). The last occurrence can be found in the Great Commission, or final words of Jesus on the day of resurrection. Having earlier said that he was "sent only to the lost sheep of the house of Israel" (15:24) and having sent his own apostles only to this group (10:6), the resurrected Jesus now breaks all boundaries. Now all those united to him must go into the *whole world*: "Go therefore and make disciples [*mathēteutheis*] of all nations, baptizing them in the name of the Father and of the Son and of the Holy Spirit, and teaching them to obey everything I have commanded you. And remember, I am with you always, to the end of the age" (28:19-20). Ultimately then, all persons who embrace the words and works of the Gospel of *Matthaios* are to be its *mathēteutheis*. As such they are to be its final redaction in the world entrusted to them. In other words, as far as spirituality is concerned, the author and the audience of Matthew converge in anyone who is discipled to Jesus in a way that allows the words of the Gospel to be translated into his/her/their lives, individually and communally.

Beatitudes as Indicators of a Culture's Code of Conduct for Household Honor

All established social settings, including that of the household, involve an order that defines a particular culture and its ethos. Understanding the culture and ethos helps us identify the sense of belonging shared by individual members or groups within that order, as well as their expectations regarding the means of right living within those communities. In other words, the cultural environment affects the ethos and relationships of individuals in a community as well as the structuring or ordering of communal relationships within it.

When we don't understand others' culture, with its unique codes determining what constitutes honorable and shameful behaviors, serious mistakes can be made. The United States learned this the hard way in Iraq after its successful invasion in 2003. It floundered in its initial effort to establish "democracy" because it did not adequately consider Iraq's traditional culture. For example, the Western value of "individual freedom" represented an alien concept to most Iraqis. According to one commentator, "More than 75% of Iraqis belong to tribes, some practicing unquestioning obedience to tribal elders. Family bonds are so strong that a person is regarded either as kin or as a stranger. And most Iraqis view political nepotism not as a 'civic problem,' but as a cultural duty." In an Iraq dominated by "identity politics" whereby ethnic and religious solidarity mean more than individual liberty, fidelity to the group trumps any "foreign" notions of individual freedom.[18] Indeed, the honor of being "free" in the West is eclipsed by the honor of being recognized as belonging to the group in the Middle East.

The social ethos of the first-century world revolved around dynamics of honor and shame. These were considered "pivotal values" in ancient Mediterranean societies and foundational for the dynamics in that patriarchal society.[19] Honor involved the socially recognized and expected attitudes and behaviors in areas where power, sexual status, and religion intersected. It contained two interconnected elements: the claim of worth by one's self or one's group and the recognition of that worth by others.[20] One's personal and/or group honor involved two dimensions: honor precedence and honor virtue. Honor precedence involved the public recognition of an individual's or group's various forms of status. Honor virtue laid greater stress on fidelity to the inner attitudes that were expressed in communally valued behaviors.[21] Contrasting the two, Louise Joy Lawrence writes: "People could attain honor or reputation not only through bold masculine daring and aggression, [via the typical forms of "honor precedence"] but also by virtuous living and adhering to affiliative norms" that would describe right living in a community, such as those prescribed in the Beatitudes. In fact, she sees these as often witnessing to a much higher value. She writes:

> It is often these moral values that are idealized and linked with the divine in Jewish tradition in a way that social strategies for gaining prestige are not. If the acquisition of honor precedence leads one to dishonor God through disregard of God's will, one stands under the danger of divine retribution. Jewish tradition honored the internal state of the heart and . . . so it promoted concerns more in line with an honor virtue ethos.[22]

From earliest history until the present, the ethos of a concrete culture or its "code of belonging" can be discovered by examining its "beatitudes." These serve to characterize right living among its members.[23] In the era of Enron and WorldCom some groups believed that "greed is good," while a code characterizing my teenage years involved the blessedness of "not getting caught." In the ways of many senior citizens you are "blessed" if you know where the "early bird specials" can be found, for you will save lots of money. Many politicians seem to be blessed simply if they win. But this is not what the term means scripturally, which is our purpose here.

"Beatitude" is derived from the Latin word *beatus*; the concept is expressed in Hebrew as *ashrey* and in Greek as *makarios*. In classical Greek literature, the "happy" or "blessed" person is the one "who takes cognizance of the essential harmony which binds him to society and to the world."[24] The ethos reflected in beatitudinal living revealed the way individuals and especially groups embraced the core values of the culture of that society and world and one's standing in that culture.

While we find few beatitudes before the exile (e.g., 1 Kgs. 10:8), in postexilic writing they become more abundant.[25] In selecting the Greek adjective *makarios* to render the Hebrew *ashrey,* the Septuagint's translation of the notion suggests a happiness that flows from justice, or from having a right relationship with God.[26] In contrast to *eulogia, w*hich connotes a cultic blessing that accomplishes what it pronounces for the one who is blessed, *makarios* refers to those considered fortunate in the standing of the community. *Eulogia* was a "top-down" form of recognition for right living; it came from God. Someone *makarios* was a person from "below"; it represents communal recognition of valued/honorable behavior.

K. C. Hanson, whose understanding of the honor/shame dynamics in cultures led him to helpful insights about "makarisms," notes that biblical makarisms (*makarioi*) are "fundamentally different" from blessings (*eulogiai*) in at least five ways: "1) Makarisms are not 'words of power.' 2) They are not pronounced by God or cultic mediators. 3) They only refer to humans, and never to God or non-human objects. 4) They do not have their setting in ritual. And 5) one does not pray for a makarism, or refer to oneself with a makarism."[27]

Beatitude refers to humans rather than God. Indeed, God is never called *makarios* in the New Testament, except in 1 Timothy 1:11; 6:15; nor is the term applied to nonhumans. Almost two-thirds (28) of the forty-four beatitudes in the New Testament are in Matthew and Luke; thirteen of these are found in their "Beatitudes" from the Sermons on the Mount and the Plain.

As we examine the notion of beatitude in Matthew, we need to be clear about how Matthew's concept differs from that of Luke, even how he seems to translate "*makarios*" differently. Unfortunately, I believe that too many commentators, Hanson included,[28] have reached their conclusions from a simplistic transposition onto Matthew of the four Beatitudes and four woes in Luke's Gospel. However, nowhere in Matthew is any form of *makarios* connected with the word for woe, *ouai,* as in Luke's Gospel. For a stronger argument, it seems more appropriate to link *ouai* with *eulogia* or with those curses that come from God for cultic aberrations rather than with any "curse" or dishonorable form of rejection coming from humans.[29]

Since the context for Matthew's *makarioi* is the "house," it seems more fitting to find their antithetical notions related to *skandalon,* meaning "that which is dishonorable" or "that which creates a stumbling block to healthy community." This connection is found at least twice in Matthew (11:2-6; 16:17-23). *Skandalizein* and *makarios* appear in the critical passage highlighting Jesus' self-definition as the Messiah (11:2-6) and the need for his disciples to understand this (which will be examined at the end of this chapter). Traditionally the concluding verse has been translated as "Blessed are you, if you are not scandalized in me" (11:6). The one who takes no offense in Jesus, his message, and his life will be honored in the community of disciples. Consequently the passage might also read, "If you are not scandalized by me, honored are you!"

L. Michael White shows that "giving offense" (*skandalizein*) "represents tensions at the boundaries of the community, both internal and external, in the midst of some sort of crisis."[30] He shows that, of Matthew's ten uses of the word *skandalizein*, eight refer to dynamics of individuals in relation to the community (5:29, 30; 11:6; 13:21; 18:6; 24:10; 26:31, 33) while only one refers to "giving offense" to the Jewish leaders (15:12) or the collectors of the temple tax (17:22). The five uses of *skandalon* (13:41; 16:23; 18:7 [3x]) all refer to communal situations. Thus, in Matthew, it is clear that the notion of "giving offense" is related not to the wider environment but to the members of the household itself. As we will see in the remaining chapters, essential to an understanding of the beatitudinal way of life for disciples is an equal insight into those kind of behaviors that create stumbling blocks or obstacles to the way that is honored as followers of Christ.

The Beatitudes as a Code of Honor for Living Justly in Matthew's Household

If there are different interpretations regarding the meaning of the Beatitudes as a whole, there are almost as many ways to translate "*makarios*" itself. Consequently, we find it as "blessed" (King James Version, Revised Standard Version, American Translation, and Moffatt), "how blest" (New English Bible, New American Bible), blessings (Schweizer), "Oh the bliss" (Barclay), "happy" (*Today's English Version*), "*how happy*" (Phillips, Jerusalem Bible), and "fortunate" (Anchor Bible). All of these have merit. However, realizing that the household was the context for beatitudinal living in that honor/shame culture[31] and that Matthew's use of the term seems more related to "honor virtue" than "ascribed virtue," it seems most appropriate to translate the word *makarios* and those considered the *makarioi* as "honored" and the "honorable." This refers more to the attitudinal approaches honored by the community rather than to any particular circumstances which, in themselves, referred to being on the "outside."[32]

The Matthean Beatitudes outline a code of communal approval for behavior that is honored and approved by the members of his households. They articulate "which forms of human behavior are worthwhile"[33] or, as Wolfgang Schenk notes, "conditional affirmations" that characterize membership in the Matthean community; they are "conditions of admission" to the community of the new age.[34] More specifically, Leland J. White goes even further in articulating what uniquely should characterize this honorable way of living. Recognizing that the word "honor" appears neither in the Sermon on the Mount nor in the Beatitudes, White highlights the indispensable role of justice as the ethos that should characterize the Matthean community.[35]

Such a justice, we will see, involves those communally acknowledged forms of household behavior that are meant to characterize the household of Jesus' disciples of all time.

Given how I began this section, noting some of our "empire's" beatitudes (as well as the way religion too often limits the images to its clergy class), the implications for living as disciples today should not be lost on the reader. In other words, we all need to ask: What is the honorable way we are called to be disciples today? Even more, how can we create communities that again will value and reward such behavior?

The Challenge of Structural/"House" Analysis for a Spirituality of the Beatitudes

Just as in the first-century world of Jesus, to be at the heart of a world with its own "good news," we must proclaim another gospel: that of God's reign. To proclaim Jesus' gospel effectively demands that we analyze the countervailing "gospel" proclaimed by society. This implies that we under-stand our society's various levels—the individual, the interpersonal, and the infrastructural dimensions—if we are to "make disciples of all the nations" (28:19) in a way that will promote justice, peace, and the integrity of that fourth level of the world, creation itself, that is, the environmental level of the world. In the process at times we will find ourselves "at home" and at other times "not at home" at one or the other level. Consequently, I believe we need to develop a contemporary understanding of the gospel's primary metaphor—the house—and determine how this applies to our lives today.

In spirituality, the notion of "house" or *oikia* can be applied to all four levels of our world. At the first level, that of our individual lives, psychiatrists and psychologists have long recognized images of the house in dreams as symbols of dynamics within our own personal lives. When it comes to spir-ituality, the same image applies to the soul's grounding in God. In one of the most revered works of mysticism, John of the Cross writes in his opening verse of *The Dark Night:*

> One dark night,
> Fired with love's urgent longings—
> Ah, the sheer grace! —
> I went out unseen,
> My house being now all stilled.[36]

Moving beyond the word *oikia/oikos* for our individual lives, anyone familiar with the history of economics knows that *oikonomia* means "the ordering of the house," that is, both the persons and the resources available to them in the household. In a parallel vein, we know that, before the Constantinianization of the church in the early fourth century, almost every "church" was found in the household, beginning with the description of Cornelius and "his household" in the tenth chapter of the Acts of the Apostles. These economic and religious notions of house refer to the interpersonal level of our life in community.

However, living at this second level finds us, individually and communally, affected for good or for harm in ways that become a blessing or a stumbling block in our relationships with the wider world. This Matthew (and only Matthew) calls the *oikoumenē*, or the whole inhabited world. At times, as the U.S. Bishops noted in a recent pastoral letter on "Faithful Citizenship: A Catholic Call to Political Responsibility," "some Catholics may feel politically *homeless*, sensing that no political party and too few candidates share a consistent concern for human life and dignity."[37] This will be even more the case with issues of basic rights related to life itself and a just ordering of relationships within the political *oikonomia* and *ekklēsia*.

The first and second levels of gathering people and groups into institutions find them, as well as the earth's resources, arranged in certain ways. When we do not find ourselves "at home" in these social arrangements, it will likely be because they are unjust. These unjust "isms" organize people according to race, sex, age, and nation, as well as in oppositions such as cleric/lay, powerful/powerless, gay/straight, and so on. Resources are arranged according to technological know-how, producers or consumers, military prowess, and the ability to capture global markets. Each of these social and resource arrangements is legitimated through an ideology or worldview that is nurtured by education and promoted by the communications media as the "only way." Because of the power of ideology in defining the "isms" in the institutions, what we would consider "unjust" will often be canonized as "just" in a way that often claims the sanction of religion, as it did in Jesus' day (5:20). The interrelationship of institutions, "isms," and ideology is what I call the *infrastructure*. The infrastructure constitutes the underlying, systemic order that sustains all else.

The first three levels of life (the individual, the interpersonal, and the infrastructural levels) are part of the ebb and flow of that level of life that is the context as well as the ideal sustenance and nurturer of the first three: the environmental level. This is the *oikologia* itself. How we relate at all three levels, in this interconnected universe, will have dramatic consequences on the fourth level, as environmental issues are making us inscreasingly aware. The four levels of the world and their parallel notions related to "house" can be depicted as follows:

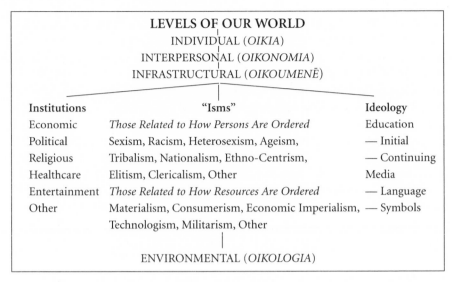

LEVELS OF OUR WORLD
INDIVIDUAL (*OIKIA*)
INTERPERSONAL (*OIKONOMIA*)
INFRASTRUCTURAL (*OIKOUMENĒ*)

Institutions	"Isms"	Ideology
Economic	*Those Related to How Persons Are Ordered*	Education
Political	Sexism, Racism, Heterosexism, Ageism,	— Initial
Religious	Tribalism, Nationalism, Ethno-Centrism,	— Continuing
Healthcare	Elitism, Clericalism, Other	Media
Entertainment	*Those Related to How Resources Are Ordered*	— Language
Other	Materialism, Consumerism, Economic Imperialism,	— Symbols
	Technologism, Militarism, Other	

ENVIRONMENTAL (*OIKOLOGIA*)

In the past, the gospel and spirituality have too often been limited to the first and second dimensions of life (individual and interpersonal); however, if Jesus' gospel had been limited to just these we would not be here today as his disciples. It was because his gospel threatened that "gospel" of the empire with its religious reinforcement coming from entrenched Jewish leaders that he was persecuted for justice to the point of his death, which has become resurrection for us.

Even though Matthew viewed individuals in terms of the whole generation (12:39-43), we have not taken sufficient cognizance of the impact of the infrastructure on our spiritual lives. If our call as disciples is to go into the whole world (see 28:18), our spirituality must flow from an awareness of the infrastructure and the impact of social sin on people and groups that go largely ignored in our country and in other developed nations. As a consequence of this ignorance, we have been unable to promote seriously the cosmic change demanded by the gospel.

In 1971 Roman Catholic bishops from all parts of the globe gathered for a Synod in Rome. They brought with them experiences of poverty and wealth, famine and luxury, malnutrition and throw-away societies, and racial and national conflicts. Their analysis of these realities convinced them of the need for a revitalized gospel message. They said: "Scrutinizing the 'signs of the times' and seeking to detect the meaning of emerging history, while at the same time sharing the aspirations and questions of all those who want to build a more human world, we have listened to the Word of God that we might be converted to the fulfilling of the divine plan for the salvation of the world."[38]

Having made this "social analysis," they did some theological reflection. This led them to make a dramatic conclusion:

Even though it is not for us to elaborate a very profound analysis of the situation of the world, we have nevertheless been able to perceive the serious injustices which are building around the world of men a network of domination, oppression and abuses which stifle freedom and which keep the greater part of humanity from sharing in the building up and enjoyment of a more just and more fraternal world.[39]

The underlying theme of God's plan for the world found in Genesis showed that all people are to image God by having access to the earth's resources. However, if their analysis is correct—that people's freedom was being stifled and the greater part of humanity was not sharing in the earth's resources—then our world stands in direct opposition to God's plan for creation. As long as people are not free, they cannot image God as fully as they should. As long as the goods of the earth are not shared with equity, people cannot easily increase, multiply, fill the earth, and subdue it or enter into a relationship of care with the goods of the earth. This is a condition of social sin. This "network of domination" is the infrastructure of institutions and "isms." It includes the ideology that must feel the impact of a call to conversion if God's plan for the earth will be realized.

We are part of society's institutions, its cultural patterns and social arrangements. We are touched by its ideology. Many of us in the church of the developed world are the beneficiaries of the injustices that are part of this network. Not to develop a model of evangelization that brings Matthew's Gospel spirituality to bear on this part of the world is to deny the very commission given us at baptism (28:19). This is especially important for many of us in the First World who benefit from the infrastructure. In this sense we are challenged to conversion in the same way as was Matthew's rich young man. Our spirituality and hermeneutics (i.e., understanding of the scriptures) must find us grounded in solidarity with all those who are poor (19:21); it must intimately connect us with everyone and everything in that universe we call the household of God.

Sharon Daloz Parks writes that the notion of "house," whether economic (*oikonomia*), ecumenical (*oikoumenē*), or ecological (*oikologia*) reflect dynamics that should compel

> our attention to the fact that we dwell in a profoundly interdependent world. Each of these words is rooted in the Greek word *oikos*, meaning "household" or "habitat." Each of these dimensions of life is teaching us to be attentive to home—our small planet, the dwelling place of the human family, the domain for which we are responsible, a responsibility which we cannot defer to others, a responsibility from which we have no escape.[40]

To live authentically what we mean by "spirituality," the Spirit-at-work-in-us must find us letting the scriptures be expressed in our lives in a way that this word will transform our world at every level. These levels must include the individual, the interpersonal, and the infrastructural if this gospel is to impact the fourth level, the universe itself, with "good news." Consequently our gospel must continually proclaim two powerful principles: the dignity of every person in the *oikia* from the womb to the tomb as well as the parallel demand that we find greater equity in the way the resources of the universe are shared among all, especially those structurally denied access to them.

If Sharon Parks is correct in saying that "home-making" is "a primary activity of Spirit" and if I am correct in saying that "house" is a primary metaphor for Matthew's community of disciples, the spirituality that is necessary for our whole world is a new way of recognizing that God is dwelling "with us" and that we must dwell with each other as brothers and sisters. In this sense I resonate theologically and spiritually with the conclusion of Sharon Daloz Parks:

> We humans are being invited anew to dwell together, to enlarge the boundaries of "home" so as to embrace our earth, to meet new relatives, and to practice the arts of hospitality. We are being invited to inhabit new symbols, and thereby to discover that we *are* home. For it is here that *creator spiritus* meets us, in the midst, in the present, now in this dangerous moment, inviting us to be home-makers, to be co-creators of a space in which we—the whole human family—can dream and thrive.[41]

The Challenge of Matthew's Beatitudes for Contemporary Discipleship

Unless contemporary interpreters are conscious of the original concerns that the message of Matthew tried to address, their hermeneutics will remain wanting and lifeless, academic and sterile. According to Russell Pregeant, "these existential questions belong to human existence per se." Life's concerns cannot be divorced from biblical interpretation or biblical spirituality. "This must be so," he says, "if they are intelligible to all interpreters willing to question their own lives."[42]

Matthew's community experienced religious upheaval, conflicts of authority and interpretation of law, as well as cultural clashes within its imperial world. We have seen that, almost two thousand years later, the same problems touch the experience of our church and society. To discover how we can address these problems in the first years of the third millennium, we can return to the Matthean community for our direction. As we do so, we need to probe more deeply the meaning (hermeneutics) of the text and its relevance for us in our contemporary households.

Again, quoting Russell Pregeant, "a hermeneutical method that reveals the text's relationship to its own present and past, but ignores its thrust toward the future, violates that text's very nature to the extent that it implies that the true meaning of the work is thereby exhausted." Indeed, according to him all hermeneutics, if it is to offer us "meaning" in any life-giving way, must fulfill two goals: (1) by its reflection on the past, current problems should be able to be addressed (2) in a way that enables us to take authority over them in a way that will find us creating hope-filled alternatives.[43]

Good biblical hermeneutics leads to evangelical living modeled on authentic gospel spirituality. In his own spirituality, Jesus was the fulfillment of the scriptures themselves, according to Matthew and the other Gospel writers. In Jesus, orthodoxy (right teaching) became orthopraxy (right living). Indeed, as Mark Allan Powell writes so clearly: "There is not a single instance of nonconcurrence between what is revealed through Jesus' speech and what is revealed through his actions, motives, or values."[44] As Jesus' words to John's disciples about reporting to him what they "heard" and "saw" attest (11:2-6), orthodoxy should be concretized in orthopraxy, and vice versa, if the scriptures are going to be fulfilled in our lives.

The hermeneutic or method that has best enabled me to bring the scriptures to bear on the existential questions of my life and world—and which also faithfully reflects the approach Matthew seems to have used with his questioning community—is based on that model proffered by Juan Luis Segundo in his book *The Liberation of Theology*.[45] I find in his "hermeneutic circle" (or the "circle of meaning" or "faith cycle") an approach that makes sense to me about my world and God's word. At the same time I have discovered that each of us, in our own ways, must go through this hermeneutic circle if the scriptures are to be translated in our lives by our profession and practice:

WORLD   WORD

1. I have an experience that jars   4. This reveals to me a new
the worldview that has   understanding of God, who now
previously formed my values   is revealed as part of my experience
and behavior.   for my life and the world's.

2. This leads me to call into   3. Rejecting this former concept
question the very ideology that   of God, I return to the scriptures to
once reinforced my worldview,   search for similar experiences
including God.   others have had.

As I consider a key passage in Matthew's Gospel—11:2-6, regarding whether or not Jesus would be understood by a questioning people to be the Messiah—I not only find it to be an exemplification of the key elements of the Beatitudes (insofar as it is based on Isaiah 61); I also find all the dynamics of Segundo's hermeneutic circle at work.

In the chapters preceding 11:2-6, Matthew has built the foundation and set the key building stones for his house of disciples. After rejecting society's temptation to live according to its ways (3:1-4:11), Jesus begins preaching the in-breaking of God's reign (4:17). Knowing that proclaiming this gospel would be considered subversive-unto-death, he immediately called disciples (4:18-22), who begin to witness him teaching "in their synagogues," preaching the *euaggelion* of God's reign and "curing every disease and every sickness among the people" in a way that begins to make him famous (4:24-25).

After contextualizing the Jesus phenomenon, Matthew shows how Jesus began teaching a new ethics in the Beatitudes (5:3-6) and the rest of the Sermon on the Mount (5:1-7:29) in a way of authority (*exousia*) that astounded his audience. From here he goes on to show how Jesus' deeds of power or *exousia* would meet the needs of broken people (8:1-9:38). In 10:1-11:1, however, Matthew shows that these forms of Jesus' *exousia* are to be extended into the life of the house churches. The life and ministries of the community of Jesus' time are to become those of any community living under *exousia* (28:18) and wisdom (see 28:20) until the end of the world.

The "works" that John had heard about while in prison (11:2) were not just Jesus' teaching and healing in the past. More importantly for Matthew, these works were those that the community was to perform (see 9:8). By placing questions and doubts in the attitudes of the disciples of John, Matthew seems to have made the Baptizer a type for those raising questions in his community. According to Eduard Schweizer, Matthew "wants to make the point that the same authority to perform miracles is also given to the community. Jesus' response to the disciples of the Baptist is thus also the response of the community to adherents of the Baptist in the period of the evangelist. Jesus' authority can still be seen at work in the Christian community. It answers all doubting questions."[46]

As I interpreted John the Baptist's search for authentic spirituality, his doubts offered an invitation for Matthew's questioning community to journey through its own hermeneutic circle; its own crisis of meaning. It parallels the spiritual journey we are invited to undertake when we begin to question and especially when the traditional understanding that has reinforced our political, economic, and religious worldview (including our understanding of God's own nature and ways) is shaken to its core. Consequently, the questions of John (which expressed the concerns of Matthew's community) can be seen as reflective of my questions and those of many concerned friends about the future of our lives in this church and culture.

In prison, John experienced the jarring shock of incarceration. The hermeneutic circle began. In this jarring experience he heard about "the works Christ [note to the reader: it is "Christ," not "Jesus"] was performing" (11:1). Examining these works against his previous theology, John then called into question everything about his previous worldview and method of evangelization. Had he done the right thing or was it all in vain? This represented his position at step two of the hermeneutic circle. Not willing to despair, he moves to the third level: he sends disciples to ask Jesus: "Are you 'He who is to come' [add: "to be with us"] or do we look for another" (11:3) to bring an answer to our doubts and alienation?

Jesus' response to John became Matthew's invitation to his community to reread the scriptures about the Messiah and to experience the third step of the hermeneutic circle. This other part of the third step invited a reexamination that might lead to a rediscovery of that authentic spirituality Jesus not only preached about but *brought* about: "Go back and report to John what you hear and see: the blind recover their sight, cripples walk, lepers are cured, the deaf hear, dead men are raised to life, and the poor have the good news preached to them" (11:4-5). The "poor" in this context are in the same category as those others having been restored to health: they are not just blind, crippled, deaf, and materially poor; they are marginalized from the "system" insofar as they are "sinners, those whose way of life has put them outside the pale of observant Judaism."[47]

On hearing these words wherein Jesus articulated his mission in terms of "the Christ," the community of Matthew, grounded in God's word, immediately would recall Isaiah 61. It would understand that Matthew's Jesus was saying to his disciples for all time: authentic spirituality must incarnate in concrete history the promise about the coming Messiah predicted by Isaiah 61. The fourth step of the hermeneutic circle is profession and the practice of the good news itself, especially insofar as it impacts those who are poor.

In many ways, the pericope of John in prison is central to Matthew's Gospel spirituality. To individuals and communities once quite sure about spirituality, Matthew showed that there could be but one authentic spirituality. Authentic biblical spirituality fulfills in the personal and communal biographies of people the theology of revelation itself. Jesus' spirituality fulfilled Isaiah's revelatory theology about how God would be with the people. Now Matthew's theology about Jesus offered the church a spirituality for all ages and places. Within the church of our era, our spirituality is called to manifest Matthew's theology about Jesus. This is the only spirituality the world has a right to expect from us (11:3).

How we make this "gospel" our own in the way we identify with the poor (11:6) in a world that will be blessed rather than scandalized (11:7) demands critical individual and communal discernment. While applications may differ, all of us are called to go through this hermeneutic circle, this cycle of meaning, if the scriptures are going to be fulfilled in us. As we do so within this wider circle of meaning, we often will find that we never stop having jarring experiences that will continually invite us to call into question even our most cherished convictions in order to have the gospel message of God's word be translated in our lives and, through us, into our world.

Just before the first edition of this book was published, I learned the truth of our need to pass continually through the hermeneutic circle. A few weeks before its release, I had three jarring experiences; all were connected to a high school that my province operated that was committed to bringing "good news to the poor." Just before Christmas, the thirty-eight-year-old heir apparent to the rector died suddenly in front of the staff who had gathered for a staff party. Three weeks later a friar committed to tutoring disadvantaged students was found dead in bed. Three weeks after that a popular freshman died of Reye's Syndrome. The accumulation of these jarring experiences led me to step 2: I called everything into question. I wondered if I believed anything, including that which was about to be published. I even wondered whether I should call Orbis and tell them to cancel the book.

At that point I realized my need to put into practice what I had written about the need to go through the hermeneutic circle when faced with such a crisis of faith. Recognizing these events had brought me to stage 2: calling into question everything (including my received ideas about God), I knew these events were inviting me to move into stage 3. I needed to examine the Word again. This led me to reread Matthew's Gospel from the beginning.

I got through the infancy narrative without any lights coming on. Jesus' baptism offered no more help. But then it happened at Jesus' temptation in the wilderness. It dawned on me that, as followers of Jesus, we in our province were being led by the Spirit into the desert. There we could play "God" as did the devil (4:3-9), trying to define how we were to submit to the dynamics of being in the wilderness of the unknown, with our lack of power in the face of such trying situations, or we could say to such forces that come from other "gospels" what Jesus did: "Away with you, Satan! For it is written, 'Worship the Lord your God, and serve only him'" (4:10).

This new understanding of the need to be totally abandoned to God alone demanded the parallel need to be free of those gods that can only drive us further into the wilderness. In embracing this God, I found a measure of peace. It did not make the problem go away; it just enabled me to realize that there are times we may be in the wilderness a lot longer than we would want. There the only question will be the one facing Jesus in the midst of Satan's temptations. Give in to them or remain faithful to the vision of what must be the gospel of God's reign: that God alone and the reign of that God only must we serve.

This brings us now to examine how this gets expressed in moving into the blessedness of becoming poor in spirit in such a way that God's reign will be ours.

CHAPTER TWO

Whose Is the Reign of God?

Many spiritual directors recommend reading the last part of the collected works of St. John of the Cross before the first part. They feel that the beginning books can be best understood in light of the final section. A parallel can be found as we try to develop a "spirituality of the Beatitudes." This is particularly true as we approach the first Beatitude. We can understand the first part better if we know what the last part means. Once we understand the last part of the first Beatitude—those whom "God rules," as Mark Allan Powell translates the text[1]—it is much easier to approach questions raised about those who are poor in spirit.

The image of the "kingdom of heaven" or the "reign of God" bookends the eight Beatitudes. Since Jesus came proclaiming the gospel of the reign of God (also meaning "the kingdom of heaven" or "eternal life" in Matthew), it can be concluded that the Beatitudes held together by these bookends explicate what it means to live in the church baptized into God's reign and what it means to live in our empires as citizens of another reign.

This chapter begins by considering the Matthean text to determine what it does not mean to be under the reign of God. Then I will investigate the cosmology about the "heavens" and the "reign of God" that colored the first audience of Matthew's Gospel and how this cosmology has changed with findings from contemporary science and astronomy. From there I will show how Matthew's approach to Jesus' proclamation of God's reign serves as a call to discipleship, a call to which we all must respond. After defining what it means for a person, community, and institution to live under God's reign by sharing in God's own power (*exousia*), this chapter will describe the central project of the society in which we live and its attempt to bring us under its reign. I will explain how this "reign" is diametrically opposed to the central project of God's reign as expressed in the parables. Consequently, we must choose which central dynamic will become the basis for our individual, interpersonal, and infrastructural lives. Living under the power/influence of one central project or "reign" will automatically put us at odds with the primary thrust of the other. Such a life demands ongoing personal, communal, and collective conversion.

What the Reign of God Is Not
in Matthew's Gospel

Matthew's favorite phrase indicating the reign of God is "kingdom of heaven" (*hē basileia tou ouranou*). While the meaning of the reign of God will be discussed more fully in the last chapter, we can say here that it exists personally in Jesus (3:1-17; 4:17; 10:7; 11:2-6; 13:16-17) and his message (4:23; 9:25) as well as spatially in the community gathered in his name (18:20; 28:20). However, before examining how this reign of God must come on earth as it is in heaven (6:10), we need to be free of false notions about its presence and functioning.

A deeper examination of Matthew's Gospel makes it clear that God's reign cannot be limited to any specific institution or ideology, to any certain rules and regulations, or even to one dimension of spirituality (especially the inner grounding) without an external expression.

God's Reign Cannot Be Limited to Any One Institution and/or Ideology

The beginning years of the third millennium witnessed a never-to-be-expected surge in religious fundamentalism. This involved the effort of its proponents to destroy those perceived outside their "reign" or influence. Such a "reign" cannot be found in Matthew; God's reign cannot be limited to some kind of once-and-for-all participation in any specific ideology or institution. "Mark what I say," self-assured members of the community were warned. "Many will come from the east and the west and will find a place at the banquet in the kingdom of God with Abraham, Isaac, and Jacob, while the natural heirs of the kingdom will be driven out into the dark. Wailing will be heard there, and the grinding of teeth" (8:11-12).

Weeping and gnashing of teeth refer to the apocalyptic breakthrough of God's reign into concrete historical situations (13:42, 50; 22:13; 24:51; 25:30), criticizing those realities in light of the wisdom of God's word. While traditional exegesis presented the "natural heirs of the kingdom" as the Jews, recent scholarship has extended this passage to include those in the church. In a special way it referred to those leaders who think they are beyond criticism because of their position in the church. The fact that one is a Jew does not mean that one is automatically part of God's reign, Matthew's Jesus declares. But equally, membership in the church does not assure a place in the reign of God, even for a leader.

Matthew raises this theme about not identifying God's reign with any human reality in various places. Nowhere does he address it as strongly as in the parable of the tenants. He portrays a Jesus who makes it clear that the very one excluded from the kingdom, probably in the name of God (21:31), would be the first to enter it (21:42). "For this reason, I tell you, the kingdom of God will be taken away from you and given to a nation that will yield a rich harvest" (21:43). When we consider those who tend to limit God's reign to any one institution, it's good to know that people in the church or the Jewish community are not, by that fact, automatic heirs. Even though baptism and circumcision signify entrance into the community, remaining a full member of the community requires more. Matthew says that many different people not considered part of the community (8:11; cf. 2:1f.) will come within God's reign if they submit to the gospel. Often they will be members without realizing it (25:38, 44).

Many years ago, Alan McCoy, O.F.M., then president of the Conference of Major Superiors of Religious Men, displayed a visual representation of what the reign of God is not. He drew three interlocking circles, labeling them "world," "church," and "kingdom." Such a visual aid makes it clear for our church what Matthew was saying to his community: some in the world who are not official members in the church will be part of God's reign. In the same way, not everyone in the official church, including even those who make a great protestation of their faith (7:21), will share in God's final reign. Only those who perform wisdom's deeds of goodness will be recognized by the good God as those with spiritualities reflecting the divine goodness.

God's Reign Cannot Be Limited to Rules and Regulations

Another thing Matthew's Jesus disassociates from a simplistic identification with the reign of God involves our observance of rules and regulations, especially when they might be viewed as ends in themselves or where they fail to bring about authentic justice. Matthew's Jesus warns his followers: "Unless your righteousness exceeds that of the scribes and Pharisees, you will never enter the kingdom of heaven" (5:20).

The religious leaders incurring the retort of Matthew's Jesus stressed observance of God's law as a way of achieving community identity after the fall of Jerusalem. The law would help keep people faithful to Yahweh. In the process of articulating this goal, the leaders' zeal got out of hand. They were enslaving and binding the community to observe their own subjective interpretations of the law. These "laws" controlled others while protecting the leaders in power. As almost all of chapter 23 makes clear, Jesus saves his worst condemnation for those in authority who control others through self-serving legislation. While such interpretations definitely protect human power, positions, and prestige, they may have little to do with the true will of God.

In institutionalized Catholicism, through centuries of councils and catechisms, dogmas and decrees, norms and traditions, the leaders' power and ability to control were beyond question—until the pedophilia scandals of recent years. Until then, God's will was often equated with the will of humans who made the rules in what I call "the church of Matthew 16." Thus, when I was in college, the people in charge of the infrastructure that affected my life were part of my Capuchin religious institution in Indiana. During my senior year, I repeatedly asked to visit my father, who was slowly dying of heart disease. Repeatedly I was told: "It is God's will that you stay here. You can do more good for your father by obeying than in doing what you think is right." Paradoxically, at the same time, my Capuchin brother Dan was allowed to go home each month from our theologate in Wisconsin. Evidently, God had a change of mind somewhere around the Illinois border!

In such situations, authority is often buttressed by the subjective belief that it truly is articulating what God wants. Be that as it may, it still incurs the retort of Matthew's Jesus, who says: "Why do you break the commandment of God for the sake of your 'tradition'? For God said, 'Honor your father and your mother' . . ." (15:3-4).

Another example: the exclusion of women from the fullness of resource sharing in the Roman Catholic Church dishonors their dignity as images of God and is a stumbling block to church unity, and yet the push for change is resisted at almost every level of the patriarchal institution, including that of its ideology. Yet these "man-made" rules are seen as "God's will."

I experienced yet another example of this after the first edition of this book on the Beatitudes. I was commenting at a lay-run program at a Benedictine seminary. There a young monk challenged me about the "radical" ideas about God I discussed in the first edition of *Spirituality of the Beatitudes.*

"What radical ideas about God?" I asked as we met at the library of the seminary.

"You say God is neither male nor female. But the Trinity is constitutively patriarchal," he declared. "This has been revealed by Jesus Christ. He told us to call God 'Father' and he called himself 'Son of Man.'"

Why was this priest so angry? Why was he so defensive? Was it really because he was that convinced God was male? Or was it that, to preserve his place in a patriarchal church, God *had to be male?* Would it be the only way this male cleric could maintain his elite position in this sexist institution? Centuries of ideological reinforcement supported his network of beliefs. Yet, if he had analyzed the way dogmas about God's sexual identity had evolved to become ideology, he would have found that the only persons who had the power to make the declaration at such places as Chalcedon and Nicaea were males!

During his short pontificate in 1978, Pope John Paul I said that God is "more" mother than father.[2] Our angry priest would probably not agree with the pope's judgment. Undoubtedly this priest probably prayed daily for God's reign (which will have no such distinctions) to come on earth as it is in heaven (5:10). Why would he only remember that we are to call God "Father"? While differences, distinctions, and discrimination may be used to reinforce certain power relationships, Matthew's Jesus contends that they have little to do with God's true reign.

God's Reign Cannot Be Limited to One or the Other Dimension of Spirituality

As noted earlier, by the time the Gospel reached its final editing, one of two approaches seem to have prevailed regarding the way the early disciples of Jesus put his teachings into practice. The first group stressed what he *did* as the basis of their practice; the other concentrated on what he *taught.*

Matthew addressed the problem that arose in the community over these two viewpoints; we find him doing so at the end of his first and last discourses. Opting for the choice of those who chose to do God's will by putting Jesus' core teachings into practice (7:24-27), he has Jesus declare: "Not everyone who says to me, 'Lord, Lord,' will enter the kingdom of heaven, but only the one who does the will of my Father in heaven. On that day many will say to me, 'Lord, Lord, did we not prophesy in your name, and cast out demons in your name, and do many deeds of power in your name?' Then I will declare to them, 'I never knew you; go away from me, you evildoers'" (7:22-23). In other words, the charismatic gifts take second place to the practice of Jesus' teachings.

Prophecies, exorcisms, and miracles signify the reign of God breaking into the world (12:28). Yet these must be accompanied by a deeper sign: the witness of our lives committed to those in need. Without this witness, we can expect to hear: "I never knew you. Go away from me, you evildoers [*anomia*]!" (7:23). Evildoing here means not being involved in good-doing. Doing good is God's will, not just going to a prayer group seeking God's will or experiencing the various gifts.

Here and in other places in Matthew, there is no question about the authenticity of the prophecies, the exorcisms, or the miracles done in the name of Jesus. What is rejected is a spirituality that stresses charismatic activity to the exclusion of that obedience to God's will that must be translated in the work of justice (see 11:3ff.).

Yet invariably, when I have given retreats on the Beatitudes and speak about this way we can limit God's reign to the inner dimension of spirituality without translating Jesus' teachings into contemporary practice, I find some in the charismatic renewal get upset. They find it difficult to accept a critique of the ways many in the renewal limit the charismatic gifts to their own prayer group without an accompanying social concern.

In defense of those in the renewal who are trying to make the connection with social justice, I love telling the story of being part of a huge gathering of people in the renewal years ago. At a gathering of thousands of people in St. Louis, the Jesuit John Kavanaugh and I had been asked to offer comments concerning social justice. Quite a few of the leaders were skittish, not just about what we would say, but about the idea of linking social justice with the renewal. However, everything fell into place when a young woman on the team got a prophecy as we gathered for prayer before one of the events. She was led to Isaiah 58:6-10, which promised that the wounds of the hearers would be healed if they would be committed to heal the wounds of others.

"Maybe we need to hear God telling us," she wondered, "that we have been concentrating too much on our own hurts and needs. Maybe if we are concerned about the greater needs and hurts of others, our own wounds will be quickly healed."

Her prophecy became the turning point in the alleviation of many fears.

Paradoxically, the other time, aside from the end of the Sermon on the Mount, when people who consider themselves loyal disciples are rejected can be found in the Last Discourse. At what is popularly called the "Last Judgment" scene (26:1) those who sincerely call Jesus "Lord" as did the ones with the charismatic gifts (7:22) find themselves displaced in God's reign by those who may have never known who Jesus was but actually did the works (25:34-40) that defined him as God's anointed one (11:2-6). These are the just ones.

God's Heavenly Rule in Matthew's World;
God's Trinitarian Rule in Ours

In Matthew's time the cosmology ruling people's worldview as well as their understanding of God's heavenly reign was depicted by a flat world that stood on gigantic pillars (or huge turtles) at its corners. Above the earth were the "heavens," which contained the stars, the sun, and the moon. Beyond the firmament of these heavens was the heavenly dome. Periodically this dome would open to let down the upper waters in the form of rain, sleet, and snow. Beyond this was "heaven" or the "kingdom" of God.

In Matthew's world, the "kingdom of heaven" (3:2; 4:17; 5:3, 10, 19, 20; 7:21; 8:11; 10:7; 11:11, 12; 13:11, 24, 31, 33, 44, 45, 47, 52; 16:19; 18:1, 3, 4, 23; 19:12, 14, 23; 20:1; 22:2; 23:13; 25:1; see 6:33) was synonymous with the "kingdom of God" (12:28; 19:24; 21:31, 43). Whether it was the "kingdom of heaven" or the "kingdom of God," both were the places one entered (or was denied entrance) for "eternal life" (19:16, 19; 25:46). Thus "kingdom of heaven," "kingdom of God," and "eternal life" were/are synonymous. It was "into" such a place-defined reality that Elijah went (17:10, 11) only to return again (see 11:14; 16:14; 17:12; 27:49).

Besides these spatial notions connected to the place where God dwelt, Matthew portrays Jesus as proclaiming a gospel or "word of the kingdom" (13:19) that does not say it is of "heaven" or even of "God" (4:23; 9:35; 24:14). This kingdom, which Jesus prayed, taught, and lived as though it would come on earth as it was in heaven (6:10) seems to be in contrast to all the "kingdoms of the world" (4:8) with all their potential for violence (see 12:25; 24:7), especially that imperial reign centered in Rome. It is this notion that now has come to move our understanding of God's reign from a place to a presence, from somewhere specific to everywhere, from a kind of heavenly earth to a way of relating on earth as it is in heaven.

We have come to know the "heavens" as part of the Milky Way galaxy, which astronomers tell us came to be when an infinitesimal but highly compressed speck of matter exploded ten billion years ago into an ever-expanding cosmos that now holds one hundred billion galaxies, each having one hundred billion stars.[3] "Heaven" can no longer be found in a place; the kingdom of heaven where God rules must now be found in a fuller notion of what it means to "enter" or be part of God's reign. This is what the late Bishop Kenneth Untener alluded to in a talk in 2003, noting the need for a notion of God's reign that would account for the expected future of the universe.[4]

Today other words for God's *reign* are God's reality, actuality, presence, dynamic, being, force, strength, existence, subsistence, truth, life, energy, and power. Entering that reality and proclaiming its "gospel" now are the task of the disciple and those of Matthew's house of disciples constellated around Jesus, the Christ. Entering that reign demands that we come under its power, live in its power, and proclaim this power as the ultimate reign that rules the universe. Not only must everything in this universe reflect its maker; it must do so in a way that makes its various households of relationships a manifestation of the reign of God.

For Matthew's house churches, this meant that they must break from their understanding of God's presence with them in exclusivistic terms defined by blood ties and circumcision to one much more inclusive, grounded in a new understanding of God's universal reign at work in the world. That world was defined by the notion of limited good, in which, as Bruce Malina notes, "an individual, alone or with his family, can improve his social position only at the expense of others." That attitude finds an echo in today's language of "zero-sum economics."[5] Given the limited allocation of the earth's resources, any significant improvement among one family or kin would be "perceived not simply as a threat to other single individuals or families alone, but as a threat to all individuals and families within the community, be it village or city quarter."[6]

To mitigate this understanding of a world constituted by "limited good[s]," Malina notes, there arose "an informal principle of reciprocity, a sort of implicit, non-legal contractual obligation, unenforceable by any authority apart from one's sense of honor and shame."[7] General reciprocity or extreme solidarity involved the sharing of resources among household members without expectation of return. Balanced reciprocity, or *quid pro quo* exchanges, took place among neighbors who helped someone out knowing they could count on that person/group to help them when they were in need. Negative reciprocity, or extreme unsociability, demanded that one do to others what one would *not* have them do to you. Negative reciprocity involved hostility toward and warfare with non-kin or enemies.

When Jesus preached the dynamics of the "kingdom," he totally collapsed the second and third notions of reciprocity into the first: "You have heard that it was said, 'You shall love your neighbor and hate your enemy.' But I say to you, Love you enemies and pray for those who persecute you, so that you may be children of your Father in heaven: for he makes his sun rise on the evil and on the good, and sends rain on the righteous and on the unrighteous" (5:43-45). If all house ordering is to reflect the reign of God, then the limited notion of the *oikia* and the *oikonomia* demand that we live in the whole inhabited "world," or *oikoumenē*, as brothers and sisters. Now nobody can be excluded from this household. When someone is marginated or in poverty, the new reciprocity demands solidarity with them to alleviate their need. Such a way of being "kin" evidences that we are in the "kingdom" of God. The kingdom of God becomes the "kindom of God." For reasons such as this, reflecting our changed understanding of cosmology and science, I believe that we should now use the word "kindom of God" for "kingdom of God."[8] This approach is supported by one of my favorite Matthean scholars, Warren Carter. Given our new understandings of our world, he has argued for the need for "alternatives" in our way of thinking—"not just of language (e.g., 'kin-dom'), but of the very conceptual and metaphorical frameworks by which we imagine and verbalize God's salvific" presence in our world.[9]

Through the centuries we have come to understand the kindom of God's reign, reality, and power as the "trinity" that is at the heart of all being and must be reflected in everything. And, although this may not have been the trinity of Father, Son, and Holy Spirit of Matthew's Gospel (28:19) we know from a fuller understanding of the word of God that, indeed, it is. While Jane Schaberg has spent a whole volume discussing Matthew's approach to this "trinity,"[10] my approach to the trinity is more like the interpretation of the scriptures that has been articulated by Sandra Schneiders in her very helpful book *The Revelatory Text*: "Consequently, there is no such thing as *the* one correct interpretation of a text. Texts are susceptible of endless new interpretations as different interpreters, with different questions and different backgrounds, interrogate the text about its subject matter. There is also no one correct method or constellation of methods for interpreting a text."[11]

From this fuller understanding of interpreting what we mean by "God's reign," therefore, we can say that God's Trinity is the reign of God and that the reign of the Trinity is how God has designed to rule our universe. As a result, when we talk about the reality, actuality, presence, dynamic, being, force, strength, existence, subsistence, truth, life, energy, and power of God, we are talking about the reality, actuality, presence, dynamic, being, force, strength, existence, subsistence, truth, life, energy, and power of the trinity, which must be sustained in and reflected in all that is. It must ground and be at the height of all that is, it involves a trinity of persons in relationship with each other— a household (*oikonomia*), in which all resources are shared in a way that ensures a divine commonwealth. If this is God's reign, then everything in the universe must be ruled by this trinitarian dynamic, since everything in the universe exists because of its relationality.

Given our understanding of how the "heavens" are the "earth" and the smallest on the earth contains all the heavens, it follows that *oikia, oikonomia, oikoumenē*, and *oikologia* are all interconnected. From the perspective of faith, all are charged with the trinitarian presence of the reign or dynamic of the God we address in Jesus' prayer as "Father," realizing that any attempt to reduce this "Father" to the male dynamics of patriarchy undermines the integrity of all four households. Our ministry is about integrity—not buttressing patriarchy.

Thus, at the individual level of our own *oikia* and that of others, a more therapeutically oriented ministry of healing works to make sure that we are whole and healthy within ourselves. At the interpersonal level of life, in an *oikonomia* that defines our relationships, community must be stressed in ways that ensure reconciliation among all members. However, this reconciliation must be grounded in underlying dynamics of justice. Consequently, at the infrastructural level, if the underlying power is skewed so that one institution with its "isms" and ideology offers a counterwitness to the trinitarian reign of God's household, prophetic integrity demands that such power be challenged. The ultimate goal of all is to work toward ever-widening circles of compassion that bring more and more into unity, so that creation itself will find right relationships in the *oikologia* itself. The chart below describes how these areas interconnect.[12]

LEVELS OF WORLD	ECONOMY INVOLVED	MINISTRY EFFORT	AIM OF SPIRITUALITY
Individual	*Oikia*	Therapeutic	Healing
Interpersonal	*Oikonomia*	Community	Reconciliation
Infrastructural	*Oikoumenē*	Justice	Prophetic
Environmental	*Oikologia*	Union	Compassion

It is into this "whole world" that we must proclaim God's reign; every level of the universe must come under its domain. But we are not called to proclaim this gospel and live our spirituality on our own; we have been empowered to do so by our share in God's reign of *exousia* itself.

How Matthew Links God's Reign with *Exousia* in the House of Disciples

In no fewer than three places (4:23; 9:35; 11:1, 5), Jesus is portrayed as inaugurating the apocalyptic age in his teaching, preaching, and curing. All these are manifestations of the reign of God's power. At the heart of this reign was Jesus' exercise of that power in the form of *exousia*. The word appears ten times in Matthew.

Its first appearance is found at the end of the Sermon on the Mount: "Now when Jesus had finished saying these things, the crowds were astounded at his teaching, for he taught them as one having *exousia,* and not as their scribes" (7:28-29). He next shows it when the centurion acknowledges Jesus' authority as greater than his (see 8:9). After that Jesus heals a paralyzed man as well as forgives him his sins; both actions of healing are manifestations of his *exousia* (9:6). Aware that the "harvest" was plentiful but the laborers were "few," Jesus extended his power to "his twelve disciples" (10:1).

His own exercise of this power put Jesus in direct opposition to the "power" of the religious leaders. Thus we find the word *exousia* used four more times in one small section (21:23-27) after Jesus cleanses the temple.

In the ninth use of the word for "authority" we find it shared with the community of his house churches (9:8). Following the cure of the paralytic, Jesus showed that "the Son of Man has authority on earth to forgive sins" (9:6). Matthew shows Jesus doing the curing, yet the crowds "praised God for giving such authority to human beings" (9:8). According to James Reese,

> The comment of Matthew focuses attention not on the physical cure but on an ongoing expression of the authority of Jesus that was not limited to his earthly existence. . . . It portrays the wonder of the primitive community at sharing in the divine saving power of forgiving sin.[13]

It is true that Matthew does not explicitly state the transfer of authority until the final scene of his Gospel. Yet the organization and dynamism of his presentation tell readers that this transfer is uppermost in the intention of Matthew.

Earlier Matthew's Jesus summoned his twelve disciples to give "them authority to expel unclean spirits and to cure sickness and disease of every kind" (10:1). Now, on the mountain where he promised to be with his disciples and in the world through them, all who are baptized share in the authoritative presence of God by the same power of *exousia* (28:16, 18). God is with us in power! This is the reign that must always remain our "bottom line." It is the reign that must invite to conversion every power, at every level of the world, that fails to reflect the trinitarian reality of the Godhead.

God's *Exousia* Contrasted with Those
Who Make Their Authority Felt

If the trinitarian reign of God's power is manifest in *exousia*, it stands opposed to the forces of empire and religion intent on preserving and expanding their own forms of power. In the eyes of Matthew's Jesus, the power wielded by these forces of control—which makes its authority felt—could be found in various forms of imperial and/or ecclesiastical control (see 20:25; 10:16-18). The temptation of every disciple, then or now, is to be seduced and/or to succumb to the kind of abusive authority found in the reigns claiming imperial and infallible power rather than to come under God's rule. How does this happen?

In the United States we have witnessed, especially since the fall of the Berlin Wall, a kind of manifest destiny of unrestricted markets cloaking and justifying the ever-expanding power of the U.S. brand of capitalism. Despite the fact that the *Catechism of the Catholic Church* teaches that regulating the economy "solely by the law of the marketplace fails social justice,"[14] the average Christian and Catholic in the United States fails to see the contradiction. Indeed, as Edward M. Welch, professor in the School of Labor and Industrial Relations at Michigan State University, wrote in *America* in late 2003:

> It has become the accepted wisdom that government regulation is in itself bad and must be reduced in every possible way, that as many functions as possible should be taken away from government and turned over to for-profit businesses, and that the control of our society should be turned over to the forces of the marketplace. . . . Today we just assume that what is good for business will somehow result in good things for people.[15]

Even if the dynamics of the market-driven political economy might not always be good for *all people*, especially the poor, the average citizen (and, therefore, the average Christian and Catholic as well) somehow does not care. Despite the fact that Welch shows that the ever-increasing gap between the rich and the poor comes not from the poor being gouged but from the middle class being diminished, a high percentage of people do not care. They have been duped into believing either that they are in the upper echelons of the wealthy or that they will be there one day. A *Time* magazine survey found that 19 percent of people in the United States believe they already have incomes within the top 1 percent while another 20 percent believe they will be in the top 1 percent sooner or later.[16] The result of such thinking is a sclerosis of the heart that infects people at every level of life; by ideologically controlling the average individual and family in their thinking that they are "better off," the institution and its "isms" can remain unchecked. Despite the hard data showing the present form of globalization to be unjust, such people end up with ears to hear and eyes to see, but keep from acting on this information and accepting its consequences, because their "heart has grown dull" (Matt. 13:15).

When it comes to the *ekklēsia,* the same situation of hearts being dulled prevails. Here, however, as it was with the religious leaders of Jesus' day, it is not so much the hearts of the people, the *laos,* as those of the clerical group, especially its leaders. A classic case revolves around their willingness to ignore the cries of frustrated people in the pews and to see the declining numbers of thinking Catholics rather than consider having noncelibate men and women preside at the Eucharist. Despite the fact that there is nothing in the scriptures against women being ordained and in the face of the centuries of evidence of married people being priests, church leaders seem willing to destroy the church to preserve their patriarchal, celibate system. For this injustice rendered against the church I believe they incur not only the name "hypocrites" but the indictment that they might honor God with their lips, "but their hearts are far from me; in vain do they worship me, teaching human precepts as doctrines" (15:7-9). Donald Senior, a member of the Pontifical Biblical Commission, notes that these words cannot be limited to a "judgment on past generations of Israel's leaders, but to scorch false leadership in the *Christian* community."[17]

If the average citizens in the United States have developed hearts that are hard, what has hardened the hearts of our religious leaders in Catholicism to have moved in a direction that seems so "far from" Jesus and his evangelical vision? While false expectation may have driven the former, I believe it is fear that blinds our religious leaders today. To be controlled by fear or anxiety (*phobos*), Matthew's Jesus reminds us, is to keep one's self from the reign of God (6:25, 31-33).

Fear is a basic, if not the most primitive, human emotion; it involves our deepest needs of survival and security. In the patriarchal system known as Roman Catholic curialism and clericalism, fear is found at every level of those in its hierarchy. Everyone at the lower level is afraid of how the one above will use *his* power of control in ways that might deprive *him* of that security. Such dynamics, I have argued elsewhere, have revealed Roman Catholicism, in its organizational structure, to be addictive and abusive.[18] Both the addict and the abuser, whether an individual or an institution, are sustained by fear.

Anne Wilson Schaef, an expert on the addictive and abusive dynamics of dysfunctional systems, insists that "all of the characteristics" of such systems "are rooted in fear." She explains:

The illusion of control, crisis orientation, dishonesty, abnormal thinking processes, denial, dependency, negativism, defensiveness—each is born out of fear. When we do not know our own boundaries, when we perceive the world as either for or against us, when we never have enough of anything, we cannot help but be fearful. The only way we can hope to survive is by controlling what others think, do, and say, and minimizing their effect on us.[19]

Whether of the imperium or the religion, when addiction and abuse define the dynamics, hardness of heart will not be far behind. The consequence of the negative use of power in the addictive and abusive forms of domination and control, whether of politics and markets in the imperium or of women and laity in the *ekklēsia,* will be the eclipsing of God's reign by those who make their authority felt. Such dynamics demand conversion. However, given the hold on the mind (albeit illusionary) and the emotions (especially through fear), such a conversion will not be easy. It involves coming under a higher power; it demands that we choose to live under the power and reign of God and serve the purposes of God's rule or be given over to the control of the addictive and abusive powers of other "gods."

The Call to Conversion:
Seeking, Finding, Selling, and Buying

"To serve" or "to be given over to" in Greek is *douleuein* (6:24). The Latin word for addiction—*addicere*—means the same thing: "to be given over to" or to be "under the control of" a force outside oneself or one's group. One can tell what rules people's lives by discovering what they are "given over to"; this can be determined by discovering what preoccupies their hearts. Discovering this "treasure" will define where the heart of a person or group may be (6:21). Thus, after telling the people not to "worry about your life, what you will eat or what you will drink, or about your body, what you will wear" (6:25, 31), Matthew's Jesus invites his readers to seek first "the kingdom of God and his righteousness, and all these things will be given to you as well" (6:33). "Seeking first" to come under the reign of God implies conversion from other forces that can rule us, our groups, and our institutions.

The Matthean Jesus consistently links announcement of the kindom to the call for conversion of life: one must repent (4:17); one must sell all to purchase the kindom's pearl (13:45); one must let go of other treasures to buy the field in which the treasure of the kindom is buried (13:44); the dead must be abandoned for the way of life (8:22); entangling riches must be given away to free one for the way of discipleship (19:21).

In retreats I often ask participants: How many of you think conversion is easy? Invariably I get nervous laughs. In response I say in my limited Spanish: "*Depende*; it depends." Conversion from one rule to another, from being "given over to" one set of gods or ultimate authorities to the reign of God is all a matter of focus. If anyone knows this it is the advertisers.

Our whole market economy is based on the advertisers who seek new markets. When they find them, they begin their various forms of persuasion to get people to sell what they have (especially in money transactions) to buy the good or service the advertisers are promoting. Say we are looking for a certain item of clothing that we feel we need. When we find something on which we set our hearts, we are willing to buy it—if the price is right. Marketers have already done the research to determine the price.

The dynamic of conversion promoted by the marketers has created the "Wal-Martization" of our lives. We want to get something at the best quality for the cheapest price. So Wal-Mart satisfies this drive by giving us cheaper goods made in places that will pay the lowest wages. We join the poor going to Wal-Mart.[20] We get what we want for the cheapest price, not caring what this may be doing to the workers who made the goods as well as to the employees of Wal-Mart, who are continually blocked from organizing for higher wages. It becomes a vicious circle, but we continue to be caught in it because we have been given over to the marketers.

When I give retreats and workshops on conversion, after I establish the dynamic of coming under the reign of the market economy as defined by seeking and finding, selling and buying, I then ask someone to read the summary of all the parables in Matthew's Gospel (13:44-45). It describes the process of coming under the influence or power of God's reign. They read:

> The kingdom of heaven is like treasure hidden in a field, which someone found and hid; then in his joy he goes and sells all that he has and buys that field. Again, the kingdom of heaven is like a merchant in search of fine pearls; on finding one pearl of great value, he went and sold all that he had and bought it.

The people are shocked to realize the dynamic of conversion that gets us to go to Wal-Mart is the same as that demanded for us to enter the reign of God and to come under God's authority. Seeking and finding, selling and buying are the processes of conversion to the market economy or to the reign of God. Which becomes the object of our heart's desire will determine which force we are "given over to."

Continuing my invitation to my listeners to probe more deeply the dynamics involved in authentic conversion, I ask them to examine the stories of two people who have come into contact with Jesus: the man called young and rich and the man called "Peter."

Entering the Reign of God:
The Rich Young Man and Peter

The main character in the story of the rich young man is anonymous, a Matthean tactic to get the audience more "into the story." He "came to him and said, 'Teacher, what good deed must I do to have eternal life?'" (19:16). After Jesus makes an initial riposte typical of that honor/shame society, he tells him to "keep the commandments" (19:17). When the "young man said to him, 'I have kept all these; what do I still lack?' Jesus said to him, 'If you wish to be perfect, go, sell your possessions, and give the money to the poor, and you will have treasure in heaven; then come, follow me'" (19:20-21). At that we find the young man unable or unwilling to follow through on following Jesus. Why? Matthew tells us "he had many possessions" (19:22). After Jesus tells how "hard" it is "for a rich person to enter the kingdom of heaven" (19:23), "Peter said in reply, 'Look, we have left everything and followed you. What then will we have?'" (19:27).

In the persons of Peter and the rich young man we find two models of conversion revealing two different approaches to the process of seeking and finding, selling and buying. This can be diagrammed in the following way:

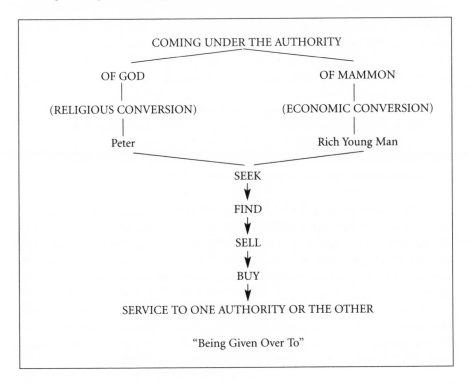

If Peter had been closed to seeking, he would never have been open to hear Jesus' invitation to follow him. In this sense Peter "sought" Jesus, as did the rich young man. Both "found" Jesus to be a significant power in their lives. However, the rich young man would not "sell" what he had "found." Peter would. Why?

Ultimately we discover that nobody sells anything unless it is for the sake of something perceived as more important, a greater "treasure," to use the image of Matthew's Jesus (6:21). When the rich young man was told that the way of perfection demanded "selling" what he possessed and reordering his household on behalf of the poor, "he went away grieving" (19:22).

The reason for the rich young man's departure, I am convinced, rested not on Matthew's rationale that "he had many possessions" (19:22) but on the fact that he treasured them more than discipleship with Jesus; he was "given over to them" more than he could imagine being "given over to" intimacy with Jesus. The young man's "many possessions" had some kind of addictive reign over him. Somehow the holding power of his possessions was more significant than the power of Jesus' way of discipleship.

Conversion implies a change of our heart's desire; a change of loyalty, a change of gods. It involves "selling" to "buy." But we will never "sell" unless what we have "found" is perceived to be better. The rich young man did not experience Jesus as better than his possessions. How else can one explain his inability to come under the influence of Jesus?

Coming under a Higher Power, Committing to a Nobler Rule

This process of entering God's reign will be impossible unless we go through each step of conversion from those forces that reign over us, our groups, our political economy, and our church. The process begins with seeking and finding, experiencing the living God in such a powerful way that God's authority is desired above all. Once embraced, God's trinitarian rule demands a reversal of any thinking or acting that does not reflect God's purposes. This is especially difficult if we are not poor.

Just as his community grappled with the contradictions of living gospel spirituality in an increasingly affluent and urbanized situation, Matthew's Jesus invites us to a solidarity with the poor that will bring about the reign of God in our lives in the way patterned on Jesus (11:2-6) and expressed in meeting others' needs (25:31-46). This demands a justice that will define our lives, not by our individual and institutional wants, but by the needs of those denied what they desire because of the way we "strive" for so many forms of wealth (6:32).

Matthew's Jesus was not willing to mitigate the demands of true biblical spirituality to win his contemporaries' favor. He alone, of all the Synoptic writers, used the word *teleios,* or "perfection," as the sign of authentic disci-pleship. In the culture of Matthew's day, *teleios* related to completing some goal, such as a race. For Matthew's Jesus, however, *teleios* was the goal of the spiritual life. Being perfect in the way God was/is perfect (5:48) demanded a reordering of one's personal, communal, and collective life in a way that would bring good news to the poor (19:21). Fidelity to such a way of perfec-tion promised everlasting life, participation in God's reign.

The first two of the three times Matthew used *teleios* can be found at the end of the antithesis statements, which challenged a purely legalistic approach to spirituality (5:21-47). Inviting his hearers to develop a spirituality that would set them apart from society, he presents Jesus issuing a new command that involves a cost: "In a word, you must be made perfect [*teleioi*] as your heavenly Father is perfect [*teleios*]" (5:48).

In the past, retreat directors and spiritual writers let us off the hook of costly discipleship by telling us, "We can't be as perfect as our heavenly Father is perfect; that isn't what the passage means." However, contemporary exege-sis indicates that Jesus was not asking the impossible when he issued this evangelical command. It also shows that this passage does not allow us to think that we can enter some sort of once-and-for-all state of perfection set-ting us apart from our society. Matthew shows that our share in the perfec-tion of God is both possibility and process.

First of all, it is possible to be made perfect in the way that God is perfect, especially when we are convinced that, as Jesus tried to convince Peter and his compatriots, "for God all things are possible" (19:26). God's plan for perfec-tion assumes that everyone is an image of God able to share in the earth's resources. Whoever lives under this authority of God's reign is also "made perfect" in the way of the trinitarian God. Becoming perfect as God is perfect is impossible on our own. Sharing in the *exousia* of God's Spirit, who makes all things possible, enables Jesus' words to become a realizable goal.

Second, Matthew showed that *teleios* reflects that process by which we can become people living in God's reign. Within such a dynamic we are able to reflect, as closely as possible, God's presence, reign, and perfection within an affluent society. Jesus addresses the young man with many possessions: "If you wish to be perfect [*teleios*], go, sell your possessions, and give the money to the poor, and you will have treasure in heaven; then come, follow me" (19:21).

Just as the underlying dynamics of the market economy are driven by the process of seeking and finding, selling and buying, and just as the parables reveal that the same process is demanded in order to come under the rule of God, so we find in Matthew a Jesus who directly counters the dynamic of society's reign with his own way of perfection. This too consists of seeking and finding, selling and buying. The only additional comment Matthew's Jesus makes to the young man (a symbol of the church as it grew in affluence) was the phrase about giving possessions to the poor.

Possessions, the wealth we have in the form of power, property, and prestige, are to be used to reverse those conditions of poverty in the world that most contradict the breaking in of the reign of God. This contradiction denies God's image in the poor who lack resources. However, once this reversal takes place in converted hearts and converted communities, which have found the joy of living under a new authority, an automatic experience of God's reigning presence is revealed: "you will [*then*] have treasure in heaven" (19:21). Having treasure in heaven is predicated on making the good news of that reign come on earth in a way that will bring good news to the poor.

Aware that societal controls keep this essential requirement of authentic spirituality from occurring in our lives, Matthew's Jesus lets us know that he, too, realizes the problem we face. "Truly I tell you, it will be hard for a rich person [group or nation] to enter the kingdom of heaven" (19:23). To convert to God's reign is hard enough; to reorder our lives on behalf of the poor is even more difficult.

This became abundantly clear to me in 1979 when I watched a previously enthusiastic crowd in Yankee Stadium that had greeted Pope John Paul II. When he began talking about the responsibility of those who are rich toward the poor, the crowd became eerily silent. None rushed to applaud his challenge. In the United States, we are not accustomed to applying the scriptures to all levels of life, especially the structural arrangements that call for conversion. Yet this must be done, as the pope indicated: "Within the framework of your national institutions . . . you will also want to seek out the structural reasons which foster and cause the different forms of poverty in the world and in your own country."[21]

With great difficulty will the United States and the institutional Roman church enter the reign of God. We seem unable to give anything of our power, possessions, and prestige for the greater good. To such a degree we are not yet a people under God's reign despite our prayers for God to "bless America" and our teachings that say patriarchy in our church is "God's will." We have political leaders who regularly play the "God card" but never challenge our lifestyle; indeed we commit ourselves to preemptive strikes in order to preserve it. In our church we do not yet have enough leaders who, from the depth of their faith experience, can speak with authority and invite others to this costly commitment of discipleship. We have not yet sold very much. Those of us in leadership seem too much in need of power, possessions, and society's prestige. But into this very situation, into our communities and families, into our individual lives, Jesus' invitation again can offer us a new kind of security: "your heavenly Father knows that you need all these things. But strive first for the kingdom of God and his righteousness, and all these things will be given to you as well. So do not worry about tomorrow, for tomorrow will bring worries of its own" (6:32-34).

CHAPTER THREE

Blessed Are the Poor in Spirit

When I was writing the first edition of this book, I happened to be talking to someone very involved in liberation theology and social justice. I mentioned that I was developing a spirituality for First World Christians, using Matthew's Beatitudes. "Why Matthew's Beatitudes?" I was challenged. "Luke is much more concrete because he just says, 'Blessed are the poor.' When Matthew talks about being poor in spirit, it shows he's already begun to sell out to his situation."

My research over the years has convinced me that, far from selling out, Matthew makes demands on his house churches far beyond what one would expect. In this I am reminded of what I would say to a Capuchin liberation theologian from Central America: "It's a lot easier for you to preach 'good news' to those who are poor in your area than it is for me to preach 'good news' to the poor to a people who are prosperous."

While Luke blesses those (the "yous" of his audience) who were poor at that time, Matthew has a different version. He declares that God's rule will come to those who are "poor in spirit" (*ptōchoi tō pneumati* [5:3]). Unfortunately, the prevailing explanations of what the term means are, in my opinion, too often colored not only by the Lukan version, but they also reveal themselves deficient in understanding one of the fundamental components of spirituality itself.

If poverty is not an honor in the theology of Matthew's Jesus, being "poor in spirit" is precisely that; consequently, those who are poor in spirit will be honored in Matthew's house church as "blessed." Thus Eduard Schweizer notes:

Only to one who can hear the Beatitudes and hear in them his own lack do they make sense: such a person knows very well that being poor necessarily means being "poor in spirit." By his amendment of the phrase Matthew has made a most significant change—his version points out the danger of thinking that poverty is an honor. Poverty is not a virtue; it should no more be boasted about by the poor than despised (and upheld) by the rich. Matthew has been more insightful about what Jesus said than Luke, who merely translated Jesus' dictum literally into Greek. In Luke the statement becomes simply the legalism that in heaven all conditions are reversed, so that the poor become rich and the rich poor. Matthew, by contrast, has retained the point that this saying becomes true only when the mystery takes place that the Old Testament calls an event of the "Spirit."[1]

Unfortunately, most commentators are still locked into an interpretation of "poor in spirit" that sees it as a kind of "spiritualization" of Luke's Beatitude that blesses the "you" who are poor (economically and socially). Consequently this summary of all the Beatitudes and, therefore, spirituality, often is misunderstood. In an effort to address this problem, Hans Kvalbein, an international editor of *Themeleios,* did a thorough analysis of the current interpretations of the phrase and came up with three conclusions. These were contextualized from his effort to consider the text as part of the overall thrust of the First Gospel, rather than to look at the text in isolation. As a result he offers an excellent summary of what it means to be "poor in spirit." After discussing the current scholarship on the "blessedness" of those who are "poor in spirit," he concluded:

1. Poverty in the material and social sense of the word is *neither a hindrance nor a condition for salvation. . . .* Poverty is never idealized. It challenges us to relieve it and work for justice. Therefore the church cannot remain passive or neutral when fellow men suffer from poverty.
2. *Salvation is given to those who are poor in themselves.* Notice now that the word "poor" is used in a transferred sense. The kingdom of God can only be received by empty hands. Jesus warns against (a) worldly self-sufficiency: you trust yourself and your own resources and don't need God; (b) religious self-sufficiency: you trust your religious attitude and moral life and don't need Jesus.
3. *The people of God are sent to the poor, to suffering and oppressed fellow men.* The empty hands receiving salvation are not made lame! They are strengthened and filled to serve the neighbour, to meet his need for bread, health, social security, justice. (1 John 3:16-18).[2]

Following Kvalbein's tripartite approach, the first part of this chapter will elaborate on these three themes by showing (1) since poverty is not a value in Matthew's Gospel, being "poor in spirit" must be dissociated from the social condition called poverty; (2) being poor in spirit demands a recognition of our inner poverty as individuals and a people; (3) in a way that demands that we "do good" to those who are in need. From here I will argue that an analysis of the addictive and unjust dynamics expressed in the world in which we live demands that we create alternative communities to support this spirituality. I will suggest that the Twelve Steps identified with addressing addictions can be a contemporary model.

Dissociating "Poverty in Spirit" from Poverty in Matthew

Most commentators on Matthew's Gospel say that it was written for a Jewish audience. Though finally redacted in Greek, it was steeped in Hebrew thought processes, which did not separate body and spirit. Hebrews viewed the person in totality. The Hebrew mentality neither "spiritualized" nor "materialized," but united the two. While one or the other might be stressed at various times, the person's body and spirit were not in opposition but were somehow brought together in a unified whole.

Only later, under a more sophisticated Greek philosophy, were distinctions between body and soul, or body and spirit introduced. Reflecting the Hebrew influence, Matthew does not say that you can be poor in body and rich in spirit (but he does not deny it either). Neither does he say you can be rich externally as long as you are poor in spirit. Matthew presents at the core of his spirituality a God who lacks nothing. Thus, a lack of anything essential to life is a denial of the image of God. Poverty simply is not good. It is ungodly.

Matthew does not canonize the poor or poverty as ends in themselves. Neither are the rich or riches blessed. Being "poor in spirit" does not sanction poverty as a social condition. Neither is it an idealized state of life to be valued. Poverty never glorifies those who suffer its misery. Yet today we are saturated with simplistic clichés (often coming from those who have not directly experienced poverty and the poor): "Isn't that beautiful—the uncluttered life of the poor!" Or, "I wish I could be so carefree!"

There is nothing beautiful about poverty. It is miserable; just ask a street person here or a slum dweller next to a busy highway in Johannesburg, Manila, or São Paulo. Poverty elicits repulsion. We automatically resist and reject poverty. We create social programs to eliminate it.

A core reason we reject poverty involves something very deep in our psyches as well as in our understanding of the "rule" or "trinitarian reign of God." In itself, poverty denies the trinitarian nature of God. In the *oikonomia* of God there is no poverty; thus poverty in itself denies the perfection and goodness of God. God's goodness has always been revealed precisely in the elimination of those conditions that reflect poverty and need (Exod. 3:7-8).

Present poverty is not sanctioned for the sake of a future reward. Such a poor-now/rich-later approach is rejected by Matthew, especially in light of his extensive discussion of the final judgment (25:31-46). Here any future share in heaven is equated precisely with our ongoing effort to alleviate various forms of poverty. Furthermore, in no way does this Beatitude reinforce a concept that says it is God's will that there be poverty. On the contrary, poverty is a sign that God's plan is not being fulfilled; the authentic proclamation of the gospel demands that "good news" be brought to the poor (11:5; see 26:6-13). Therefore, if the proclamation of the "good news" of the reign of God is to have any impact on the world today, it has to be nurtured by people striving to reflect God's perfection (5:48) in a way that works to reverse the conditions of poverty (19:21).

In some earlier parts of scripture, poverty was viewed as the responsibility of the person who was poor. This attitude cannot be found in Matthew's Gospel. Jesus never judged how the poor and the outcasts, the prostitutes and the tax collectors, the lepers and the sinners, got that way—nor even why they remained that way (unless he addressed the structures that contributed to that condition [see 21:12-16]). He responded directly to them in their need. This unsettled the people who so easily could judge why the poor were poor. Jesus' attitude created consternation in the rich elite, who felt they had a right to reject the poor from their neighborhoods and communities, and even those places identified with God's presence (8:4).

People accustomed to a Lukan "spin" on Jesus (such as that promoted by Francis of Assisi) are surprised when I say that nowhere in Matthew's Gospel until 26:3ff. (which narrates the final days of Jesus) do we find Jesus poor, promoting poverty as a value, or inviting people to "leave all things" to be his disciples. A quick comparison of the two Gospels highlights their differences.

Luke identifies Zachary and Elizabeth, Joseph and Mary as members of the community of the poor, the *anawîm*. Conversely, Matthew's "account of the genealogy of Jesus the Messiah" (1:1) makes Jesus a member of the royal household. Whereas the Lukan Jesus, as a child, is found by the shepherds (a group living in poverty) in "a manger, because there was no place for them in the inn" (Luke 2:7), in Matthew, highly educated wisdom seekers find him not in a manger but in "the house" (*oikia*, 2:11).

In Matthew, when Peter is called to discipleship, he and Andrew "left their nets and followed him" (4:20), still allowing for Peter to keep his own *oikia*, wherein Jesus will later heal his mother-in-law (8:14-15). Because Luke will have Peter leave "everything" to follow Jesus (Luke 5:11), he has the healing of Peter's mother-in-law placed before Peter's call to discipleship (Luke 4:38).

Luke as well as Matthew tells the story of the scribe who approached Jesus saying: "Teacher, I will follow you wherever you go," with Jesus saying to him: "Foxes have holes, and birds of the air have nests; but the Son of Man has nowhere to lay his head" (Matt. 8:19-20; Luke 9:57-62). Yet it can be argued from Matthew that Jesus himself maintained a house in Capernaum (9:10, 28; 12:46; 13:1, 36; 17:25), that at no place do we read that Jesus or his disciples did not have a place to "rest their head," and that, finally, Jesus never demanded that those who followed him leave "everything" as does Luke (Luke 5:11; Matt. 4:18-22). Whereas Luke seems to make poverty an end in itself for the missionary journey, Matthew envisions a different kind of household (*oikonomia*). Here those sent need not take "gold, or silver, or copper" as well as "no bag for your journey, or two tunics, or sandals, or a staff" (Matt. 10:9-10a; Luke 9:3). There is no need in the Matthean *oikoumenē* for them to be so encumbered. His world is one where resources are not denied but shared. Thus, just as his evangelical workers share their resource of the "good news" of peace, so, in exchange, they will receive the food and shelter they need. In Matthew, such "laborers deserve their food" (10:10b); indeed, they have a right to it. Luke links the laborer deserving food in connection with entering the house (Luke 10:7).

Later in this chapter we will see how Matthew's story of the rich young man (not the rich ruler of Luke) does not find Jesus telling him to "sell all" he had and give it to the poor as in Luke 18:22, but only to "sell your possessions, and give the money to the poor" (19:21). We will also consider how, in Matthew, the woman who shares her alabaster jar of very expensive ointment is highlighted as the model of discipleship (26:6-13), in contrast to Luke's portrayal of the woman as a sinner (Luke 7:36-50).

Despite such data, some commentators on Matthew still view the Gospel through the lens of Luke, which blesses people for being poor and makes it a characteristic of "house honor" for Jesus' disciples to be poor. They still argue that Matthew added the phrase "in spirit" to "spiritualize" the notion.[3] This suggests that poverty is a value and that Matthew's rendering represents a kind of "watering down" that would mitigate any challenge to Matthew's more prosperous house churches.

If this is not what "poor in spirit" implies, how might we understand it? While the exact phrase "poor in spirit" does not occur in the Old Testament, it can be found in Qumran's *War Scroll.* In the context of the Qumran commentary, as well as Isaiah 61:1ff., those who are poor or broken in spirit are so because they are the ones who do good to others. Such persons constitute the just ones. They belong to Matthew's *anawîm,* that community of disciples dedicated to realizing God's will in their lives. In this sense Matthew's "poor in spirit" (*ptōchoi tō pneumati*) represent neither a particular social or economic class nor people suffering from actual physical want, but those disciples who hear Jesus' teaching about the will of God, understand its implications in the depths of their being and put it into practice by good deeds of justice toward the poor. Those who realize their own need to reorder their lives toward God and who dedicate their lives to working for a reordering of God's creation are poor in spirit. In the depth of their being, at the core of their lives, their lives bear witness to their wholehearted dedication to God, to God's will, and to God's work. Matthew's vision of the reign of God given to the "poor in spirit" is predicated on relationships and resources being ordered in a manner that fulfills God's plan. Any such group of persons dedicated to that will of God will inherit God's reign (6:10; 7:21). Given an understanding of the mentality behind Matthew's Gospel, we can say, then, that the poor in spirit are those who have turned their lives over to God and, in the power (*exousia*) of God, work for the fulfillment of justice on behalf of those who are poor.

From this perspective we discover two significant factors related to being "poor in spirit." First, by their knowledge of God's reign in their lives, the "poor in spirit" recognize their own need for God. Recognizing their dependence on God, they assume an attitude of abandonment; they trust in God's loving care to meet their needs. Second, by their awareness of the Spirit of the Lord given over to them (see 27:50), they accept their responsibility to image God by working to reorder creation. As images of that God who brought light out of darkness, they commit themselves to "do good" in a way that shows they are blessed (Gen. 1:1-2, 26-31). They commit themselves to cooperating with God in renewing God's household on the earth at all levels of life; in effect, they become "abandoned to God." The passive dimension of abandonment or being "poor in spirit" involves the admission of one's need before God; the active dimension recognizes God's need to use humans to continue the divine creative activity of bringing about the original order envisioned by God.

The Poor in Spirit as Those Who Turn Their Lives Over to God's Will

If being poor in spirit is not a "spiritualizing" of poverty but more a recognition of one's poverty and, therefore, dependence on God, how does one go about becoming "poor in spirit"? A first step comes to us from Isaiah 66:2 (which interprets the meaning of the poor who appeared earlier in his prophecy at 61:1).[4] It declares: "But this is the one to whom I will look, to the humble and contrite in spirit, who trembles at my word." If such a person is blessed (*makarios*), then it would follow that the greatest *skandalon* or stumbling block to the experience of being in God's reign or under God's rule would be spiritual pride. Such an attitude builds for oneself, one's group, one's nation or church, a separate "kingdom" instead of an inclusive kindom. In the name of God we make ourselves, our group, or this or that institution like God. This is our way of realizing the great promise of the serpent in Genesis: "you will be like God" (Gen. 3:5). When this happens, we put ourselves outside the reign of God's kindom. Why is this so?

First of all, the poor in spirit are those who acknowledge God as ultimate source of power, life, and meaning in their lives. Having found the pearl of great price, they reorder their personal, communal, and collective lives on behalf of the poor (13:44-46). With the possession of this pearl of great price, they gladly part with those things that offer them false security, all those things that the unbelievers of the world are running after, until their security is found elsewhere, in the reign of God's presence (6:32-33).

A corollary of recognizing, acquiescing to, and living under God's power as the ultimate source of meaning in one's life, is to "let go" of those forces that have controlled our hearts until now and turn our lives over to the rule of God. In traditional spirituality this "letting go" and "letting God" is called *kenōsis*. Grounded in Paul's Letter to the Philippians, those who are abandoned to God have "let the same mind be in them" that was in Christ Jesus, who, though he was in the form of God, did not regard equality with God as something to be exploited, but "emptied himself" (*kenōsis* [Phil. 2:5-7]). An examination of almost all the great spiritual disciplines from Christianity to Buddhism, from psychoanalysis to the Twelve Steps, will reveal the critical need for their adherents to go through this process of "letting go" in order to be transformed.

The Buddhists stress the elimination of desire while various Christian spiritualities call for the equivalent, whether in the "embrace of Lady Poverty" for us Franciscans, entering into *nada* or nothingness for the Carmelites, "renunciation" for the Josephites of the Medaille tradition, or "detachment" for Ignatian spirituality. Psychoanalysts like Freud and Jung talked about the need to get rid of the false self or persona, while Twelve Step spirituality has shown the utter necessity of "bottoming out" and recognizing a higher power if one will be free of the negative forces (addictions) that can control our lives. In seventeenth-century French spirituality this "letting go and letting God" was called "abandonment." It has its deepest roots in the person and message of Jesus.

The Servant Jesus' Disciples Abandoned to God's Will

Matthew was highly influenced by certain texts from the Hebrew Scriptures. The author of the First Gospel saw these fulfilled in the life of Jesus. Central to many of these passages were servant themes from Second and Third Isaiah as well as ones from the first eleven chapters of Isaiah (which were written in light of the exile). Here we find references to the one anointed with God's authority as the poor servant filled with the spirit becomes dominant (see Isa. 6:7f.; 11:2f.; 42:1f.; 49:3f.; 53:4f.; 61:1f.). Although Matthew refers directly to Jesus as servant, *pais,* only once (12:18), the above Isaian references show that Matthew presents Jesus as preeminently God's servant who is poor in spirit because he has let God's spirit pervade his being and guide his steps.

Totally given to God's rule in his life, Jesus became radically poor in the depth of his being. So oriented to God, Jesus desired above all to accomplish what had been revealed to him by the one he called his heavenly Father (11:25-27; 26:39, 42, 44). His life would become true worship because of this commitment. This would be done in a way that would fulfill the vision of a person (or group) under the power of the Spirit as envisioned in Isaiah 61. In a special way the opening verses of chapter 61 indicate what kind of spirituality results when this Spirit takes over in one's life and what the consequences will be in one's world:

> The spirit of the Lord God is upon me, because the Lord has
>   anointed me;
> he has sent me to bring good news to the oppressed,
> to bind up the brokenhearted,
> to proclaim liberty to the captives and release to the prisoners;
> to proclaim the year of the Lord's favor. . . . (Isa. 61:1-2a)

The sixty-first chapter of Isaiah, like many other passages written in this postexilic book, outlined the characteristics of a social group who were radically committed to God within an alien culture. These were called the *anawîm*. The majority of Matthean scholars today believe Matthew envisioned such a group when he had Jesus bless those who were "poor in spirit."[5]

The *anawîm* were constituted as a community of people who had their own experience of what we have called the hermeneutic circle. Something had happened in their world that had jarred them; this led them to feel alienated from the infrastructure of their society, including its traditional religious underpinnings. The result was a growing sense of separation from a religion whose ideology seemed to reinforce the infrastructure. As they reflected on God's word, they found that they were to allow its power to rule over them. Living in this "reign," the *anawîm* gathered with other like-minded people, forming basic communities of reflection and resistance. They saw themselves as a faithful remnant within a wider culture of infidelity.

When I was in the novitiate, one of the books that influenced me strongly and helped mold my spirituality at that time was Jean-Pierre de Caussade's *Abandonment to Divine Providence*. This eighteenth-century classic helped me feel affirmed at a point in my life when I most needed it. I discovered that history was like a book, with each person in history constituting a letter or a word, a period, or a semicolon. Being faithful to the "sacrament of the present moment" made me aware that I could fulfill God's will by being present to the sacrament in my daily life. How great, I thought, that we all have a role in history. God did care for me, so why was I not more trusting that God would remain such a God?

At that time, my understanding of abandonment was overly concentrated on a passive waiting on God to meet my needs (which were so psychologically strong that I cannot remember caring too much about the material needs of others). Now I have come to believe that authentic abandonment or poverty in spirit realizes that God is not "out there." God is "with us," inviting us to work actively as co-creators. This challenges us to totally dedicate ("turn over to God") our lives to accomplishing the divine plan in that part of history entrusted to us for the span of our life (6:27). We are to submit to its ethic in our life and proclaim it to our world. When we wholeheartedly allow this way to penetrate our being, we become poor in spirit, anointed with God's favor in a way that also empowers us to bring good news to the poor of our world.

If abandonment to God's will constitutes spiritual poverty, and if such abandonment reflects what is meant by being "poor in spirit," I believe we also need to probe Matthew further to find out, more concretely, how we can show that we are living under God's will in our world. We can ask further how this "will of God" is exemplified in Matthew's Gospel.

Faithful to the "two source" theory that grounds my reflections in this book, both Mark (3:35) and Luke (22:42) have only one place where they highlight the notion of the divine will. Matthew not only includes these in his Gospel (12:50; 26:39-44) but adds at least three more (6:10; 7:21 and 18:14; see 22:31). It stands to reason, then, that of all the Synoptics, Matthew will show a more developed understanding of what it means to be faithful to "God's will." As Benno Przybylski declares in his *Righteousness in Matthew and His World of Thought*: "Indeed, it must be concluded that for Matthew the terminology which expresses the essence of disciples is *doing the will of God*."[6]

The "Will of the Father" in Matthew

Unlike Luke's version of what has come to be called the "Lord's Prayer" or the "Our Father," Matthew's version beseeches God: "Your will be done, on earth as it is in heaven" (6:10). The second unique time we find the notion of God's will in Matthew occurs in the Matthean teaching on house order, which begins in 17:24-27 and continues through chapter 18. Therein, after noting how members of the household are to live in the wider society,[7] Matthew has Jesus ground all discipleship in avoiding would-be power-plays that would divide the members. These involve notions of being "the greatest" (18:1-5) or behaviors that would be stumbling blocks rather than blessings to the life of the community (18:6-9). From here he shows that such communities must be grounded in the dignity of each of their members. Then, after the story of the stray sheep (18:12-13), Jesus concludes: "So it is not the will of your Father in heaven that one of these little ones should be lost" (18:14). This stress on the need to affirm the least among the community is followed by a model for household correction of straying members (18:15-20).

The "little ones" who remain faithful to what Jesus has taught are true disciples. They have been faithful to Jesus' ways, more than the religious leaders who failed to do justice. It is they, not the leaders, who are fulfilling God's will. Doing this will of God is at the core of prayer and ministry. Thus, when Jesus offers a prayer to God, it serves Matthew's overall intent: "I thank you, Father, Lord of heaven and earth, because you have hidden these things from the wise and intelligent and have revealed them to infants; yes, Father, for such was your gracious will" (11:25-26).

The only other direct reference to "God's will" in Matthew involves the story Jesus tells his opponents, the leadership group of the "Judeans." In the section dealing with the conflict between their authority and his (20:17-23:39),[8] Matthew presents Jesus posing a riddle to those who had come to challenge his authority (21:23-27). He tells the story of a father with two sons to indicate which household was actually being more faithful to God—the Judean one which said it waited for the Messiah or the newly created community of disciples who came later:

> "What do you think? A man had two sons; he went to the first and said, 'Son, go and work in the vineyard today.' He answered, 'I will not'; but later he changed his mind and went. The father went to the second and said the same; and he answered, 'I go, sir'; but he did not go. Which of the two *did the will of his father*?" They said, "The first." Jesus said to them, "Truly I tell you, the tax collectors and the prostitutes are going into the kingdom of God ahead of you. For John came to you in the way of righteousness [*dikaiosynē*] and you did not believe him, but the tax collectors and the prostitutes believed him; and even after you saw it, you did not change your minds and believe him." (21:28-33)

Clearly "the heavenly father's will" is connected with "doing good" and with "justice." In fact, as Mary Ann Hinsdale reminds us, "In Matthew, those who practice 'righteousness' or 'do justice' [*dikaioi*] (cf. 25:34-46) are contrasted to the evildoers," as in the explanation of the parable of the weeds (cf. 13:41, 43)."[9] Such an identification is the only way, it seems to me, that we can adequately understand the famous story of the one called the *rich young man*.

The Poor in Spirit as Those Doing God's Will
by Doing Good

Matthew, alone among the Synoptics, virtually identifies God's will with doing good. Doing good deeds toward others (22:39) is the way of reinforcing God's image in others. In fact, doing good by sharing resources with those in need enables a person to become like the only one who is good (19:16f.)

and to reflect in the closest way possible the very perfection of God (19:21; cf. 5:48). Actively cooperating with God's plan for the world, the way of perfection demands that the needs of each person must be met. According to Gerhard von Rad, this "includes everything that a man, in his isolation, might need: wealth and honor (Prov. 8:18, 21), guidance and security in life (Prov. 1)."

When we respond to others in need by doing good toward them, God's blessing comes upon us. Since God is recognized only in such images of the divine goodness, doing good in this way enables us to be seen by God as images of the divine nature. Within this perspective we can best understand the classic last judgment scene of Matthew. The blessing of salvation for fidelity to God's plan is linked to care for those in need (25:31-46). By doing good to others God blesses us as good, as Godlike. By imaging God who does good, by doing good ourselves, we are called by God to a deeper experience of the blessing of divine life.

Besides linking God's will with "doing good," Matthew also shows its connection to other notions: bearing fruit, producing a rich harvest, and, especially, promoting justice. These five images are facets of God's reign.

As early as Isaiah 61, in speaking of how the Spirit would impact those upon whom it rested, the terms "poor" and "justice" were interconnected. With the Spirit of the Lord upon the Servant, the poor would be liberated and justice would reign. The *Psalms of Solomon* noted the connection between the reality of the poor and the demand for justice (*Pss. Sol.* 5:2, 11; 10:7; 15:1; 18:2). By the time of Qumran, the poor in spirit were described as those with knowledge of God who were committed to supporting the weak and broken. They were the just.

One way we reflect spiritual poverty is by our detachment toward the goods of the earth to which others can easily become addicted (6:19ff.). In this sense Thomas Hoyt writes: "It seems that Matthew's beatitudes emphasized the spiritual aspect of [poverty] and he applied it to a church which was wealthy. In effect, the members are told that if they preserve a spirit of detachment in relation to their goods and do not allow their wealth to choke off the vitality of God's word (Matt. 13:22), they can share in the kingdom."[10]

In order to be faithful to the "good" that God has desired us to do in the world, being "poor in spirit" demands that we challenge—nonviolently—those dynamics in the empire and *ekklēsia* that fail to promote justice. Unfortunately few scholars writing on the first part of the first Beatitude stress this activist dimension of what it means truly to embrace God's will by being a nonviolent force for change. One of them is Nathan Williams. He has written that those who are "truly poor, in the light of the First Beatitude, include all who renounce violence and trust God for their security." He adds that the Beatitude includes all those "willing to renounce violence for the sake of the Kingdom of God." He concludes that the Beatitude is fulfilled in those who renounce violence and trust in God for their security."[11] I would add that they also trust in God's presence with them when they work for justice on behalf of the poor. This calls us to examine more closely Matthew's "spin" on two stories found in his sources about implementing God's will by "doing good" to the poor: the story of the rich young man and that of the woman who washed the feet of Jesus in preparation for his burial.

The Story of the Rich Young Man

The story of the rich young man (19:16-22) begins with the originally anonymous person asking Jesus, "What good deed must I do to have eternal life?" (19:16). This question really revolves around the desire to do God's will. After first putting the man in his place, Jesus lets him know that "there is only one who is good" but that "if you wish to enter into life, keep the command-ments" (19:17). The man responds by asking which commandments these might be. At that Jesus takes some of the last seven of the ten commandments but adds another from the levitical Holiness Code (Lev. 19:18), namely, "Love your neighbor as yourself" (Matt. 19:18-19). Like many "good" people, the man said he had observed these laws. Yet he still sensed a "lack." Jesus told him if he wanted to go beyond mere religion and its codes, he'd have to develop a way of life based on an option for the poor.

The rich young man who did good but was unwilling to accept Jesus' invitation to begin walking on the path of spirituality, the way of perfection (19:21), went away sad; he was unable to be converted from his lifestyle. Unwilling to share his resources with the poor, he remained under the con-trol of the main obstacle (6:24) to that perfection demanded of disciples (5:48). The rich young man typifies everyone with wealth who refuses to be converted.

Noting the young man's inability to change his lifestyle, Matthew applied Jesus' saying to all those who refuse to share their wealth with those in need: "I assure you, only with difficulty will a rich man enter into the kingdom of God. I repeat what I said: it is easier for a camel to pass through a needle's eye than for a rich man to enter into the kingdom of God" (19:23-24).

As a youth, I often heard preachers say that Jesus did not really mean these words. It seems that Jerusalem had a narrow defensive gate called "Needle's Eye." Camels could pass through only in single file. Jesus, they said, was not condemning wealth; since it was a bit cumbersome, if not impossi-ble, for camels to get through the Needle's Eye, his words were more an admo-nition to be careful.

In the first place, the Needle's Eye was not built until the Crusades—if ever. Second, the members of the early community *did* seem to be having a problem justifying attempts to live under the ethic of the Gospel. They were becoming more prosperous, if not exactly rich. They realized that there were poor in society. They recognized a conflict. Those in the community who were becoming more well-off realized that they were to love their neighbor as themselves (22:39). "How," they must have asked themselves, "can we evidence the gospel when we live this way?"

In response, Matthew's Jesus did not offer an opiate, a religiosity that reinforced the lifestyle his contemporaries were running after (see 6:32). Rather, he faced head-on the basic human and psychological fact about the difficulty of having wealth.

Responding to the disciples' complete shock at his declaration about the difficulty of submitting their wealth to this reign of God (19:25), Matthew shows that Jesus makes it clear that he is not asking the impossible. First of all he declares that, with "God all things are possible" (19:26), meaning that, with God's rule in our lives, all other forces are relativized. Second, such a reordered way of living within our households holds wonderful promises:

> Truly I tell you, at the renewal of all things, when the Son of Man is seated on the throne of his glory, you who have followed me will also sit on the twelve thrones, judging the twelve tribes of Israel. And everyone who has left houses or brothers or sisters or father or mother or children or fields, for my name's sake, will receive a hundredfold, and will inherit eternal life. (19:28-29)

Here, as in the last judgment scene, Matthew again connects the themes of the throne of God, the Son of Man, the reversal that reorders the life of the poor, and God's dynamic reign, with the theme of the blessedness of everlasting life (25:31-46). All these themes have overtones of wisdom literature, which always relates to ordered life in society. Such an ordered life refers to a just and righteous relationship with God, neighbor, and this world.

Jesus invited the rich young man who had observed the commandments to "go further." Recalling the three levels of moral development noted in the preface, Jesus invited him to the third level of the moral life. He invited him to go beyond patterning his life on the commandments and codes but on God's holiness in a way that involved solidarity with the poor (see 5:48): "If you wish to be perfect, go, sell your possessions, and give the money to the poor, and you will have treasure in heaven; then come, follow me" (19:21). He could not do so.

The Story of the Woman with the Alabaster Jar Who Washed Jesus' Feet

Some chapters later Matthew highlights a woman who comes to Jesus who "does good." Since Jesus said her action represents the essence of the evangelical life, any discussion of evangelical spirituality is bogus if it does not proclaim, profess, and promote what she did. The text reads:

> Now while Jesus was at Bethany in the house [*oikia*] of Simon the leper, a woman came to him with an alabaster jar of very costly ointment, and she poured it on his head as he sat at the table. But when the disciples saw it, they were angry and said, "Why this waste? For this ointment could have been sold for a large sum, and the money given to the poor." But Jesus, aware of this, said to them, "Why do you trouble the woman? She has performed a good service [*ergon kalon*] for me. For you always have the poor with you, but you will not always have me. By pouring this ointment on my body she has prepared me for burial. Truly I tell you, wherever this good news [*euaggelion*] is proclaimed in the whole world, what she has done will be told in remembrance of her." (26:6-11)

Despite the fact that Matthew's Jesus said that "what the woman did" not only should be told in memory of her, but proclaimed "wherever this good news is proclaimed," I don't know if I have ever heard a sermon preached on the implications of her ministry to Jesus. Indeed, if, as we saw in the previous chapter, the "gospel of the reign of God" was the core of Jesus' preaching, then, "what she did" by sharing her resources is a model for all disciples at every level of life.

Maybe a key reason why we never hear such homilies (since only men can give them in the Roman church) revolves around the fact that Jesus said "what *she* has done will be told in remembrance of her." However, according to the scripture scholar Mary R. D'Angelo: "For Matthew, the woman's deed resonates on two levels. First, she enacts the title 'messiah' which plays such a major role in Matthew (1:1 [11:2-6]). Secondly, she enshrines the practice of justice in a work of mercy toward Jesus," thus fulfilling at least three of the Beatitudes. "This aspect of the story is often hidden by a mistranslation in Jesus' defense of the woman," she adds. "By translating the words *kalon ergon* as 'beautiful thing,' the older RSV caused Jesus to endorse devotion to his person above care for the poor [I would add that, by translating the words *kalon ergon* as "good service," the NRSV does basically the same!]. In fact, the words mean 'good work,' that is, charitable deed, work of loving-kindness or mercy."[12]

Even though the words of Jesus tell us what should be remembered about the story (i.e., "what she did"), the passage "The poor you will always have with you" (26:11) has been used more than any other text not only to justify poverty but to justify why none of us needs to do anything about it. It has also been used to excuse neutrality by so-called religions in face of the personal, interpersonal, and infrastructural stumbling blocks that often reinforce this situation to the benefit of the wealthy. As Jesus' own words indicate, the point of the story has little to do with the poor at all. Its purpose is meant, he said, to honor a person who shared her resources with another: "I assure you, wherever the good news is proclaimed throughout the world, what she did will be spoken of as her memorial" (26:13).

What did she do? We must begin by recalling the context of what she did. It was within a house (*oikia*), the basic unit of the world insofar as the "house," as we have seen, constituted the base of the imperial structure. Here, in light of Jesus' projected need (his need for anointing for his burial) "a woman came to him with an alabaster jar of very costly ointment, and she poured it on his head as he sat at the table" (26:7). That this action took place in the house is one thing; that it took place at "the table," which exemplified the whole social ordering of the household, reveals Matthew's Jesus blessing a whole new way of house order, of *oikonomia*: women will relate to men and resources will be shared with those in need.

Unable to recognize the fulfillment of the messianic texts in the action of the woman, the disciples protested. "But Jesus, aware of this, said to them, 'Why do you trouble the woman? She has performed the work of God by her good deed [*ergon kalon*].'" Matthew's unique choice of that phrase in describing the work of the woman echoes the work of God at the foundation of creation, the work that brought about the original blessing (Gen. 1:26-31). That is why "what she did" should be remembered, rather than what is remembered today: "you always have the poor with you" (26:11).

By referring to the poor being "with us," however, Jesus is not placing a value on the fact of poverty any more than when he commented on the weather (which we always have with us also [16:2])! To imply otherwise would be counter the way Jesus responded to the poor who were always with him, even when he might have tried to avoid them (14:13). On the contrary, he directly linked the legitimation of his spirituality with the way he ministered to the poor. This ministry evidenced God's reign in him and God's concern toward them (11:3-5); he declared that it would be the basis of judgment for those who followed him if they were to be blessed in a way that would find them in the reign of God (25:31-46).

Given this background, if the disciples are to follow Jesus, they must do what he did. In this way he will be with them. With the same *exousia* in us which motivated Jesus to minister to the poor, the disciples for all time are to do the works Jesus did (11:2). The poor's presence in the disciples' midst demands an ongoing reciprocal responsibility to bring good news to them in imitation of Jesus. Consequently, interpreting "the poor you will always have with you" (26:11) in the context of Jesus' whole ministry, we are justified in concluding that Jesus could have said: "I assure you, wherever the good news is proclaimed throughout the world, its first recipients will be the poor who will recognize in the disciples of Jesus those who share in my *exousia* by calling for a reversal of ideas and institutions which will restore the poor to wholeness!" To interpret 26:11 in any other way (especially to legitimize non-involvement on behalf of the poor) is to manipulate the text so that it becomes an ideological reinforcement of the social arrangements of injustice that keep the poor in misery.

Analyzing Social Structures and Cultural Addictions

In Matthew's Gospel, abandonment to God's will by doing good and being just toward the poor is neither passive nor romantic; sometimes, as in the case of the woman, it involves opening oneself to people supposedly steeped in piety. As the woman shows, such abandonment represents both a commitment to radical discipleship and a realization that this discipleship must be exercised in the face of a very powerful infrastructure that penetrates all aspects of our world. This form of abandonment, in fact, is the only realistic approach to take when we understand, with the 1971 Synod of Bishops, the implications of this infrastructure's power. Abandonment becomes a *sine qua non* for authentic gospel response (26:13), especially when we realize that the infrastructure is part of that whole world into which we are to bring the good news (28:19). If we fail to touch this part of the world, which affects more individuals and groups than any other, we can hardly say we have developed an attitude of abandonment to bring about God's will! At the synod, the bishops said that this infrastructure had created around our world "a network of domination" that resulted in its being "marked by the grave sin of social injustice."[13] They added that this situation called forth a demand for conversion.

Some might react to such an analysis of our world with an appeal to an old understanding of abandonment that supports a passive approach to doing God's will: "If God wants to do something about it, he will." However, the bishops make it clear that our current reality demands a new kind of abandonment which recognizes both our powerlessness and our responsibility to work as co-creators with God to affect this infrastructure, this network. The bishops show that the global penetration of social sin demands a form of active resistance against any network or infrastructure that denies the image of God in people and keeps the majority of people on our earth from sharing in the resources. They wrote: "In the face of the present-day situation of the world, marked as it is by the grave sin of injustice, we recognize both our responsibility and our inability to overcome it by our own strength. Such a situation urges us to listen with a humble and open heart to the word of God, as he shows us new paths toward action in the cause of justice in the world."[14]

With the Spirit as well as the *exousia* of that new order within us by baptism, our discipleship and embrace of the call to live the Beatitudes demand that we respond in that power to create new paths toward action that will promote justice in the world (see 3:15; 5:6, 10; 21:32). Yet, aware of the fact that we are "poor in spirit," with the bishops "we recognize both our responsibility and our inability to overcome it by our own strength." In their own way, it seems they are repeating the disciples' wonderment about whether anyone can be saved, since perfection demands a reordering of peoples' lives toward the poor by the promotion of justice (19:25).

Facing this challenge, we can do one of two things: be controlled by this network's authority and then despair, or admit its power and influence as addictive. If we follow the second path, we can move into our own personal and communal recovery or conversion and go through our own Twelve Steps, beginning with the realization that "for God all things are possible" (19:26).

The previous chapter showed that the cultural addictions controlling us are myriad: racism, sexism, heterosexism, ageism, elitism, clericalism, and nationalism to name only some. These social arrangements within our addictive institutions deny God's image in some persons precisely because they are not part of the group in power. These cultural addictions also control everything in the way earth's resources are exploited by our nation through its consumerism and materialism, economic imperialism, technologism, and militarism. This mode of operating creates a "network of domination, oppression, and abuses which stifle freedom" among persons and also keeps the allocation of resources from being shared more equitably. Furthermore these institutionalized "isms" are secured by an ideology promoted in our schools and media that seduces our hearts. This infrastructural "sin of the world," consequently constitutes the very fabric of our nation. The result of this is that all of us, in varying degrees, suffer from a cultural addiction that we have not personally created but for which we are responsible, according to the bishops. This demands conversion. This conversion demands that we "let go" of their force over us and come under the reign of God. However, this conversion demands the creation of alternative communities committed to becoming aware of how easy it is to come under the addictive dynamics of the infrastructure and choosing consciously to live under the power of God's reign.

Creating Beatitudinal Communities
to Challenge Cultural and Clerical Addictions

Many people become depressed when they consider this huge global reality and the very significant part the United States plays in its negative dynamics. Truly, as they consider the notion of inevitability that has come to canonize the U.S. brand of corporate capitalism, and as they seem more and more overwhelmed by the ongoing patriarchal clericalism of the celibates running the institutional church, they feel more and more powerless. In the face of such forces, I believe the only way we can be free of their addictive pathologies will be when we, as Christians, believe we have a greater power and do something to change their influence. Building on the previous chapter's discussion of the "world" in which we live, an alternative way of living in it as disciples can be found in the following model for those who would be "poor in spirit."

The pattern that God seems always to employ in the face of the systemic, infrastructural sin of the world is to gather people, with their unique gifts, into *community.* Thus, the first thing Jesus did upon rejecting the temptations of the Evil One was to call disciples to join him in bringing about his vision of the gospel in a world with another *euaggelion.* Within this community they began to read the reality of these alienations and addictions and to realize how they could take authority over them with the power of God's word within themselves. This is called *conscientization*. Monika Hellwig has shown that "conscientization" characterized the preaching of Jesus insofar as he continually treated all people, especially the marginated people, as having an inherent dignity. Unfortunately, as Hellwig notes, when people preach conscientization today, it can threaten the "notion of peace that is more akin to the *Pax Romana* than it is to the vision of the reign of God as Jesus preached it." Consequently, to find some kind of support in the face of the inevitable opposition from the infrastructure, this conscientization demands a call "to community solidarity, [and] the constant emphasis on the responsibility for one another's needs."[15] With the support of a trusting community, such a conscientization leads to an ongoing *conversion* that is intellectual, moral, and religious. This conversion admits that the analysis we have given thus far is basically correct, that this negative part of the infrastructure violates God's norms for the world. If we try to reorder this situation we can be assured that God will be with us. Despite this, it seems so hard for us who benefit from the "network" of social sin to change in a way that brings good news to the poor.

In early 1978, it occurred to me that I might be able to apply Alcoholics Anonymous's Twelve Steps to *cultural* addictions. Possibly the steps could be used in communities of conscientization to help the conversion process of people imprisoned by cultural addictions. Then, in 1989, I went into treatment myself in response to the destructive anger that arose in me when I thought of the way that the institutions were using powerful ideologies to justify and entrench their various "isms." Through this process I came to believe that what I had found necessary for my own recovery could be applied to communities dedicated to the same desire for conversion in their own personal and communal lives.[16]

In the past it has been the role of prophets and wisdom figures who found serious disorders in their societies to begin gathering disciples around them. Probably they did so for support in the face of impending persecution as well as to assure continuance of their message. There is significance in gathering regularly with people having similar problems. The Twelve Steps of dealing with addictions can become the agenda for communities of conscientization who seek conversion from their cultural addictions. Thus, whenever the community gathers with its gifts, it can operate from a model of reflection and mutual sharing, guided by the Twelve Steps, to deal with its enslavements. Addressing these newly recognized addictions through the power "of God as we understand" God through Matthew helps us to realize that we now have the tools to facilitate a conversion process that can be applicable to the whole infrastructure of our country as well as of our church.

Each basic community can develop, as does every AA group, the way the Twelve Steps might be discussed and implemented. In the first edition of *Spirituality of the Beatitudes*, I spent quite a few pages outlining an application of the Twelve Steps to the dynamics of households modeled on the Beatitudes. I will not do that here. Suffice it to say that, having gone through the first eleven steps, I know that it is not enough to create basic communities wherein we can celebrate our efforts to be freed from these addictions. We must move to the twelfth step, with the support of the basic communities of conscientization, to bring this message of conversion to others. Pope Paul VI said that the disorder in our world demands that we awaken consciences to the drama of misery our addictions create.[17] All those who strive to bring their lives to that order which reflects God's plan for the life of the world will hear the invitation to become poor in spirit. All those who are poor in spirit realize their obligation to make come on earth that reign of God that is in heaven (6:10).

A consequence of embracing the Twelve Steps to address our cultural and clerical addictions involves simple living, taking things "one day at a time" (6:34). Leaving all things for the sake of experiencing God's presence reorders one's attitude toward everything. It results in a blessing. Since the time of Seneca, worldly wisdom has said that there are but two ways you can make people happy: you add to their possessions or you subtract from their desires. We either strive for more and more or we reorder our covetousness based on new priorities: "Remember," Jesus warned, "where your treasure is, there your heart is also" (6:21). The spirituality of this first Beatitude, the foundation of all the Beatitudes which follow, gives evidence of how we determine and direct our deepest desire: to live in God's reign.

CHAPTER FOUR

Blessed Are Those Who Mourn;
They Will Be Comforted

Setting the Context: The Need for Hope
in the Midst of Despair

For years our television screens have shown people in the Middle East in huge demonstrations of mourning at the deaths of their loved ones and compatriots. We have become used to seeing people beating their breast, tearing their clothes, even gashing themselves. Such are the rituals of many people in that part of the world that gave rise to the Jesus phenomenon. The late Evelyn Mattern noted that "these and other actions are the expected behavior at funerals and recall the grieving for Joseph by his father Jacob who 'rent his clothes, put on sackcloth and mourned his son for a long time' (Gn 37:34)."[1]

The second Beatitude touches deeply the reality of death in all its various forms. Even more, it addresses all the death-dealing forces that undermine health in our lives and world. As such, it touches the human experience like no other. Consequently it also represents the fulfillment of more of humanity's hopes than any other. Probably no Beatitude more powerfully expresses Isaiah 61 than this bit of Jesus' wisdom. Insofar as Isaiah's theology was fulfilled in Jesus, so also is it to be realized for all time within the house of disciples. Like Jesus, all the members of the church are to become ministers of messianic restoration within the world. This ministry is to flow from that experience of *exousia* which empowers each member of the church to say with Jesus:

> The spirit of the Lord God is upon me, because the Lord has
>   anointed me;
> he has sent me to bring good news to the oppressed,
> to bind up the brokenhearted,
> to proclaim liberty to the captives, and release to the prisoners;
> to proclaim the year of the Lord's favor, and the day of vengeance
>   of our God;

to comfort [*parakalein*] all who mourn [*penthein*],
to provide for those who mourn in Zion,
to give them a garland instead of ashes,
the oil of gladness instead of mourning,
the mantle of praise instead of a faint spirit. (Isa. 61:1-3a)

It should be evident from the wording of this Beatitude that it can best be understood in light of the promises of global restoration promised in Isaiah 61:1-3a (and fulfilled by Jesus, according to 11:2-6). Far from being limited by the forces of pain that too often seem to control our lives and those of our loved ones, this passage depicts the promise of Jubilee, the "year of the Lord's favor," which proclaims that the pain of the world one day will be reversed. Because Isaiah 61 was addressed to Israel while it was still in its Babylonian exile, it foretold the day when the people living in darkness again would see light. As such it invites exiles of all time to live in hope.

Scripture scholars have not been united in trying to ascertain what "mourning" means in this passage, much less who the mourning ones might be, except to make some kind of link to the feelings of abandonment that accompanied Israel's exilic experience. While some think it refers to mourning over one's personal, group, or collective sinfulness, and others argue that it refers simply to people who are burdened, oppressed, and unhappy, Mark Allan Powell shows that there may be truth in both viewpoints. But, he adds, "In its most specific sense, *pentheō* refers to grief related to death or loss" in a way that also refers, more broadly, to "sorrow in general." At the same time, he notes that "they will be comforted" reflects a divine passive, meaning that God will act so they will mourn no more.[2] Hope is always on the horizon.

As we consider the promise of Isaiah 61, we find that so much in our lives—our relationships in family and community, our local churches and congregations, our dioceses and orders—points to mourning; too many of us who consider ourselves disciples of Jesus have a kind of listless spirit and depression. This listlessness and sense of alienation spell "mourning." Mourning continually touches all levels of life. Yet, at the same time, many people witness to the anointing they have experienced in their mourning. In turn, they are ministering consolation, healing, and restoration. In place of the listlessness, brokenness, alienation, and division that too often characterize the mainline churches and communities, people are bringing hope and comfort to the world and to the remnant communities they are creating.

When I give retreats on the Beatitudes and try to show how this Beatitude touches the human condition, I make a list of words under the heading "Mourn" and another list under "Comfort." Under "Mourn" I list those words found in Isaiah 61: oppression, brokenhearted, captive, prisoner, faint spirit. I do the same under "Comfort": good news, liberty, release, the year of favor, a garland, the oil of gladness, a mantle of praise. Then I ask the participants to recall times they have experienced mourning in themselves and/or around them. I ask them to reflect on these situations and then share aloud other words, feelings, and behaviors that describe what it means "to mourn." The column fills quickly with words like: sadness, pain, anger, resentment, rejection, hurt, tears, alienation, and loneliness. Then I do the same thing with what it means to experience "comfort." Their list includes words and emotions, rituals and behaviors such as: embrace, "being there," acceptance, understanding, touch, care, consolation, compassion, presence, laughter. Indeed it seems for every form of mourning there can be a comfort; such is the promise of Isaiah 61.

Jesus, the Compassionate Healer, Touching a Broken World

Matthew presents Jesus as the fulfillment of Isaiah 61 as well as this Beatitude. Jesus' very name points not only to his identity but to his mission as well. He is the one who will "save" the people from their "sins" (1:21). Since sin was popularly believed to be the cause of human suffering and disease, the sign that he could take away sin would be grounded in his healing power (9:6-8). In fact, in the very first cures of Jesus, we have examples of human beings who not only experienced suffering and/or mourning; all of them were "outsiders" considered unworthy and unclean. Therefore, according to the religious system of the time, not only were they society's "untouchables"; the religious system considered them outside the reign of God.

The second "book" of Matthew's Gospel (8:1-11:1) begins with the narrative about powerful manifestations of the *exousia* (8:1-9:38) carrying forward the theme that had previously expressed itself in Jesus' teaching "with authority" (7:29). Here *exousia* is manifest in Jesus' healing (*katharizein*), which begins with one of the most ostracized persons in that society: the untouchable leper (8:1-4).

John Pilch has studied extensively the various degrees of pathology in the Mediterranean world. His study of leprosy in the Bible has led him to conclude that the man's "irregularity was not Hansen's disease but more like psoriasis . . . the concern of the community was not 'public health' but social integrity, community holiness—an obvious and major concern in a society where kinship is a formal institution."[3] The fact that I myself suffer from psoriasis—meaning that had I been living at the time of Jesus in that culture, I would have been labeled an "untouchable"—has had a powerful effect on me. The fact that Jesus *chose* to intervene in this man's life by stretching out his hand, touching him (which, in that society, automatically made Jesus "untouchable"), and saying, "Be made clean [*katharizein*]!"(8:3) has had an even more significant impact on my life and understanding of the phenomenon of Jesus.

The second of Matthew's triad of healings (8:5-13) is found when a centurion stationed in his hometown "came to him, appealing to him and saying, 'Lord my servant is lying at home paralyzed, in terrible distress'" (8:5-6). By calling Jesus "Lord," this representative of the imperial, occupying power acknowledges Jesus' higher power (*exousia*; see 8:9). This power in him enables Jesus to respond: "I will come and cure [*therapeuein*] him" (8:7). While the centurion seems ready to jeopardize his entire career by publicly testifying to his faith in Jesus, his witness is juxtaposed with the Israelites in a way that shows he has been restored to right relationship with God "while the heirs of the kingdom will be thrown into the outer darkness, where there will be weeping and gnashing of teeth" (8:12).

The third of Jesus' first miracles in Matthew's narration comes with Jesus healing Peter's mother-in-law (8:14-15). Again another "unclean one," a woman who has a fever, is "touched" by Jesus. This first triad of miracles (8:1-15) is brought to a conclusion by another one of the "fulfillment" passages so typical of the First Gospel: "That evening they brought to him many who were possessed with demons; and he cast out the spirits with a word, and cured [*therapeuein*] all who were sick [*kakōs*]. This was to fulfill what had been spoken through the prophet Isaiah, 'he took our infirmities [*asthenēs*] and bore our diseases [*nosos*]'" (8:16-17).

In the Mediterranean world of Matthew's Gospel, "infirmities" and "diseases" were part of a multilayered taxonomy of pathology. It was a world where invalids were invalidated by society as "sinners." The first level of infirmity and disease (i.e., the individual) involves the disease in itself, the problem in the body. This is *nosos* (4:23, 24; 8:17; 9:35; 10:1); it asks, Where does it hurt? The second level of the infirmities and disease borne by Jesus is communal. Pathology here is called "illness" (*kakōs* [21:41; 24:48]). This involves some kind of break in familial relationships. It asks, Who is to blame? The third level is infrastructural or societal. Here one's "infirmity" (*malakia* [4:23; 9:35; 10:1; see 11:8]) involves removal from society to keep it "well." In the New Testament world such people were considered to be "unclean."

Just as there were in that culture "three degrees of separation" from society, represented by the various pathologies, so there were three levels of restoration that paralleled these forms of alienation: diseases cured, illnesses healed, and people (and society) made well. Consequently, the *nosoi*, or sick ones, were cured (*therapeuein*); those who were ill or wretched were healed (*therapeuein* as well); and, most importantly, those who had been defined as "unclean," such as the leper, were cleansed or purified [*katharizein*] so that they could be restored to society. Thus Jesus' telling the cleansed leper to "show yourself to the priest" (8:4) meant that now he would be officially able to rejoin his household and society.

The chart below, while not slavish to the Greek words in Matthew that classified diseases "of every kind," highlights the interplay of the relational dynamics that took place when someone was diseased and then made whole:

LEVELS OF BEING (AN) INVALID(ATED)	LEVELS OF BEING MADE WHOLE
Sickness (*nosos*): Where does it hurt? Illness (*kakōs*): Who is to blame? Infirmity (*malakia*): How does it affect society?	Cure (*therapeuein*): the symptoms are gone. Healing (*therapeuein*): being made well. Cleansed (*kathariein*): restored to well-being in society.

When Matthew says that Jesus "cured *all* who were sick," "all" encompasses not just individuals like the leper, the servant of the centurion, and Peter's nameless mother-in-law. In light of Pilch's insight, "all" also includes everyone, every group, and every institution to the degree they have succumbed not just to the various forms of disease, illness, and sickness but to the authority of powers that are not of God. Furthermore, the fact that Jesus, in fulfillment of the text from Isaiah, *took* "our infirmities" upon himself and *bore* "our disease" represents Matthew's way of portraying Jesus as having the power to enable everyone in the world to overcome their underlying alienations—from themselves, from each other, from their institutions, as well as from God. In the way Matthew presents Jesus, the "taking" and "bearing" of these commonly known forms of sin upon himself enabled him to break their power over human life.

In embracing the world's brokenness and mourning (8:17) Jesus was able to cure all who were still under the authority (8:16) of alienation. In taking all the forms of alienation of the world upon himself, rather than running from them, Jesus redeemed and healed them. This salvation from sin in all its forms opened the possibility for all people to be restored to the original goodness intended for them by God. The fact that Matthew's Jesus exercised a new authority over the power and control of chaos evidences God's reign breaking into the world. Bringing the comfort of God's restoration (Isaiah 40) to all people and nations is the key to Matthew's Gospel of the in-breaking of God's rule and order.

Healing was at the core of Matthew's theology of Jesus. Since his christology was inexorably shaped by his ecclesiology, Matthew immediately connects 4:23-25 and 9:35-37 (and later 11:1, 5) with the disciples and the whole church. He shows how Jesus summoned the twelve disciples (10:1) and the whole church (28:16), empowering them with his authority that they might continue his ministry. The silence about Jesus teaching and preaching after 11:1 seems to indicate that the church's ministry of healing was considered part of the "authority to expel unclean spirits, and to cure sickness and disease of every kind" (10:1).

In light of Matthew's further discussion (see 9:8; 11:25-27), the whole community shares this power too. As we see people who are in need and who are broken, we too can hear their prayers and cries of complaint. In the power of God's reign, we too can heal sicknesses and diseases of every kind: internal and external, as well as personal, communal, and organizational. In Jesus' name and with Jesus' *exousia* we can stretch out our hands, touch that pain in all the ways it may be manifested, and say, "I do will it. Be cured" (8:3a).

In the Greek, Jesus' response to the leper's call for healing reflects an almost natural disposition of availability that is triggered by anyone in need. "I do will it" means "I am inclined." When we say "I am inclined," it means something within us makes us act or think the way we do. God's power within Jesus disposed him, by nature and by name, to save the people from their needs, to heal them of their infirmities.

What are our infirmities that he bore? Our brokenness and tears, our anxiety and guilt, our experience of rejection and separation, as well as our loneliness and depression. What are our sufferings that he endured? Our alienation and grief, our anger and fear, our experience of pain and disappointment, as well as our sadness and, even, our death.

Similarly, the comfort Jesus offers comes in the unity and joy, the security and peace, the experience of acceptance and restoration, as well as the new sense of meaning and enthusiasm that comes in a new, risen life. What is this healing he promises? It is the reconciliation and warmth, the comfort and consolation, the experience of tenderness and compassion, as well as the understanding and love that come in a loving, caring relationship. If Jesus bore our infirmities and sufferings, it was to bring wholeness and healing. The same mission is ours.

Denial and Hardness of Heart:
The Stumbling Blocks to Mourning

In the first chapter, I showed that Matthew's use of the word for "blessed" is *makarios*. I have translated this as "honorable." Unlike Luke's "woe" (*ouai*), the antonym for *makarios* is *skandalon*, or "that which is a stumbling block" to healthy community life. Thus, in considering this Beatitude that blesses or honors those "who mourn" with "comfort," it becomes clear that the great stumbling blocks to the consolation that is identified with being "comforted" revolve around dynamics of denial and delusion, psychic numbing, and biblical "hardness of heart."

One of the most significant insights from Elisabeth Kübler-Ross's study of death and dying is that denial keeps the process from moving into some kind of resolution.[4] Similarly, any grief therapist will tell us that denial constitutes the biggest stumbling block in the grief process. Any corporate executive who fails to address falling market share will be fired for incompetence. Yet, when it comes to addressing the areas of death that face us individually, communally, and collectively (in our nation and church), forms of denial and corporate amnesia can keep us from admitting the "exact nature" of the disease that infects us and, even more, from taking the steps that will "deliver us" from its hold on our lives.

The Israelites learned this wisdom well; hence, they seemed open to enter into mourning when they knew it could bring about their liberation. In this light, Walter Brueggemann shows that, far from being in denial about their failings and sins, the Israelites believed that these sins contributed to their economic and social suffering. He notes that the heart of Old Testament spirituality is the embrace of pain.[5] Only by accepting the pain could the Israelites address its causes. Only in admitting the causes of their suffering could they authentically proceed on the path of restoration.

When we reflect on the psyche of our nation, especially after attacks of September 11, 2001, a kind of fear-based hardness of heart seems to characterize the resistance of many Americans to admitting that we ought to change in any way institutionally (from our corporate approach to globalization to our unilateralism, to our resistance to submitting to the World Court, to our willingness to strike preemptively anywhere when we perceive "our interests" threatened).

Similarly, during the two very public rounds of pedophilia allegations in the Catholic Church in the United States, one of the main sources of scandal was not merely the numbers of priests who abused their power in a way that resulted in the sexual molestation of children; neither was it the cover-ups and secrecy that shrouded such behavior by members of the hierarchy. Rather, what created tremendous anger on the part of educated people in the pews was the cavalier way many bishops refused to consider the destructive dynamics that were part and parcel of their *modus operandi*. Denial keeps individual addicts and addictive systems from recovery. Until they are able to admit the exact nature of what is wrong, the dynamics of death will control them.

If denial is debilitating to the possibility of experiencing mourning, delusion is the biggest stumbling block to the blessing that Jesus promises to those who mourn. Delusion occurs when we become so self- and group-identified that we believe the "lie" to be "the truth." When this attitude is joined with a sense of God being "on our side," we become righteous in a way that keeps us from recovery. Indeed, facing such attitudes himself, Jesus showed that nothing can be done to bring about healing when this occurs. Thus to the Pharisees who challenged him for eating "with tax collectors and sinners" (9:11), Jesus responded: "Those who are well have no need of a physician, but those who are sick. Go and learn what this means, 'I desire mercy, not sacrifice.' For I have come to call not the righteous but sinners" (9:12-13).

I learned the truth of Jesus' words the hard way some years ago. I had been trying not to sin consciously and to pursue "the truth" rigorously. In the process I came to believe that I was no longer sinning. Furthermore, I honestly believed I possessed the truth. Then I heard Janet Sullivan, a Franciscan Sister from Allegheny, New York. At a workshop I attended she facetiously said: "We have come a long way when we no longer think we need a savior." If I wasn't sinning and possessed the truth, I didn't need any help, much less a savior. It was then I realized how sick I had become.

My own experience makes me very frightened of people of any nation or religion who believe they have "God on their side" and that they possess the truth. Such people and "group think" can create tremendous damage, even commiting acts of terrorism toward others, thinking they are and will be blessed by God. This pharisaical attitude incurred Jesus' greatest rejection.

Mourning and Comfort in Our Individual Lives

Far from denying the mourning that Jesus experienced, Matthew shows him entering into this Beatitude in his own individual life. At the beginning of his public life, because he allowed himself to experience the temptation and mourning symbolized by the desert, Jesus received the comfort of angels (4:11). This experience has led me to believe that we will never experience the angel of comfort until we can enter into the mourning.

In the garden of Gethsemane, Jesus voiced the depth of his hurt when he told his disciples, "My heart is nearly broken with sorrow" (26:38). The disciples' unconcern and inability to grasp his pain, despite earlier professions of care (26:31-35), failed to bring any comfort in his mourning. Comfort would come to Jesus only in his understanding that he had been faithful to God's plan by trying to heal a broken world. "My Father, if this cannot pass me by without my drinking it, your will be done!" (26:42). His next address to the one he called "Father" came in the outburst of despair he proclaimed at his impending death. "About three o'clock Jesus cried with a loud voice, 'Eli, Eli, lema sabachtani?' that is, 'My God, my God, why have you forsaken me?'" (27:46). Finally, when "he breathed his last," he again "cried out" (27:50).

The fact that Jesus would "cry out" and "cry with a loud voice" seems to represent more the traditional lament in the face of death than any self-pitying. In this Jesus reflected the pattern of the deepest form of lamentation: a protest at all the negative forces that are connected with innocent dying. According to Bruce Malina the mourning/weeping correlation refers to behavior that recognizes and protests evil and injustice and the need to work for a reversal of some present form of oppression. "Matthew discovers the evil requiring mourning behavior as the lack of righteousness, that is, proper interpersonal relations in the social body. Mourning/weeping behavior points to evil within the boundaries of the social body."[6] Thus, Matthew's image of Jesus is that of the person who fulfilled this Beatitude of bringing comfort to those who mourned, healing to those who were afflicted in a generation gone astray.

Matthew's portrayal of Jesus' witnessing to the power and the promise of this Beatitude invites us to acknowledge our own personal brokenness, including that sense of separation from God that comes to us when we admit our own sin and selfishness. In my life, this demanded sensitivity to the areas that excluded God. While not actually "sinning" all that much, I sensed that a deeper form of alienation had me under its power. This gnawing in me was reinforced by a prayer that came to my lips with growing frequency. It paralleled David's prayer in Psalm 51: "From my inmost sin, O Lord, deliver me." More and more I was becoming increasingly conscious that this inmost sin did not really refer to what I was or was not doing externally. It referred to that part of my life where I had not allowed God to rule. My real self was alienated from the other, from God.

External sins did not matter that much to Jesus, although he brought healing to them. What did concern Jesus was how they might reveal a deeper sinfulness in the heart. It would be there that God could not be found; it was from here, the heart (*kardia*), that "evil designs" (15:19) came forth. My *kardia,* or heart, was the center of my life; if God was not its treasure (see 6:21), to that degree I would be alienated from God.

The more I reflected on the roots of my underlying separation from God, the more I found all sorts and forms of curiosities and fantasies, questions and doubts. The more I reflected on these roots, the more I realized that they could be given the traditional names of the capital, or underlying, sins: envy, avarice, lust, sloth, jealousy, gluttony, and anger. Furthermore, as I reflected on my life, I had to admit that, within my depths, several of these underlying attitudes were deeply affecting my drives, my wonderings, and my preoccupations.

I was becoming increasingly aware that as long as I was refusing to deal with these underlying areas of my life, these "inmost sins," what Jesus said to his disciples would be totally applicable to me: "The eye is the lamp of the body. So, if your eye is healthy, your whole body will be full of light; but if your eye is unhealthy, your whole body will be full of darkness. If then the light in you is darkness, how great is the darkness. No one can serve two masters; for a slave will either hate the one and love the other, or be devoted to the one and despise the other" (6:22-24a). As the awareness of my darkness increased, so did the realization of my need to be delivered from my inmost alienation from God. This demanded that I face my mourning, my inner alienation, and admit it to another. The admission of what is deepest within us can be done only with an "angel of comfort." This angel comes to us in the appearance of a total stranger or an absolute friend.

I decided I would seek out my angel of comfort—in a friend. This angel appeared to me in the person of Fred Just. At that time Fred was a Capuchin in the Pittsburgh Province (he has since left, married a wonderful woman, and has a great daughter). Fred fulfills the definition of a friend: one who knows everything about you and loves you just the same. He would be God's angel sent to comfort me in my mourning. Fred would be God's minister sent to heal my brokenness.

The moment for this restoration to take place occurred at a time when we were both in New York for a meeting of the Interfaith Center on Corporate Responsibility, the group of religious groups using investments for corporate reform. We decided to take extra time to be together.

The first thing we did was to see Liv Ullmann, my favorite actress, who was starring in a production of Eugene O'Neill's play *Anna Christie.* The title character in this play had been sent as a motherless child from Boston to a Minnesota farm to live with her cousins. After running away from the farm she went to St. Paul to become a prostitute. In the city she becomes very ill. Not wanting to go back to the farm, she has nobody to turn to except her father in Boston. So she returns, not wanting him to know about her inmost sin. Her father, meanwhile, has been living on the barges in the harbor with one woman after another.

As the play begins, he is reading Anna's letter telling him that she will be coming. He immediately gets rid of the last woman who shared his barge. Neither does he want Anna to know his inmost sin. As the play develops, these two humans with their brokenness and hidden sins, their alienation and their hurts, start healing each other. By the end of the play they have created a deep bonding of personal care and trust.

After the play, Fred and I went to a restaurant in the area. There he started to tell me things he had been discussing with a counselor. He shared experiences from his past and present life, telling me about experiences he had had at different stages in his life. Listening to his story, I was able to understand and accept not only the experiences but Fred himself. Sharing his mourning with me became an invitation for me to reveal and admit similar areas from my own past and present life. So I started talking to Fred, admitting my inmost sins, revealing those areas of my life that had been controlling me. I told him about my cowardice in grade and high school, those sexual fantasies you get when you are growing up (which never seem to leave!), and my hidden fears. Since it was a year before our Provincial Chapter and because various brothers had been telling me they thought I might become provincial, I was able to share my emotions about that. Did I want the job or not? Was it something I coveted deep down or was I fearful of failing in this ministry as I became more and more aware of my limitations?

Whatever came to my mind, I was going to share with Fred. I was not going to leave one stone unturned. I was going to be delivered from the depth of my sin. As I shared these drives and fears, these hurts and hopes, Fred was accepting the reality of their existence. But even more so, he was accepting Michael Crosby. He was touching me as a minister of healing in the deepest part of my mourning. In Fred, Jesus was saying "I do choose. Be made clean!" (8:3).

The experience of God's forgiveness of my sinfulness in Fred's acceptance brought back a line from *Anna Christie*. It is the only line I can remember. Having shared my inmost sins and, in the process, having found myself experiencing ever-increasing release, I recalled a line toward the end of the play. Anna is on the boat by herself. She has her arms wrapped around herself in a hug, symbolizing a "glorious mantle instead of a listless spirit" (Isa. 61:3). I could identify with her emotion as she repeated over and over again, "I feel so clean; I feel so clean!"

As this Beatitude was experienced by Jesus in his own individual life, our discipleship means that it can be experienced in our lives as well. As we are ministered to in our mourning by angels of comfort, we can be those angels of comfort to others in their mourning as well. Sometimes this means we find the right word to say at a critical time; at other times it means simply "being present" to show we care.

As I revised this edition of *Spirituality of the Beatitudes*, Sr. Marce Connolly, a Dominican friend, asked what I'd recommend for her newly begun ministry at a hospital. I could not find any magic way she could be an angel of comfort to those who were at various levels of sickness and dying. I could only suggest that her presence with the people in care would be the best dose of medicine she could give. I found myself saying: "People probably won't remember anything you will say (unless it's inappropriate, which you never do); they'll just remember you showed up."

Mourning and Comfort in Our Relationships

Matthew does not elaborate on Jesus' grief at the death of a close friend like the Baptist. He does not comment on the tears Jesus showed at the death of Lazarus (John 11:35ff.), which we read about in the Fourth Gospel. Yet anyone who has just heard of or experienced the death of a loved one can identify with the emotions and grief that must have enveloped Jesus upon being informed of John's death. "Now when Jesus heard this, he withdrew [*anachorein*] from there in a boat to a deserted place by himself" (14:13a). When we lose loved ones, we just want to be alone in our pain and loss. Thus Jesus "withdrew." The word Matthew uses for this removal of himself from the situation is *anachorein*. It often refers to a strategy one uses in face of some overpowering threat, violence and/or death (2:12, 13, 14, 22; 4:12; 12:15; 15:21; see 27:5); it implies the response one makes to an experience of conflict or death over which one feels powerless—at the time. This response is made in a way that the scriptures are fulfilled in the person who so responds.

As the word *anachorein* implies, Jesus would not remain immobilized by his sense of loss. The brokenness of others again invited him not to be controlled by his own pain and grief but to continue his ministry of alleviating the hurts of others. "When he went ashore, he saw a great crowd; and he had compassion for them and cured their sick" (14:14).

The power to heal others is a gift the apostles were given for the sake of announcing the good news (10:1, 8). Matthew's theology shows that the disciples were not given the power to teach until chapter 28. Furthermore, they did little actual preaching (10:7). Especially from 11:2 on, Matthew shows that almost all of the disciples' exercise of power revolved around healing. Matthew seems very conscious of the human and psychological fact that barriers and controls must be broken and healed before people can be open to preaching and teaching. When we are in pain we cannot easily be taught or sermonized.

The healing power of the disciples flowed from the same *exousia* that enabled Jesus to heal. Yet, while they shared the same *exousia* to heal, the disciples were not always able to heal as Jesus healed. The difference was the disciples' lack of faith (17:14-21). When our healing of others does not measure up to the healing power manifested by Jesus, it is important that we examine our faith and that of the people with whom we minister.

If we are to be the angels of comfort, consolation, and restoration to those who mourn, the desire to heal must be central to our lives, as it was the core of the lives of the disciples and Jesus. Because healing was so central to Jesus' life and the acts of the early church (1 Cor. 12:9), I once was haunted by the thought that it should be more evidenced in my life. My work for the Vatican in preparing the volumes of testimony in support of the canonization of the Servant of God Solanus Casey, one of my confreres, convinced me that I might not be allowing the possible charism of healing to be manifest in me not only because of my own sins but especially because I was like the early disciples in that I lacked sufficient faith.

Writing a biography of Solanus Casey (1870-1957)[7] and working on his cause[8] have convinced me that in this Capuchin friar I had met someone who took seriously Jesus' words about asking that we might receive (7:7)—so seriously that they were fulfilled in him. Indeed, this farm boy from Wisconsin, who was rejected from a diocesan seminary on the grounds of being academically deficient, was ordained by the Capuchins but never allowed to hear confessions or preach formal sermons. But he lived in the promise of Jesus. In notes made by him during his novitiate in 1897-98, the first quotation from scripture noted by him under prayer is "'Ask and it shall be given to you' (Mt 7:7)."[9]

Because Solanus was not considered smart enough for traditional tasks of priests of that era, after his ordination as a priest in 1904 he was assigned as "Porter" at various Capuchin friaries, notably St. Bonaventure's in Detroit. There he became known as one to whom people could go with their needs. Soon word got around that this "miracle worker" could get the healing or help that you needed. Despite beginning as a skeptic regarding these "cures," it did not take me long, after talking with so many people with firsthand stories, to conclude that this simple man of faith might be the first male born in the United States to become a saint.

Solanus simply believed Jesus' words about "asking" that we might "receive." After all, he reasoned, is this not a command of Jesus to all his disciples? I love the story told by Gerald Walker, the provincial during Solanus's last days. One time, he noted:

> Faced with what seemed to me would be a tragedy, I asked him to pray that God would spare me from it. He promised that he would. A week passed by. The situation seemed more threatening. I went to see him again to ask if he was praying, as he had promised. He assured me that he was. I went back to my room.
>
> Soon there was a knock on the door, and there was Fr. Solanus, the tears pouring down his cheeks. Evidently hurting very much, he said, "Gerald, I am so disappointed in you."
>
> Paining to hear that from him, I asked, "Why?"
>
> He said, "Because I thought you had more faith than that?" Then, referring to Jesus' words in the Gospel, he said, "Remember that Jesus said, if you ask, you shall receive."
>
> It was lesson in faith I needed.
>
> By the way, I then received what I asked for.[10]

In Solanus's view, the only stumbling blocks to the power of God and God's work in us would be doubt and fear. Thus he concluded that "one of humanity's greatest weaknesses is setting a limit on God's power and goodness."[11] With God's *exousia* in us as it was in Jesus, we are called to find ways to bring healing into our broken world at its various levels. What we lack in enabling God to work in us to be such healers, Solanus would say, is our faith.

To help us in our faith, Solanus believed, the Catholic Church celebrated God's grace in sacramentals and other "means of grace." One of these, Solanus believed, was the association people enrolled in so that they could support the foreign missions. In exchange the Capuchins worldwide promised these benefactors a remembrance in their Masses and prayers.

A great story of Solanus's bringing about a kind of healing in the face of great difficulties involved the many workers at the Chevrolet plant in Detroit in the slump of the winter of 1925-26, a few years before the Great Depression. Solanus noted the story of John McKenna, who came to visit him at St.

Bonaventure's Monastery in Detroit. "He was evidently discouraged, notwithstanding his otherwise wonderful faith," Solanus noted.

"Father," he began, "I don't know what to do. I can't support a wife and family with the hours I've been working. I haven't had a full day now in two weeks. Today I had only two hours. They're always finding an alibi to send the men home." All at once, as though by inspiration, he said, "Father! Enroll the company!"

Solanus thought, "That's new," and quickly realized that this was not about a company; it was about the fears and concerns (i.e., the "mourning") of potentially thousands of people like John McKenna. Solanus answered, "All right, John."

"Yes, Father, I'll give them fifty cents" [for an annual membership in the association].

That same night, Solanus wrote in his letter, "The company received an astounding order." He concluded, "It was believed that order saved Detroit itself from bankruptcy."[12]

Such an example of how healing and hope can touch a whole organization naturally brings me to the third level of mourning and comfort: that dealing with the institutions, "isms," and ideologies that define the infrastructural level of life.

Mourning over Structures to Bring Comfort

In the Lamentations of Jeremiah, the mourning of Israel was likened to that of a lonely city and to a widow with none to comfort her (Lam. 1:1-2). "Judah has gone into exile because of affliction" (Lam. 1:3). Even the "roads to Zion mourn" (Lam. 1:4); her children have gone away (Lam. 1:5). Jerusalem remembers "in the days of her affliction and bitterness" (Lam. 1:7) and has no comforter (Lam. 1:9).

While landless Israel in its sixth-century exile was "not comforted," prophets like Hosea envisioned a day of restoration. Second Isaiah expressed the reversal of Israel's exile from its land in terms of comfort coming to the people (Isa. 40:1-2). "For the Lord has comforted his people, and will have compassion on his afflicted" (Isa. 49:13).

Continually Matthew presents Jesus as the one who had compassion on the crowds (9:36; 14:14; 15:32; 18:27; 20:34), not only when their mourning was an expression of their suffering, hunger, and blindness (14:14; 15:32; 20:34) but also when they were in debt (18:27) and "harassed and helpless, like sheep without a shepherd" (9:36). Indeed, when the word "compassion" is used, it invariably is ordered toward *groups* of people in need.

While some commentators, taking a more individualistic and "spiritual" approach to the Beatitudes, view "Blessed are those who mourn, for they shall be comforted" as pertaining to those who grieve over their sins, there are others who look at the rest of the Sermon on the Mount, as well as the whole thrust of Matthew's Gospel, and stress the community's lament (and, therefore, protest) against evildoing and injustice.[13] Indeed, Warren Carter writes that "on the basis of Isa 61:1-3," those who mourn in this Beatitude also include those who "lament the destructive impact of imperial powers such as Babylon (and Rome) which oppress God's people."[14] Probably the Franciscan Richard Rohr says it best: "In this Beatitude, Jesus praises . . . those who can enter into solidarity with the pain of the world and not try to extract themselves from it."[15]

While we have seen that Matthew uses code words to describe how Jesus confronted the destructive dynamics of the imperium (gospel, Lord, *exousia,* the passages in Jesus' Prayer[16]), nowhere do we find Jesus confronting the sinful structures of his day as clearly as the diatribe against the scribes and the Pharisees in the whole of chapter 23, which seems to have occurred within the temple itself (24:1). After being confronted with a triad of entrapments, queries, and tests (22:15-40) from all the key branches of Israel's religious leaders, Jesus gives a riposte with his own line of questioning, to which "no one was able to give him an answer" (22:46). In utter frustration at their denial, distortion, and delusion, Jesus now is at the end of his rope trying to get the leaders of his institutionalized religion to convert. Time after time they have created stumbling blocks to the promise of blessing he has proclaimed. Instead they have placed one stumbling block after another in the path of Jesus' ministry. Overtaken with frustration, Jesus lashes out at his religious opponents with a tactic used in battles between key opponents: he calls them one name after another. However, the one that is used as a thread exposing their utter injustice is "hypocrite" (23:13, 15, 23, 25, 29). This diatribe unleashed against the scribes and Pharisees concludes with one of the most pathos-filled statements in the scriptures: "Jerusalem, Jerusalem, the city that kills the prophets and stones those who are sent to it! How often have I desired to gather your children together as a hen gathers her brood under her wings, and you were unwilling! See, your house is left to you, desolate" (23:37-38). He who had spent his whole public life inviting his coreligionists and their leaders to a new kind of household under God the Father that would make them brothers and sisters not by blood but by a new vision of doing good had been a failure. His failure is expressed in his words of utter frustration. Their "house," their religious system, is bankrupt.

Although Jesus worked throughout his life for communal restoration, the infrastructure would not budge. Unable to bring about conversion because of society's sluggishness of heart (see 13:14-15), Jesus could do nothing but mourn over his people. By admitting his brokenness and frustration at society's intransigence Jesus owned the grief from his apparent failure; yet comfort would come to Jesus in this realization that he had been faithful. A restored community would be announced by an angel of comfort (28:1-7) at the resurrection, after Jesus would be taken to the depth of despair.

Jesus mourned over his own institution's infidelity. Today Jesus' Spirit in us invites us to grieve, to mourn over the brokenness and alienation within our institutions. But, we might ask ourselves, When was the last time our concern over globalization was translated into making a stand on behalf of its victims? When were we ready to pay a little more for coffee and other "fruits of the earth and work of human hands" so that those who grow and harvest them might be paid a sustainable living wage? When did we really grieve over such things as the clericalism and sexism in our churches that, in effect, is denying hundreds of millions of people the body of Christ on a regular basis? Or when has our lifestyle been ensured in a way that justifies the continued destruction of whole peoples and the environment in the name of freedom? Healing will never come within the infrastructure until we first admit the existence of the sins and cultural addictions that contribute to human and societal brokenness, and then mourn over them.

David P. Reid notes that this Beatitude "is an ecclesial stance." He writes: "When the Church proclaims, 'Blessed are those who suffer and mourn,' the Church commits itself to an involvement in all the pains, anguishes, hurts, struggles of the human family." Recalling the famous passage that says almost the same thing in the Second Vatican Council's *Gaudium et Spes,* Reid shows that, when "the Church" proclaims this Beatitude, it accuses itself. He declares:

> Just as the preaching of Jesus provoked a resistance, so, too, will the declaration of the victory of Christ in the midst of the brokenness of humanity provoke a resistance against the Church. All the more painful when the resistance is born of the Church's own lack of fidelity! Who can deny that the pain of a sinful Church bears heavily upon us? There is purgation at hand, no doubt. But, purgation can lead to newness and rekindling of the basic calling of the Church to be about the gospel.

Returning to the theme of denial that has been shown in this chapter to be the key stumbling block to the realization of this Beatitude in the institutional expression of the Roman Catholic Church itself, Reid concludes: "However, the denial and the blindness of the institution to its own sinfulness have to be acknowledged before it can be dealt with"[17] in a way that will find some degree of comfort and the beginning of some kind of resolution.

Over the years, I have tried to bring about corporate and church reform in my ministry of socially responsible investing as well as retreats, workshops, and books like this. Here I have tried to address the sinfulness that characterizes the male, celibate, clerical model of the existing Roman Catholic Church.

My efforts have been met with rejection and at times indifference. Consequently, while never "withdrawing" from this struggle, I have found much comfort by belonging to a province of brothers who are serious about societal and ecclesiastical reform. However, even in my own province, we have our own share of "mourning."

This became quite evident when we came together for the 1978 Chapter. We had to admit that, as an institution, we had brokenness among our members. Despite the great efforts made since the Second Vatican Council to achieve unity, a study showed that we had not yet achieved the agreement we seemed to have had before the council. We did not agree on which model of church we favored, how we were to live, which ministries were primary, and whether we sensed a need for a common goal. Faced with these facts about our dismemberment, some of us sensed we could no longer continue to live with our heads in the sand. We had to own the very real differences that are part of the reality of every group in the church-in-transition. We sensed a need to begin healing the wounds from that dismemberment. Admitting our dismemberment could lead to re-membering ourselves. From a re-membering we could then develop new forms of care with which we could initiate a process of patterning our lives in more unified ways for the good of society.

For several days in June 1978 we convened under the theme: "Re-Membering Our Spirit and Life." We did not seek to achieve any great decisions or resolutions. We wanted to let the Holy Spirit, the real "Minister General of our Province" (to use Francis's words about where he wanted ultimate power to rest in the Order itself)[18] bring comfort to those areas over which we mourned.

At the liturgy celebrating the jubilees of our brothers, the homilist was Rupert Dorn, a previous provincial. I never remembered Rupert as an exciting preacher. His charism seemed to be best expressed in enlightened administration. During those tumultuous years 1967 through 1973, his steady, low-keyed approach as provincial kept the province on an even keel. After leaving office, Rupert became a rural pastor. At the same time he became involved in the charismatic renewal. His homily evidenced the Spirit's power.

Rupert spoke on that occasion about the biblical concept of Jubilee—"the year of favor" that Isaiah promised to those who were poor in spirit and who mourned (Isaiah 61). He noted that biblical Jubilee contained elements of reflection, reconciliation, and freedom. He observed that we had taken time off that week for reflection. We were reflecting together on the future of the province. This reflection, the first step in bringing about a Jubilee (see Leviticus 25), would lead to the realization of our collective need for the next dimension of Jubilee: reconciliation. Only if we sought reconciliation, Rupert urged, would we be able to experience the final gift of Jubilee: our freedom as individuals and as a province.

Toward the end of the homily, Peter Kutch started to play gently on the pipe organ. The music and Rupert's words began to touch many hearts. As brothers put their heads in their hands, with some allowing the tears to roll down their faces, letting their mourning take hold of them, the once-average preacher grew in *exousia*. Inviting us to conversion in the power of God's word that touched him, Rupert concluded:

> So during these days let us in the spirit of reconciliation and unity, while we will be different in age and shapes, in thinking and lifestyles and ministry, let us be united in our expressions of love. Let us be soaked in love these days. Soaked in love.
>
> In the spirit of jubilee, we pray that through our reflections and reconciliation we will feel a new freedom. We will feel that truly the bonds that are holding us down, that are impeding the progress of our beloved province will be cut. Jesus, you said at the resurrection of Lazarus, "Unbind him, let him go free." Unbind us and let us go free. Cut the bonds of bitterness and resentment that we may harbor. Cut the bonds of self-pity and mistrust and fear and false respect.
>
> Cut the bonds that keep us from truly loving our brothers and telling them so. Lord Jesus, heal all divisions in our lives. Let us now move into that gesture of reconciliation, the sign of peace, with a warm hand clasp or, if we feel comfortable, a hug and embrace. Let our brothers know that we are happy to be present to each other. My brothers, peace be with you. My brothers, I love you.[19]

For the next ten minutes or so, the whole chapel seemed to move. Brothers sought each other out, seeking reconciliation and peace. A couple of friars came up to me saying, as they hugged me, "Crosby, I really need reconciliation with you." I did not even know there had been alienation between us! But it did not matter. That afternoon a beautiful experience of comfort touched the mourning that had formerly controlled our province as an institution. We experienced the second Beatitude: Blessed are those who admit their mourning; they will be comforted with a new-found power that enables them to be restored to authentic life.

Despite the ability to celebrate how an institution like my own province realized it had to stop denying its divisions and open itself to healing, this Beatitude cannot be restricted to our own limited, provincial institutions, be they local church or congregational. As difficult (and as futile) as it may be, the Beatitude must touch the total religious institution.

Dr. Martin Luther King, Jr., grieved over the sluggishness, the sloth of the church, in addressing its various expressions of racism. He found this capital sin of sloth deeply rooted within the churches' efforts to bring about social justice between the races. What King said regarding the "ism" of race still can be applied to our churches, but, in the case of Roman Catholicism, we can add sexism and heterosexism as well. Such sins are alienating more and more women *and* men from the church. Yet, protected with our ideologies, it seems we still will not listen, lest we be converted (13:15).

This fear of conversion became very clear to me on one occasion as I shared a reflection week for campus ministers. The dynamics of the group revealed a growing awareness of problems stemming from a clerically controlled ministry in the Roman Catholic Church. On one side were clerics; on the other were nonclerics: religious women, married couples, and single people. All of these depended on clerics for their jobs and paychecks.

One particular situation involved a very friendly but threatened young priest. A young couple had shared ministry with him at a particular Midwest campus. They were more successful than the priest in their programs and in getting students involved. To top it off, the woman in the couple was a feminist. By the time they came for this study week, the handwriting was on the wall. He who had the power could make the rules. And since this cleric not only had the power but the purse strings, he could fire the couple, with the bishop's backing, if need be. The hatchet was about to fall.

I had done much sharing with the group during the week about the new directions for community-conscientization-conversion that I outlined earlier in this book. In a particular way, I talked about sexist structures and the need to convert from them. When the last morning arrived, I sat in the back of the group listening to their reflections on what their next steps would be.

They admitted that my analysis of the sexist situation in the church was correct. That was an intellectual conversion. They even agreed that Genesis 1:26-28 cannot show the scriptures supporting, as God's plan, a form of oppression for a whole class of people. That was a moral conversion. Yet, as I saw the members of the group discuss everything except *their sexism* and elitism, I suddenly realized that this very way of discussing was keeping them from a religious conversion. This religious conversion would have been an invitation to let an old form of ministry die in order to give birth in reconciliation to new power and possibilities for the good of God's whole church.

I had been under a lot of pressure before that week and had worked hard with the group. So, when I realized that my effort would be to no avail, I sensed my emotions taking over. I quietly departed from the room and went outside. And I broke. Having spent myself intellectually and emotionally, my tears reflected the only emotion I had left within me: a sense of utter failure.

At that point of tears, the image of Jesus weeping over Jerusalem came into my mind. As immediately as I had let myself enter into this mourning, the image of the weeping Jesus became an instant angel of comfort in my grief. It brought a consolation into my depths the likes of which I had rarely experienced. I had been faithful to the process, I seemed to sense. I did whatever I could; I could do no more. That was also the pattern of Jesus' life. He had nothing to show as he went to death; yet he had remained faithful. At that very thought, the realization that he too had been powerless in the eyes of the world brought comfort and peace.

As I was experiencing this deep inner peace and joy, I felt the presence of someone nearby. It was the priest; he was standing next to me. He must have watched me, as I slipped from the room. Now, in my presence, he said spontaneously, without a word coming from me: "But Mike, I can't change." His statement was almost a plea for understanding. Even though I had said little that morning, we both recognized the unwillingness to change that had become part of him and the group. My reply to him might be restated this way: "If we don't change, then we will remain controlled. And, if we remain controlled in our fears and mourning, we will never experience the hope and comfort of the resurrection of God's power in us that has been promised."

When I consider how far from the trinitarian reign of God so much of the institutional dimensions of our empire and *ekklēsia* appear to be, I get discouraged but never depressed. As I experience myself increasingly in exile within these institutions, I find Isaiah's words comforting. The only thing that will keep us from admitting "the exact nature of our wrongs" will be when we remain in denial about their destructive dynamics for people and the planet. But it need not always be so. Thus, as the continuation of Isaiah 61 promises: "You shall no more be termed Forsaken, and your land shall no more be termed Desolate; but you shall be called My Delight Is in Her, and your land Married; for the Lord delights in you, and your land shall be married" (Isa. 62:4).

Mourning over the Despoiling of Our Universe: Comfort as Protest

At the time of Jesus and Matthew, spirituality assumed the comfort of being part of an ecological balance. Today we cannot afford to make the same assumption. Part of life's unity came from the birds in the sky (6:26); today oil slicks wash them ashore, and we are broken. Wild flowers and grass in the field (6:28, 30) brought spontaneous joy; today the fact that chemicals leave the land barren makes us weep. Jesus spoke in parables about picking grapes from thornbushes, figs from prickly plants, and good fruit from decayed trees (7:16-18); today cash crops from the poor nations support the lifestyle of rich nations like ours and create for us a harvest of shame. Jesus assumed that foxes had lairs (8:20); today we cannot assume that many species of fox will survive, and we experience guilt as we wear our fur coats. Jesus multiplied loaves and fishes and brought comfort to the crowds (14:13-21; 15:32-38); today malnutrition and hunger increase on a global scale while acid rains suffocate streams and lakes as far north as Great Bear Lake.

We have become alienated from creation itself. What Hosea said of general infidelity to God's plan can be applied to this ecological situation; God's warning can no longer fall on deaf ears, closed eyes, and hardened hearts:

> Hear the word of the Lord, O people of Israel;
> for the Lord has an indictment against the inhabitants of the land.
> There is no faithfulness or loyalty, and no knowledge of God in the
>   land.
> Swearing, lying, and murder, and stealing and adultery break out;
> bloodshed follows bloodshed.
> Therefore the land mourns and all who live in it languish;
> together with the wild animals and the birds of the air,
> even the fish of the sea are perishing. (Hos. 4:1-3)

As I prepared this new edition of this book, I found that, over the score of years since the first edition, my eyes have been opened dramatically and, I hope, my heart has been changed by the awareness of what the imperial power of the United States is doing to undermine the integrity of the universe. Just as I was rewriting this chapter, article after article detailed the ways the president of the United States had worked to undermine environmental regulations so as to benefit the oil, coal, and timber industries that contributed to his election and party.

At the same time, the *Washington Post* carried a column that sounds like a scientist's contemporary lament over what Hosea had forewarned. The column reported on what researchers discovered in the first study of its kind in a range of habitats including northern Britain, the wet tropics of northeastern Australia, and the Mexican desert. They discovered that global warming at currently predicted rates will drive 15 to 37 percent of living species toward extinction by mid-century. Dismayed by their results, the researchers called for "rapid implementation of technologies" to reduce emissions of greenhouse gases and warned that the scale of extinctions could climb much higher because of mutually reinforcing interactions between climate change and habitat destruction caused by agriculture, invasive species, and other factors.[20]

As this was being reported, the world's largest petroleum company, ExxonMobil, continued to remain in denial. It refused to admit that global warming exists, that human factors contribute to this, and that the burning of [its] fossil fuels is a key factor in this reality that is devastating the ecological balance. As the corporation buttressed its position by citing this or that individual scientist (often persons who had received funding from ExxonMobil itself), one body of scientists after another not only offered more data to support the findings of the study but urged immediate changes in our lifestyle for the integrity of creation. Even more a cause of mourning is the fact that my province has been challenging ExxonMobil on this issue since the 1980s, along with many other religious institutions and concerned share-holders, only to be dismissed by the company and the vast number of share-holders. Why? The company returned very good dividends to their portfolios.

However, while mourning over the earth's despoliation and its despoilers needs to continue in our protests, we can always live in the faith that a restored people seeking first God's reign can take a new authority over creation itself. Creation can stop quaking in death (see 27:52). We can proclaim life and a new solidarity with humans who realize creation too has rights that must be respected as part of God's plan. Extending care to inanimate creation brings good news into the whole world. Such is the promise of Jubilee: an entire creation restored to its original purpose.

CHAPTER FIVE

Blessed Are the Nonviolent; They Will Inherit the Earth

In my world "meekness" is not "blessed." Often it seems more a "stumbling block" to "making it" in the land. We consider "meek" people doormats, people you can "walk over." They are timid and submissive, easily dominated and exploited. When Charles Keating headed Lincoln Savings and Loan, he sent an in-house memo that said: "Remember, the weak, the meek, and the ignorant are always good targets." While Keating's statement went unchallenged—until he was jailed for his part in the savings and loan *skandalon* of the 1980s and '90s—Matthew's "meekness" (*praüs*) is anything but passive capitulation.

One time I heard a preacher suggest that we have someone read us the eight Beatitudes. We were to be especially sensitive to any stirrings in our heart that might indicate that one or another Beatitude was challenging us about something that needed to be changed in our lives. When I went through this form of "discernment" I discovered that, without a doubt, "Blessed are the meek, for they will inherit the earth" (5:5) was inviting me to live in a different way.

Letting one of the Beatitudes or something else in the Sermon on the Mount challenge us to transformation is the first step in personal conversion. Leo Tolstoy discovered this when he was "convicted" by the passage from the Sermon inviting him to a nonviolent stance in his world. This came from the admonition by Matthew's Jesus not to "resist an evildoer" (5:39).

Tolstoy was the kind of person who was obsessed with finding "the meaning of life." As he looked for models around him, he discovered that people either lived unreflectively, like animals, or were so preoccupied with getting power, making money, or maintaining a good name for themselves that they failed to go deeper to life's ultimate questions about meaning. Unable to find answers from the world around him, he came upon the Sermon on the Mount. There, just before Jesus told his followers to "be perfect . . . as your heavenly Father is perfect" (5:48), he instructed that one of the key ways to achieve this perfection was to practice nonresistance in the face of evil (5:39).

Tolstoy could not accept the judgment of scholars who claimed that

Jesus' teaching could not be practiced. And so he was left with a huge dilemma. Either believe that Jesus' counsels were impossible to be fulfilled and live in mediocrity or try to translate them into practice and face rejection by other devout believers and religious authorities. Realizing that the first course would annihilate "the whole doctrine of Christ completely," he ultimately chose to put the words of Jesus into practice. In so doing, he knew he "would be forsaken, miserable, persecuted, and sorrowing, as Christ tells us his followers would be." He wrote that, "if I accepted the law of man, I should have the approbation of my fellow-men,"[1] but if he did not, he would be putting himself outside the way of perfection as it was outlined in the Sermon on the Mount.

Just as Tolstoy came to realize about the Sermon that the "whole force of the teaching lay in the words, 'Resist no evil,' and that all the context was but an application of that great precept,"[2] so I found the third Beatitude challenging me regarding how I would live in my world knowing that "all the context" of my world would militate against it.

While meekness is praised as nonviolence in the *Acts of Judas Thomas*,[3] the notion of "meek" as "nonviolent" seems first to have been stressed by Schalom Ben-Chorin in 1969.[4] Since then, especially in German circles, this idea seems to have gained ascendancy, especially when the German equivalent of the English *Good News for Modern Man* (*Einheitsübersetzung*) translated the blessedness of the *praüs* as "Blessed are those who do not employ violence."[5]

Of all the evangelists, Matthew is the only one who uses *praüs*. In all three places where we find it, *praüs* as Jesus' way stands opposed to the prevailing ways of imperial control and infallible religion. The first reference to *praüs* is this Beatitude itself; the second is when Jesus contrasts his yoke that gives "rest" with the violent yoke of control under which people "labor" (11:28-30). The third is in the context of Jesus' nonviolent entrance into Jerusalem, which is contrasted to that of the imperial forces with their tacit support of the religious leaders (21:5).

Setting the Context for an Understanding of Meekness: The Biblical Meaning of "Land"

Matthew's Beatitude about the "meek inheriting the land" repeats the same words found in Psalm 37: "the meek shall inherit the land [*gē*]" (Ps. 37:11); "those blessed by the Lord shall inherit the land" (Ps. 37:22). The whole psalm contrasts the two ways that people live with themselves and each other in the land: through violence or meekness. As such it offers a wonderful examination of conscience for those trying to grow in the spiritual life. Seeking security in excessive desire for power, material things and honor results in various forms of worry and envy (Ps. 37:1), anxiety (Ps. 37:7), anger, wrath (Ps. 37:8, 12). This false security leads to evildoing and various forms of wickedness as a way of protecting our position whether we be individuals, groups, or organizations. The psalmist warns against making such land-based attitudes the foundation of our lives. Rather, the psalmist urged, "Trust in the Lord, and do good; so you will live in the land, and enjoy security" (Ps. 37:3). In a society dominated by concerns about national security to the degree that preemptive strikes are "blessed" in order to ensure that security, this Psalm and Matthew's canonization of it for disciples sound strangely "other worldly."

Psalm 37 offers those who pray it, sing it and try to translate it into their lives a nonviolent way of living. However, before showing how Matthew took this notion and made it Jesus' third Beatitude, I find it best first to discover what the terms "land" and "earth" (Greek *gē*; Hebrew *'eretz)* meant in the context of Matthew's world.

Scripturally speaking, "earth" was synonymous with "land."[6] While they might both have the same scriptural meaning, "earth" and "land" at the time of Jesus, as well as in our own time, had quite different social implications. When people talked about "earth," they were speaking about something that was God's. The earth was the Lord's; it was God's "possession," part of God's household. Consequently it was to be ruled by the divine householder. As Walter Brueggemann notes, "In affirming that the earth belongs only to God, Israel's faith means to deny ultimate ownership to any other."[7] However, Brueggemann goes on to show that, while God might be acknowledged as the house-orderer who controlled the earth (Ps. 24:1), the Israelites, especially after the exodus, gradually came to distinguish between the earth as "God's" and the land as "theirs." Just the fact that we ourselves say "the earth is the Lord's" and "the land is mine" shows how we make a similar distinction. When the land is mine and not yours, it must be defended; thus the inherent potential for violence.

As noted earlier, Psalm 37:11, the foundation for this Beatitude, said that the meek would inherit the land. The *Didache*, which some believe first appeared in house churches in Antioch between 50-70 C.E., urged its followers: "Be meek, since the meek will inherit the earth (land)." While it may be debated about how this passage reached the redaction of Matthew as we have it now, the fact that Matthew wrote to his house churches less than a score of years later and quite probably at the same place—Antioch—makes this Beatitude all the more significant. It is especially relevant when one considers the conflictual situations that characterized the Matthean house churches, especially regarding people's power, claims to property, reputation, and prestige (see 5:38-47; 6:14-15; 18:15-20). This need for meekness becomes even more important when we consider how being landed, as described in Deuteronomy, can tempt us away from living under God's rule and plan.

Deuteronomy's Warnings about "Occupying the Land"

Israel was about to cross the Jordan. Moses realized that, once there, the nation needed to remember its past so that it could live rightly in the future. Once the people "occupied" the land, it would be difficult for them to seek Yahweh first. So that the people would depend on God's word to have all the resources they needed in the world (6:33), Moses stressed the need for symbolic reminders. These symbols would help the community always to remember, from its past experience, that its ultimate security had to be placed in God's word. To help it never forget its need to base its love and loyalty ultimately in God (see 6:4-5), Israel was given no fewer than nine different ways to remember not to forget: "Keep these words that I am commanding you today in your heart. Recite them to your children and talk about them when you are at home and when you are away, when you lie down and when you rise. Bind them as a sign on your hand, fix them as an emblem on your forehead, and write them on the doorposts of your house and on your gates" (Deut. 6:6-9).

Once we get into the land of the condominium, the job, the position, the neighborhood, the education degree, the second and third car, the honor, the tenure, it will be easy to forget that it was God, not ourselves, who *brought* us to this point in our lives. The land is always inherited; it is not taken. It is not ours to take, but God's to give. Thus we have no absolute right to it. Our "inheritance" of any land ultimately demands fidelity to God's vision for the household, how we are to live in the land. In this sense Deuteronomy continues:

> When the Lord your God has brought you into the land that he swore to our ancestors, to Abraham, to Isaac, and to Jacob, to give you—a land with fine, large cities that you did not build, houses filled with all sorts of goods that you did not fill, hewn cisterns that you did not hew, vineyards and olive groves that you did not plant—and when you have eaten your fill, take care that you do not forget the Lord, who brought you out of the land of Egypt, out of the house of slavery. (Deut. 6:10-12)

In Deuteronomy's eighth chapter, Moses made it clear that all resources of the earth that were considered fundamental, basic human needs of that era (such as food, water, and mineral resources), would be given in enough abundance so that no one would lack anything. Continuing in the same vein as the chapters previous, God promises to provide all the resources they can imagine if only they order their households according to God's rule as shown in the commandments (see Deut. 8:6-9).

Why does Yahweh spend so much time telling Moses these things at the entrance to the Promised Land? Because, when Israel will occupy the land, the land will preoccupy their hearts; it will become their treasure, their "bottom line." Therefore, God warned Israel not to forget how it got to this point in its history, lest it become proud of heart, getting amnesia about how it inherited the land. When this delusion would take over, the people would declare: "My power and the might of my own hand have gotten me this wealth," forgetting that it was "the Lord your God . . . who gives you power to get wealth" (Deut. 8:17-18).

In his classic *The Affluent Society,* John Kenneth Galbraith offers an interpretation of what the Bible called "land" in his notion of contemporary *wealth.* Wealth is the sum total of all our financial resources; while income is that which we derive from our wealth. Thus, when we speak of land, we are talking about all financial resources, about wealth. "Broadly speaking," Galbraith writes: "there are three basic benefits from wealth. First is the satisfaction in the *power* with which it endows the individual. Second is the physical possession of things which money can buy. Third is the *distinction* or *esteem* that accrues to the rich man as a result of his wealth.[8] In other words, power, possessions, and prestige are our contemporary equivalents to what the Israelites meant by "land" and "wealth."

How Jesus Approached "The Land"

Under the Roman occupation at the time of Jesus, land was often a key source of conflict and various revolts. To be sheltered from taxes, liquid assets were quickly converted into land. As a result riches were often identified with land; sometimes rich landowners were often absentee or away from their households for extended times (21:33-46; 22:5; 25:14-30; see 20:1-16). In a stratified society where wealth was not accumulated, some became rich because they had inherited land and amassed it. Most household land was passed from one family generation to the next. Such property holdings constituted the basis of one's "possessions," as in the case of the young man who "had great possessions" (19:22). "Since land was ancestrally owned," Walter Wink has noted, "the wealthy had to find powerful means by which to pry tracts loose from their owners. One way was cash; the more frequent was the foreclosure for debt."[9] Not surprisingly, because the records for such foreclosures and other forms of indebtedness were kept in the temple treasury, the first act of the Zealots at the outbreak of the Jewish War in 66 B.C.E., according to Josephus, was to burn the temple treasury to destroy the records. Since Brueggemann has noted that "every settlement of the land question must be a conflictive one,"[10] it is not surprising that much violence during the Jewish–Roman War was based on conflicting land claims.

The relation between *praüs* and the land as envisioned by Matthew's Jesus thus turns upside down the prevailing ideology of society. This way of thinking also seems to have penetrated Matthew's households. What had happened to Israel throughout its history was now occurring in Matthew's house churches: the land was becoming an end in itself; the pursuit of wealth was taking precedence over seeking God's reign. The ordering of the house, its economics, was being used to give more to those who already had. Consequently the landless were being kept out. While some households were prosperous and quite well-off, many more people were poor, homeless, and marginated.

Bruce Malina shows that divisions between the wealthy and the poor involved exploitation and injustice.[11] Thus, in a situation wherein some were landed and housed at the expense of others, reciprocity was violated. In contrast to this violence, Matthew shows how Jesus, in his deeds and words, offered another vision: a reordering of such violence to create households of the *praüs* that would find them living in "the land" (*tēn gēn*) in a way radically different from the prevailing ways that were seen as "blessed." Rather than in greed or violence, the new order would be grounded in an attitude of *praüs* or meekness (5:5; 11:29; 21:5; see 18:1-10; 19:13-15; 20:20-28; 23:8-12).

Looking at Jesus' deeds, we find him rejecting as temptations what the world offered regarding land. This begins with the three temptations that Jesus faced at the beginning of his public life, when he "was led up by the Spirit into the wilderness to be tempted by the devil" to succumb to a way of living in the land that would be defined on the devil's terms (4:1-11). The three temptations refer to the forms of power, possessions, and prestige that constitute our contemporary meaning of wealth itself. Jesus knew where he came from. Thus, at the end of the triad of his temptations to "possess" the land rather than to live under the power of God's reign, he said to his tempter: "Away with you, Satan! For it is written, 'Worship the Lord our God, and serve only him'" (4:10).

During his public life, especially in his parables, Jesus talked about a new ordering in the land, especially vis-à-vis the received understanding of right social ordering. In his book *The Land*, Walter Brueggemann explains how Jesus called into question the traditional house ordering of that system, along with those norms and values which served to enfranchise and disenfranchise. He writes:

> Jesus and his gospel are rightly received as a threat. The new enlandment is a threat to the old arrangements. And he evokes resistance from those who wish to preserve how it had been. A proper understanding requires that we discern the socio-political, economic issues in the religious resistance which forms against him. A threat to land-

holders mobilizes his opponents; land here understood both in literal and symbolic senses.[12]

At the end of his ministry, when Jesus came into Jerusalem, he "entered" a constellation of possible personal and political conflicts related to power, possessions, and prestige. However, when Matthew wrote his Gospel, Jerusalem had already been destroyed (see 24:1-2). Until that time, Jerusalem had been recognized as the center of Jewish institutional life. It was the arbiter of the people's social arrangements or, what I call the "isms." It also served as the ideological link with God. The real political, economic, and religious power in the Western world at that time may have been in Rome. So the people in Matthew's time considered Jerusalem to be the center of their universe. Whoever would be given Jerusalem would inherit all the land—the whole infrastructure containing all the institutions, "isms," and ideologies. Those who would give up Jerusalem would be relinquishing their authority (in the forms of love and loyalty, reinforcement and acclamation) to the new authority.

In contrast to the imperial rulers and their surrogates who "entered" the lands they had conquered or ruled in mighty chariots or on powerful horses in a way that would ensure their dynasty, Jesus came "mounted on a donkey" (21:5) in a way that would fulfill the scriptures. While he came in a spirit of nonviolence or meekness (21:5; Zech. 9:9) in a way that "the crowds that went ahead of him and that followed were shouting . . . 'Blessed [*makarios*] is the one who comes in the name of the Lord!'" (21:9), those with economic and religious power (the "landed") saw it as a *skandalon*; they perceived it as a threat to their power base. They became indignant (21:15). Consequently, they concluded, violent force would have to be used to silence him (see 21:45-46). Jesus' teachings threatened all their land arrangements—their possessions, power, and prestige—for they owed their possession of much of their "land" to the Roman occupiers, and Jesus' words and ministry were perceived to be undermining that Roman system from which they benefited.

When we consider Jesus' words, especially his more formal teaching found in the five discourses, nonviolence becomes a key theme as well. Matthew's Sermon on the Mount advocates for a way of nonviolence in the face of both the imperial patterns of domination and exploitation and prevailing interpretations of the law that reinforced dynamics of control by the religious leaders. Thus, at least a third of the antithesis statements in the Sermon contrast a prevailing pattern that would be considered "violent" with a disarming way that would be considered nonviolent. Whether addressing society's justification for retaliation (5:38-42) or reciprocity (5:43-47), nonviolence is highlighted as the way the disciples of Jesus will move toward true justice (5:20) as well as the perfection that characterizes the reign of God (5:48).[13]

Understanding What It Means to Be "Landed" Today

Once the Israelites entered the land, their temptation was to believe that
they had "obtained" all their "wealth" by their own power. Today, such
"wealth" is concretized in our ability to have access to power, possessions, and
prestige. Land as power, possessions, and prestige can be approached in one
of two ways: meekness (or nonviolence), which grounds all life in God, or
violence, which bases all life on greed and obsession for more power and prestige. In a society whose great ones made their authority felt (*katexousiazein*
[20:25]) through control of the "land," the *exousia* of heaven and earth given
to Jesus' followers (28:18) was to be exercised differently. Rather than maintaining the existing order, a new order was to be proclaimed and practiced.

Some time ago I discovered that Israel's experience of coming into the
land and becoming proud of heart had become replicated almost perfectly in
my own life. The unique history that we have inherited from our ancestors
(which we so easily forget once we get "landed") came home to me when I
was in Ireland for the first time in late 1978. At the request of Pax Christi, I
was invited there to give workshops on corporate responsibility and the
future of religious life.

It had always been important for me to be Irish. My family attended St.
Patrick's, an Irish parish in Fond du Lac, Wisconsin. I went to St. Pat's grade
school for eight years. I was part of the annual St. Patrick's Day play. During
those years I even dreamed of marrying Kathleen McKelvie.

At the end of one seminar which I gave that was attended by major superiors from many orders throughout Ireland, I was principal concelebrant of
the liturgy. During the silence after communion, I became distracted with the
thought: "Wow, Crosby, do you realize what's going on here? Here all these
religious leaders have come to listen to you. You aren't just the first from the
family to come back to Ireland like any tourist; the leaders of its church are
accepting what you have to say!"

In my distraction I also mused: "Wouldn't it be great if I could go back
and tell Mother and Dad [both dead now] about this and share this great
experience with them, knowing how proud of me they'd be." My musing
turned into a deeply powerful experience. "But you are here aren't you? You've
seen it all. You're in the communion of saints that have gathered around this
altar!" But the realization of my parents' presence, the role they played in my
past life, which had brought me to this time and place, came to me as a gift:
"If it weren't for you I wouldn't be here. If it weren't for the way you shared
your life with me, I wouldn't have the educational and psychological background that brought me to this point in my life." It was not only *my* parents
but *theirs* and *all* my ancestors. It was the genealogy of those instruments of
God's plan from Cork and Mayo, Donegal and Kilkenney who came across

the ocean to the towns of Colby and Mitchell, Wisconsin. In this latter township, I only recently discovered that one of my Murphy ancestors was the "second white man" born there.[14] This made me wonder if violence might have been involved in the way they got their "land" from the natives who had inhabited that land for centuries. It made me aware of how easy it is to forget, especially if we don't know our real history.

At any rate, all this genealogy resulted in two blessed people, Blanche Bouser and Hugh Crosby. They came together from all "those others." From their loving union I was born in Fond du Lac, a city midway between Milwaukee and Green Bay. There they nourished me and my three brothers. With their blessing I had moved from home. Now, with thirty-eight years of more people and many other experiences, I was at this time and place in Dublin.

Such ruminations now bring me to consider how we, as members of groups, can make ourselves landed in the way we perceive our social location as the center of the universe. For people like me (able-bodied, educated, white, straight, male, American, Roman Catholic cleric), looking at others and my world from this position of privilege can be deeply problematic. At times it can do violence to the truth, especially when I consider the lens through which I view my world to represent universal truth. This is reflected in the continual data that show how people living in this country are unable to understand why people in other countries dislike us so much and consider us so violent.[15] We find it in a system whose "god" sanctions patriarchy.

When we see how our individual narcissism is justified in our collective "isms," especially nationalism and patriarchal clericalism, we can begin to see how violent we can be as a people. If meekness reflects the way God's word in us enables us to relate to the land, then violence is the way society's word deals with power, possessions, and prestige. This fact is very important to consider when we try to develop biblical spirituality for the United States. Our land was conceived in violence related to property rights and their unequal distribution among people.[16]

If we are the meek in this land, we have to be the ones who change the direction of spirituality in our country that legitimizes, by its violent silence, the continued division among social groups. We have to be the ones who convert so that we never forget that we are no more the images of God than anyone else and that our stewardship of the earth's resources cannot support structures and relationships that deny others their right to those resources. We have to be the first ones who no longer wonder why the poor might need what we want. Instead we should begin to ask ourselves if we really have a right to what the poor may need. We have to be the first ones who understand the connection between the land and wealth. We should be the first to realize that we have been invited, as was the rich young man, to use our resources on behalf of the poor (see 19:16-22). We have to be the ones who bring the full implications of this Beatitude to bear upon every level of our lives.

When we consider how the Roman Catholic Church became landed under Constantine and took on the trappings of the imperial court, we have to admit that we have come a long way from Capernaum. According to the standard New Testament lexicon, *praüs* was to be a quality "required of church leaders."[17] Having such an attitude in their hearts, the leaders would not evidence the desire to be first or to be served but to serve, even to the point of laying down their own lives (20:27-28). When bishops and cardinals are called "Your Grace," "Your Excellency," and "Your Eminence," and even priests are distinguished between "Reverend," "Right Reverend," and "Very Reverend," it's a little hard to imagine calling them "Your Meekness," "Your Humility," and "Your Gentleness." Jesus even warned against wanting to be called "father" or "teacher," because both might be ways we try to exalt ourselves (23:9-12).

Today our leaders seem unable to fathom how much this system of celibate, patriarchal clericalism does violence to their ability to proclaim the good news to our world today. As the pedophilia *skandalon* has shown so clearly, to "protect their [land] interests," the bishops were willing to allow children to be abused, even ruined. Even after they supposedly created systems to keep such violence from happening in the way it did before, they were unable to see how their very social location separated them from "their" people. Until this changes, violence will continue to characterize too much of the dynamics of leaders in the church, since, by the bishops' own definition, violence is any way one uses to control another through fear and intimidation.[18]

This notion of violence as any way one uses to "control" others brings me to a deeper consideration of the second of the three times Matthew uses the word *praüs* in his Gospel.

Learning the Nonviolent Way of Jesus

Once in the land after the exodus, Israel could easily succumb to haughtiness and lack of concern for others. Jesus found this same culturally learned and sanctioned behavior in his coreligionists, but his words and deeds offered an alternative. His approach to the land and its resources reveals how easily we can end up being "given over to" (*douleuein*) their addictive power in ways that find us serving wealth rather than God (6:24b). However, precisely because we have come to a deeper understanding of how we become "landed" individually, communally, and institutionally, there is all the more reason for us to examine more deeply the notion of meekness or nonviolence (*praüs*) in Matthew.

Matthew 5:4: "Blessed Are the Praüs, *for They Will Inherit the Earth"*

Until now I have spent quite a bit of time reflecting on the word *praüs* in Matthew. Given this background, it might be good to contrast this honorable way of being a disciple with the stumbling block (*skandalon*) that comes into our world when we are *a-praüs* (since "*a*" in front of a Greek word means its opposite). If the "land" means "wealth" and if wealth involves our power, possession, and prestige, we will either approach these legitimate human needs in ways that are *praüs*, nonviolent, or *a-praüs*, violent. I have found it helpful to chart it in the following way:

MAKARIOS	the PRAÜS	they will inherit	the WEALTH
SKANDALON	the A-PRAÜS	they will "possess"	the Power, Possessions, Prestige

Almost all of us have some kind of wealth. The issue regarding our spirituality is not that we have wealth (since a "rich man from Arimathea, named Joseph, also was a disciple" [27:57]); it is how we are willing to share our resources with those in need. Therefore it is important for us in the United States (which has the highest amount of accumulated wealth in the world), to bring a biblical spirituality to bear on life—individual, communal, and collective. This is not easy, especially when everything is ordered to "making it" in the land, and when our wealth makes us look on the poor as a threat.

"Lord," St. Francis said to a bishop who pressed him to acquire property as a means of greater security, "if we had any possessions, we would need arms to protect them because they cause many disputes and lawsuits. And possessions usually impede the love of God and neighbor. Therefore we do not want to possess anything in this world."[19]

The way we "defend" our possessions parallels other ways we "protect" our power and reputation. Returning to the way Matthew portrays "Satan" offering Jesus a similar temptation, we again can see how easily we give in to temptations to let legitimate needs become our gods.

While the first two temptations deal with property and prestige, Jesus' final temptation, which reinforces society's values, involves the use of power itself. On the mountain, the two authorities, the two manifestations of power, meet face to face: "Again, the devil took him to a very high mountain and showed him all the kingdoms of the world and their splendor; and he said to him, 'All these I will give you, if you will fall down and worship me'" (4:8-9).

Because Jesus remained conscious of the power he experienced in the depth of his prayer (4:2), Satan was unable to seduce him to live by land arrangements that would be contrary to that experience. Thus, Jesus said, "Away with you, Satan!" Quoting Deuteronomy again (Deut. 6:13), Jesus made clear that all spirituality is to manifest a lifestyle that submits every land arrangement to the power of God: "For it is written: 'Worship the Lord our God, and serve only him'" (4:10).

Matthew 11:29: *"Take My Yoke upon You, and Learn from Me, for I Am* Praüs *in Heart"*

One of the best-known passages in the New Testament, again from Matthew, deals with Jesus' way of living in the land: "Come to me, all you who are weary and are carrying heavy burdens, and I will give you rest. Take my yoke upon you, and learn from me, for I am *praüs* and humble in heart [*kardia*], and you will find rest for your souls. For my yoke is easy and my burden light" (11:28-30).

Matthew's Jesus begins by inviting "*all* who are weary and are carrying heavy burdens" to come to him and learn his way of living in the land. It will bring them rest instead of weariness; the yoke of his discipline for disciples will be a yoke that "is easy" and a burden that "is light."

When I give retreats on the notion of *praüs* as we live in the "lands" of our various social locations, I use the chart presented above. Only now I add the images from this passage connected to living in our land with the wealth that is expressed in our power, possessions, and prestige. The chart is now expanded to address the consequences of dealing with the land in a way that will be a *makarios* or a *skandalon*:

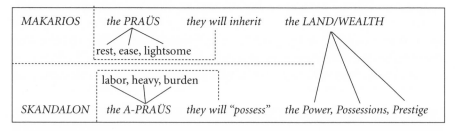

At this point, I ask the participants to reflect on their lives and relationships, especially where they may be conflicted. I ask them to close their eyes and think of what is going on in their hearts. Then I ask: "Is there any relationship you are in that is creating weariness for you? Are you finding yourself saying: 'I'm sick and tired of . . .' whatever? Do you feel especially burdened by someone or something?"

Then I randomly say to someone: "I don't want you to tell me any details at all, but, can I ask if you found yourself in a situation or relationship that was creating this kind of pain for you?" Almost inevitably the person nods in assent. Then I say, "I'm not going to ask you for anything else but to answer this question: 'Might this situation or relationship be defined by control?'" Again without exception, the person nods in assent.

Reflecting on this Beatitude from the perspective of Matthew 11:28-30 has made me realize that, when our hearts (our thinking, feeling, and act-ing—that is, our very "souls") are weary, heavy, and burdened, we will not experience the blessing of living the wisdom of this Beatitude. Rather, we will be in a situation of *a-praüs*. I have "learned from" this wisdom of Matthew's Jesus that a heart that is *a-praüs* will not only be in a dynamic of violence, but this violence will be grounded in the need to control some aspect of "our" power, possessions, and prestige. Most often, but not always, it revolves around the abuse of power.

The need to control not only represents the abuse that is making victims of innocent children as well as the earth itself; it is the source of all violence in the world. Such a perspective on the source of violence may not have the sophistication of a René Girard;[20] however, I find it resonates with our day-to-day life. Violence arises from the need to control. Indeed the U.S. bishops, as I have already noted, define violence as any way one uses "to control" another through fear and intimidation.[21]

Carrying this burden, we are invited to come to Jesus in our weariness. Each of us can bring the burden of running after so many things, without finding meaning. Each of us can walk through our first steps of the hermeneutic circle and admit that we are not really trusting in God's word as in the past. Each of us again can be touched by the refreshing, the strength-ening experience of God's presence. In saying, "Come to me," Jesus is saying that we do not need to go to the power, the possessions, the prestige defined as "blessed" by our society and above all to the empty promises of an ideol-ogy that has held us in the yoke of such myths as "survival of the fittest," "the more, the merrier," "greed is good," and "at the end of the game, the one with the most toys wins," or, vis-à-vis our church, "just submit."

Jesus says, "Come to me," not "Come to the Law [Torah]." Life cannot be found in a law, only in a person. Come to me, not to your elites, to your scribes and Pharisees with their theologies, their academic controls, and their teaching. Come to me for the wisdom that has been revealed to me by my God and yours. Come to me and be refreshed by God's plan of life for you and the world. I have received this plan from God; now I freely share this plan with you (11:25-27).

In coming to Jesus, to that Jesus whom we have sought and found (13:44-46), we can more easily sell all those things in our individual and interper-sonal lives, as well as those parts of the infrastructures of our life—those yoking institutions, "isms" and ideologies—whenever they do not reflect God's trinitarian rule. We can be free of their yoke by submitting to a new authority, a new yoke. In taking the yoke of Jesus upon our shoulders we learn from him in religious experience everything that has been revealed to him (11:27).

If we are going to "come" to the way of Jesus' nonviolence, two things are involved: (1) We must realize that the way of control that defines the dynamics of *a-praüs* are destructive of our soul—whether that soul is our core being, the character of our groups, or the raison d'être of our nation or church. As long as we remain under its yoke we can never be "at rest." (2) We must unlearn the patterns of behavior that have perpetuated the *skandalon,* these stumbling blocks to right relationship in our households, and heed Jesus' words: "Learn from me" (11:29a).

This is especially difficult to do in this country when, as we have seen, so many people think they are among its wealthiest or one day will be.[22] They have taken on the yoke of delusion that the wealth they have puts them among the richest 1 percent of people in this country. If such ones are to come to Jesus, they must embark on a new way of thinking, a change of heart. This demands right thinking, it demands conversion.

Our efforts at conversion will be compounded because we are the inheritors of a national religion that subtly reflects a civil religion. Civil religion tends to equate religion with "making it in the land," in a way that is blessed by God.[23] We have created institutions to enable a faster and more secure access to the land's limited resources. We have justified our actions in the name of God. We reinforce this ideology, with God on our side, supporting our social arrangements. Ads in our diocesan papers and religious magazines often seek to convert us to the "American Way" of consumerism. This ideology is reinforced also when we often spend over 50 percent of our parish budget on schools that help our children make it in the land, even as we say that these schools are an alternative to the "American Way."

We seem afraid to critique our media or education from the viewpoint of that justice which reorders all institutions to reflect the divine will. Yet the Synod of Bishops in 1971 made just such a critique; as such it cannot be divorced from our spirituality: "Part of the human family lives immersed in a mentality that exalts possession. The school and the communications media, which are often obstructed by the established order, allow the formation only of the man desired by that order, that is to say, man in its image, not a new man but a copy of man as he is."[24]

This statement from the 1971 Synod of Bishops addressed the ideology in media and education that often reinforces the attitudes of our nation's infrastructure. When this mentality or ideology, which supports consumption, on the one hand, and clericalism, on the other, is questioned in magazines or newspapers, people write in and cancel their subscriptions. Some letters are signed "True American" or "Loyal Catholic."

Regarding our own Catholic schools (to which parents often pay many thousands of dollars annually for their children's education), it is interesting to observe the numbers of parents who threaten to pull their children from our schools once these institutions develop a curriculum geared to education for justice and nonviolence, that is, the Beatitudes. Even though the 1971

Synod of Bishops said this is the purpose of Catholic education and even though the 1977 Vatican decree on the proper purpose of Catholic education and schools stated the same, the average U.S. Catholic does not seem ready to financially support a school system that would take seriously such moral development.

At the time the Vatican issued its decree on Catholic schools, stressing the truly "alternative" approach to education envisioned, Nicholas von Hoffman commented:

> The Vatican says that church schools ought to be helped "in face of materialism, pragmatism, and the technocracy of contemporary society." According to Rome, parochial education is alive with "those who are building a new world—one which is freed from a hedonistic mentality and from the efficiency syndrome of modern consumer society."
>
> Any school system dedicated to imparting such values is worthy of support. But by their fruits you shall know them, and the products of Catholic education in the United States seem as enslaved to hedonism and the efficiency syndrome as Jews, Baptists, and pagans.
>
> The failure of American Catholic education is that it has made its students socially docile and politically conventional persons. Far from being models the rest of us can look up to, they bear a depressing resemblance to everyone else.[25]

Even though the 1971 Synod of Bishops said we must develop forms of conversion on the individual and social levels in the face of the infrastructural use of the media and education, Catholic behavior, as noted by von Hoffman, shows how little we have moved. Preaching or teaching with *exousia* pointing out the need for such conversion is seen as a threat to the system.

This understanding now brings us to consider more fully the implications of the third incident in Matthew's triad of *praüs,* Jesus' triumphal entry into the heart of his "world."

Jesus, the Praüs, *Inheriting the Land* (Gē)

Upon Jesus' entrance into Jerusalem, with a "very large crowd [*ochloi*]" before him and after him shouting his blessedness and laying down their cloaks (symbolizing their willingness to come under Jesus' authority or reign), Matthew tells us that "the whole city was in turmoil, asking 'Who is this?'" (21:10). At the beginning of Matthew's Gospel the civil leaders in the person of Herod were "frightened, and all Jerusalem with him" (2:3) to such a degree that he would resort to violence with nary a protest from the people

(2:16-18). Later in the Gospel, the disciples of John asked whether Jesus was the Messiah expected to come (11:3). This question, we have seen, was their point of entry into the depths of the hermeneutic circle. This happens when a jarring experience shakes your worldview, including your received notions of religion, even God. Now "the whole city was in turmoil"; could it be that this "Jesus from Nazareth in Galilee" is indeed the prophet (21:13)? Would this mean an end to the existing institution(s), their "isms" and the ideologies that had sustained them for centuries?

The city was shaken to its depths just as creation itself would later be shaken at the divine presence that burst forth in Jesus' death (27:52). So deeply shaken would those in the infrastructure be at the coming of true authority that they would take collective action to preserve their way of life. This is evident in the response they made to those who called Jesus the blessed one, to his "cleansing" of the temple, and to the healing of those blind and lame people who now felt free to "come to him in the temple" from which they had previously been ostracized: "they became angry" (21:15b). Rather than joining the crowd and the children shouting Jesus' praise and being ready to come under his authority, the chief priests and the scribes resorted to the "honorable" action they had learned in such conflictual situations: attack. They retorted: "Do you hear what these are saying?" (21:16a). Faithful to the prevailing dynamics of honor and shame, Jesus retorted with his own question: "Have you never read, 'Out of the mouths of infants and nursing babies you have prepared praise for yourself'" (21:16b).

The anger shown by the religious leaders at the thought that they might lose their closely guarded power, possessions, and prestige is typical of all of us who see another authority or rule as a threat rather than an invitation. When our anger arises in response to a threat, this often means we are insecure. When we are insecure we get our individual and collective "backs up"; we need to protect ourselves (as well as our institutions, their "isms," and the ideology that have become our "way of life"). When we need to protect ourselves we make defenses to keep any threat from undermining our security. We live in fear. Consequently, when we live in fear (*phobos*), to that degree we have not come under the presence and reign of God.

Bill Cunningham, the former director of justice education for the National Catholic Education Association, used to say, "If you and I are alone on an island and you have the loaf of bread, you will never sleep." In other words, to protect our consumer-selves, we must keep our defenses up. The link between consumerism and militarism can be extended beyond individuals to groups. It affects races and sexes, the rich and the poor, the North and the South.

Despite many downfalls, I have been trying to live by this wisdom ever since. I don't know how successful I am in my efforts. I do know that Matthew and I don't have our "backs up" when we are together, and the men in my province don't either. In the process, I don't think I am quite as weary as I used to be; I have found a glimmer of rest.

Despite God's promise to be with us to meet our needs, we still seek to find security in our own resources. Often we are so controlled by our need to be in charge that we make ourselves gods. We cannot leave anything to God's provident care. We have to be *sure*. We cannot trust that God will be faithful to these promises. All these attitudes evidence some lack of faith. Our security rests in our wealth in its various forms. However, good social analysis will sometimes show us that our effort to proclaim the gospel to individuals and groups can be undermined by the very infrastructures that sustain our own life. These too need to be invited to conversion.

I discovered this during the civil war in Nicaragua when the dictator Anastasio Somoza was still in power, backed by the United States. Nicaragua was the "mission" of my province; we had at least twenty men there at the time.

After the Second Vatican Council the friars embarked on a pastoral approach that involved "liberation theology." Thus, as more catechists, delegates of the word, and deacons were educated, they were conscientized to bring about change in that nation. As a result, many were killed or threatened, or they just "disappeared." Soon the men realized that the main obstacle to their pastoral mission was President Somoza. Meanwhile he continued to renegotiate his debts, backed by U.S. monetary agencies and banks. He strafed his own civilian population, backed by U.S.-trained armed forces.

In an effort to be in solidarity with our brothers and the people of Nicaragua, some of us in the province who were involved in social justice had been lobbying Congress and praying for peace there. Then, in late 1978, during a chance conversation, I discovered that one of the banks that had loaned Somoza millions of dollars was Bankers Trust in New York. Much to my surprise, the province, whose portfolio exists to help our brothers, including those in the Nicaraguan ministry, had five hundred shares in Bankers Trust! While the province was involved in the Nicaraguan mission by way of our ministry and prayer for justice on the level of the individual and group, it was unwittingly investing monies to reinforce the third level of the infrastructure, which systematically countered our effort to bring justice and peace to Nicaragua! Structurally and institutionally, we were a stumbling block to any blessing coming from our pastoral thrust with individuals and groups.

Immediately we began a process with Bankers Trust. After initial dialogue proved futile, we filed a shareholder resolution asking the bank to disclose its loans to Somoza and to make no more loans to Nicaragua until the Somoza regime and its ideology were replaced. Had we not taken this action (which subsequently resulted in Bankers Trust agreeing to our proposal), we would have been praying and ministering with one institutional hand, while our other hand benefited from structures of oppression. Had we remained uninvolved on the structural level, as an institution, we would have been saying, "Lord, Lord."

This story points to the need to do adequate social analysis about the forms of violence in our "land" if our spirituality and pastoral action are to be truly evangelical. This brings me to the final section of this chapter.

Biblical Spirituality in Our Land

Another form of irresponsible spirituality often occurs when our notion of God confines God's activities to working for a just order, leaving little or no room for transcendent religious experience. Many times people working to change structures and promote justice seem embarrassed to pray together, yet they quote the scriptures to justify the kind of just world they struggle to create. It almost seems that God and the scriptures are often used to justify a certain world order. Particular economic structures that are based on a concrete economic or political analysis become ends blessed by God. I have found that both those on the right and those on the left can do this.

Prayer and ministry are equal dimensions of spirituality. Jesus' spirituality was no more authentic when he healed the sick than when he departed to be alone with God. Both had their proper time and place in his spirituality. When either prayer or ministry absorbs the one without enabling the other to be given its proper order, unsound biblical spirituality results.

We can no longer afford to say which takes priority—prayer or ministry, religious experience or social justice, charismatic activity or ethical obedience. From the example of Jesus, Matthew articulates the need for his community to develop a spirituality that integrates both the Mount of the Transfiguration (17:1-8) and the Mount of Final Commissioning to bring God's total plan into the whole world (28:16-20). The need for such balance is particularly acute today as we reflect on our past history as people who say we are committed to Yahweh and to God's vision for all creation.

From our examination of the blessedness of the way of nonviolence, in contrast to the stumbling blocks that come with control, Matthew's story of Jesus' words and deeds is simply saying that a life based on ultimate trust in God makes us poor in spirit and *praüs* in such a way that our basic wealth in all its forms rests securely in God. All the human expressions of wealth must be oriented to others to promote God's reordering of our world in justice. Manifesting such a spirituality brings about the reign of God's presence along with its secure protection. If, for the sake of this divine plan, we orient our wealth on behalf of the poor, God will always provide.

When people challenge me regarding such ideas, I often ask them if they know people who (for the sake of God's reign) have oriented their lives to promote God's plan but who are now in need. I have never heard of anyone, who, for the sake of God's plan, has worked for justice, who has not found inner security and even peace, even if their personal troubles continue or they still find themselves in external tensions. The same psalmist that promised "the meek shall possess the land" also comforted the people with the wisdom gained of such experiences when we read: "I have been young, and now am old, yet I have not seen the righteous forsaken or their children begging bread. They are ever giving liberally and lending, and their children become a blessing" (Ps. 37:25-26).

Having been blessed themselves, their children inherit their blessing. You can't leave a greater legacy than that!

The way of nonviolence is not only being free of the need to control; it is expressed in "the land" as a way of care. As such it can do much to heal an uncaring world that busily runs after power, possessions, and prestige. Nonviolence should be able to touch every aspect of our lives. It can enter our attitudes and our behavior. It can reflect a new way of wisdom and meekness that arises from our sense that God is God, that we are God's people, that the land is God's, and that the land is ours to use responsibly.

Meekness can be extended to stewardship for the resources of the land itself in contrast to the violence we have done to the earth. Injustice and disorder in the way we pollute land, sea, and sky point to desecration of God's plan for all creation. The central good news of Matthew's spirituality tells the world that God is with us (1:3; 28:20). Yet we often fail to evidence this fact of God's presence in our midst in the way we exercise stewardship over the land and the whole ecosystem. Instead, we violate the command given Israel by Yahweh as it came into the land: "You shall not defile the land in which you live, in which I also dwell; for I the Lord dwell among the Israelites" (Num. 35:34).

If we honestly believe God is with us, our spirituality will reflect that faith in meekness toward God, humans, and the land itself. It simply is unrealistic to believe we can continue to exploit false gods, dehumanize people, and pollute the earth without suffering consequences. Therefore, wisdom would tell us more than ever that we need a good dose of spiritual realism as we consider how we will live on the land within a limited ecosystem.

CHAPTER SIX

Blessed Are Those Who Hunger and Thirst for Justice; They Will Be Satisfied

Dikaiosynē, or justice, sets Matthew's Gospel apart from the other Gospels. In the context of the world of Matthew's audience, *dikaiosynē* also sets apart the Matthean community from the "justice" practiced by the imperial powers and the justice practiced by the leaders of the synagogue households. Leland White argues that justice was to be the code of honor that would define membership in the Matthean church. "The Sermon on the Mount contains norms that serve to set Matthew's community apart from its environment as the righteous from the unrighteous." In fact, White insists, the traditional Mediterranean notions of honor and shame, as far as Matthew's vision for his house churches is concerned, "is played in the higher key of righteous/unrighteous." In line with the argument I made in the introduction for translating *makarios* as "honorable," White shows that *dikaiosynē* was an "honor term" that makes Matthew's Gospel unique and Matthew's house churches equally unique. He writes: "Although the noun *honor* does not appear in the sermon or in Matthew, the term *dikaiosynē/righteousness* occurs seven times in the Gospel and five of these are in the sermon (5:6, 10, 20; 6:1, 33). While its meaning is much debated, there is a scholarly consensus that this is an important concept in the Gospel of Matthew."[1]

Matthew portrays Jesus as founder of an alternative household of disciples, committed to justice; a kind of semi-egalitarian community[2] within a patriarchal system that was unjust. The corresponding Beatitude in Luke honors those who hunger, but Matthew's households seem not to be hungry. But at the same time they are not especially concerned about those who are. Thus, he shows that honorable living in those households would be constituted by a hunger and thirst for the kind of order that God wants—at every level, including justice toward the poor (25:31-46). Such an attitude put the members of Matthew's increasingly prosperous house churches in opposition to those in the world around them.

That the audience in Matthew's households is to be defined by justice becomes even clearer when we realize that Matthew's Gospel stands unique among the Synoptic Gospels in the way it uses the word *dikaiosynē.* While

Mark, who served as the main source for Matthew's text, never uses the word and Luke's only use of *dikaiosynē* seems to have come from a source in the liturgy—the word is found in the Prayer of Zechariah ("that we . . . might serve him . . . in holiness and *dikaiosynē* [Luke 1:75])—Matthew uses the word seven times (3:15; 5:6, 10, 20; 6:1, 31; 21:23), a number related to perfection.[3] Indeed, these seven uses of the word have become embedded so deeply in our understanding of evangelical spirituality that the 1971 Synod of Bishops declared that "action on behalf of justice" is a "constitutive dimension of the preaching of the Gospel" itself.[4]

In the final analysis, according to Jacques Dupont, one of the foremost commentators on the Sermon on the Mount, all the Beatitudes are concerned about one subject: justice or righteousness.[5] This should not be surprising, if we are mindful of Jesus' earlier words about his very existence on earth as being the fulfillment of "all justice" (3:15) such as was found in the law and the prophets (5:20). His justice, as well as that outlined for his house churches, however, would have to be radically different from that of the religious leaders of his day.

When we contextualize Matthew's Beatitudes and Sermon on the Mount within the wider Gospel, it becomes evident that those who would translate *dikaiosynē* as "righteousness" might be "spiritualizing" the notion with ideas about justification that arose more than 1400 years after the Gospel was written. Consequently, Mary R. D'Angelo argues: "it also tends to evoke the narrowly individualistic version of sin and justification that is often the focus of post-Reformation interpreters (both Protestant and Catholic), obscuring the communal concerns with God's justice and the demand for moral rightness and equity, especially economic equity for the poor; that are central to early Judaism and Christianity." Instead, she concludes: "The sermon is about the practice of justice; the good deeds of the disciples enlighten and preserve the world; the justice of those who enter heaven's reign must be greater than that of the scribes and Pharisees."[6]

Despite differences about the meaning of *dikaiosynē* in Matthew, the First Gospel never calls the members of his house churches "just." Rather, White argues: "They are called to righteousness, but not called righteous, and they are enjoined to conceal their righteous deeds from public view. . . . Nonetheless, by proposing a righteousness higher than that held by those called righteous, they imply that they are a superior community of the righteous."[7]

Setting the Context for an Understanding of *Dikaiosynē* in the Old Testament

The fourth Beatitude expresses concepts faithful to the Old Testament notion of justice. The responsibility of the wealthy class toward poor and needy people was described in Hebrew as *tsedāqāh* and *tsedeq,* "righteous-ness," "justice." When the prophets spoke of the need of the rich to hear the cry of the poor, they talked in terms of "righteousness" and "justice" rather than charity or love. When the Hebrew Scriptures were translated into Greek, two interconnected meanings resulted: *eleēmosynē* (mercy or care) and *dikaiosynē* (justice or right relationships).

Matthew's honoring of those who hunger and thirst for justice seems to have some connection to Isaiah 49:10, which speaks of God leading the peo-ple in ways so that "they shall not hunger or thirst" but will be led to "springs of water" that would satisfy them. In a special way, however, this Beatitude, as well as the whole Matthean Gospel, reflects the understanding of justice that runs throughout Isaiah 61. As this messianic passage about Israel's restoration indicates, the fullest expression of justice contains both a constitutive and a normative dimension. With "the spirit of the Lord God" anointing us (Isa. 61:1), we are clothed with a robe of justice; we are wrapped in a mantle of jus-tice (Isa. 61:10). The robe and the mantle of justice enable us to experience God in the depths of our being as *our* justice. Constituted in God's justice, God uses us to "cause righteousness and praise to spring up before all the nations" (Isa. 61:11).

Justice is the authority of God which must rule the world. Hence, the goal of justice, people like Jeremiah believed, was to reorder the world's chaotic alienation, or *tohu wabohu.* Consequently, "the days are coming, says the Lord, when I will raise up a righteous shoot to David. As king he shall reign and govern wisely, he shall do what is just and right in the land. In his days Judah shall be saved, Israel shall dwell in security. This is the name they give him: 'The Lord is our righteousness" (Jer. 23:5-6).

Jeremiah and Isaiah before him show that the constitutive dimension of justice begins with a personal experience of God's care for us in our disorder and need. In our need, God empowers us so that we can give evidence of the righteousness within us by living under the normative ethic of justice. In the power of that experienced justice, Israel was called to a similar ministry of justice. Since Israel's religious experience and ministry are the archetype of our spirituality, when the world sees our ministry of justice it should also be able to say of us:

> They will be called oaks of righteousness,
> The planting of the Lord, to display his glory.
> They shall build up the ancient ruins,
> they shall raise up the former devastations;
> they shall repair the ruined cities,
> the devastations of many generations . . .
> as a bridegroom decks himself with a garland,
> and as a bride adorns herself with her jewels.

For as the earth brings forth its shoots,
and as a garden causes what is sown in it to spring up,
so the Lord God will cause righteousness and praise
to spring up before all the nations. (Isa. 61:3b-4, 10-11)

Isaiah also wrote to the people in the context of the exile. At this moment of weakness, the Israelites said they would have been happier with the security of enslavement. At least they could rely on a structure of oppression to feed them and give them drink in abundance. Isaiah was trying to give them hope by recalling that the God of the exodus was a God of justice. He wanted to give them hope rather than allow them to descend into despair as the Israelites had in the desert.

From an economic perspective, hunger and thirst constitute the basic needs or appetites of the human race. In the desert, without productive land, Israel depended on Yahweh to meet all of its basic needs, especially food and water. Despite its dependence on God in the desert, the people were not satisfied with the provisions offered. Wanting to control the land rather than depend on Yahweh who had promised always to be with them (Exod. 3:12), the people grumbled. "If only we had died by the hand of the Lord in the land of Egypt, when we sat by the fleshpots and ate our fill of bread," they said to Moses and Aaron, "for you have brought us out into this wilderness to kill this whole assembly with hunger" (Exod. 16:3). Despite the people's grumbling, God showed fidelity to the promise to be with them not only spiritually but economically as well. Life's basic resource of food would be provided: "I am going to rain bread from heaven for you. In that way I will test them, whether they will follow my instruction or not" (Exod. 16:4).

During the period when Israel was homeless it was invited to trust that Yahweh would meet its basic need for daily bread. The sign of its trust would be a concrete manifestation of its response to God's word; Israel would not hoard what was given: "And Moses said to them, 'Let no man leave any of it over until the morning'" (Exod. 16:19). Israel failed the test; the people were not satisfied with enough (Exod. 16:17)—they wanted more: "But they did not listen to Moses; some left part of it until the morning, and it bred worms and became foul" (Exod. 16:20).

The Deuteronomist's recalling of Israel's experience in the desert (especially in chapters 6 and 8) was used as a figure for the temptation facing Matthew's house churches: the tendency to store up for themselves rather than to prove their trust in God by sharing with others in need. Thus Matthew's Jesus warned his households as Yahweh earlier had warned the Israelites (Exod. 16:20): "Do not store up for yourselves treasures on earth, where moth and rust consume and where thieves break in and steal, but store up for yourselves treasures in heaven, where neither moth nor rust consumes and where thieves do not break in and steal" (Matt. 6:19-20).

We considered in the last chapter how easily we can be seduced by the land and its promise of bread. By giving only bread enough for each day, God would give Israel daily portions so that the community continually would realize its need for God. "They so gathered that everyone had enough to eat. Moses also told them, 'Let no one leave any of it over until morning. But they did not listen to Moses; some kept part of it until morning, and it bred worms and became foul'" (Exod. 16:18-20). The bread became wormy and foul because Israel did not need it. Then, as now, enough was enough! Israel was like all of us: we always want more than enough; we can never be satisfied.

Another basic need that every economic system must supply is for water. In the desert Israel experienced severe thirst: "there was no water for the people to drink" (Exod. 17:1). Rather than trusting in God's promise, the people let the land control them: "The people quarreled with Moses, and said, 'Give us water to drink'" (Exod. 17:2). Again, in the desert, the Israelites' "treasure" was in trying to supply themselves rather than trusting God's promise to be with them in their need. "The place was called Massah and Meribah, because the Israelites quarreled and tested the Lord, saying, 'Is the Lord among us or not?'" (Exod. 17:5, 7).

"Is the Lord among us or not?" This is the perennial question arising from the human condition that needs to be sure and to control. Yahweh has shown throughout Hebrew history, and Matthew makes clear for our histories, that God is in our midst (1:23) for all days (28:20). In response God asks us to believe our needs will be met: "Your heavenly Father knows all that you need" (6:32). God knew what Israel needed when it was in the desert; God knows what we need.

Following the prophetic tradition, Matthew links "knowing" God with the "doing" of justice. Matthew presents justice in its constitutive ("knowing") and normative ("doing") manifestations. However, before examining this "spirituality of justice" found in Matthew's Gospel, we need to see how this notion of "justice" is at the heart of Matthew's message. In using *dikaiosynē*, Matthew does not seem to have appropriated the word from the traditional sources available to him. Rather, he inserted it in the Gospel in each of the seven instances (3:15; 5:6, 10, 20; 6:33; 21:32).

Jesus on John the Baptist's Mission: Not Satisfied until Justice Is Fulfilled

The first and last times Matthew uses *dikaiosynē* involve John the Baptist. The first time is connected to Jesus' "inaugural statement"; the passage also marks the first words of Jesus in the Gospel itself. If the theory is true that we should pay attention to the first words Jesus speaks in each of the Gospels, then "justice" will be a notion we must probe at length. John's baptism was to be the sign of reform that would show that Jesus was committed to letting God's reign dominate his life. In submitting to John's baptism, Jesus said, "Let it be so now; for it is proper for us in this way to fulfill all righteousness [*dikaiosynē*]" (3:15).

As the Gospel proceeds, Matthew presents Jesus as one who evidenced in his spirituality everything found in the Hebrew Scriptures—"the law and the prophets." The word and way Matthew showed this is *plērousthai;* it refers to Jesus' *fulfilling* the law and the prophets. Matthew would use the same word a total of twelve times throughout his Gospel, all referring to the fulfilling of the scriptures in Jesus' life. One of these times is in Jesus' inaugural address (3:15). At the time of his baptism Jesus said: "Let it be so now; for it is proper for us in this way to fulfill [*plērousthai*] all righteousness [*dikaiosynē*]." Justice fulfills God's whole plan for the world. Justice is essential to spirituality. This spirituality of justice is expressed in fidelity to law; yet all law must serve justice.

Justice is the fulfillment of God's will, of God's demands. Jesus' words about the purpose of the baptism summarize everything we have said thus far. In commenting on 3:15, Donald Senior states:

> There are two key words in the sentence: To "do all" (literally to "fulfill," the same Greek word Matthew so frequently uses regarding Jesus' fulfillment of Old Testament prophecies) and "righteousness," or justice. The latter term has a double layer of meaning in biblical thought. *God's* justice is his saving activity on behalf of his people. *Human* justice, or righteousness, is the effort we make to respond to God's goodness by carrying out his will.
>
> It is possible that both levels of meaning are present in this keynote statement of Jesus. God's justice, or plan of salvation, is fulfilled by the very presence of John and Jesus in world history. At the same time, Jesus is a model of *human* righteousness as well, because he carries out God's plan of salvation by his loving fidelity to his Father's will. This emphasis on obedience to the will of God, on obedience perfectly modeled by Jesus, is a hallmark of Matthew's portrait of Christ.[8]

All those who hunger and thirst for the justice that Jesus personified in his life, all those who will not be satisfied knowing that God's plan for the world is still not fulfilled will show in their spiritualities Matthew's portrait of Christ. Their biographies will become models of the theology of justice that Matthew found fulfilled in Jesus.

The seventh time *dikaiosynē* is used refers to John the Baptist's preaching. "For John came to you in the way of righteousness [*dikaiosynē*] and you did not believe him, but the tax collectors and the prostitutes believed him; and

even after you saw it, you did not change your minds and believe him"
(21:32). Because the tax collectors and prostitutes repented, they experienced
God's justice; in that justice they made normative the way of Jesus for their
lives. Consequently, Jesus added, "Truly I tell you, the tax collectors and prostitutes are going into the kingdom of God ahead of you" (21:31). The challenging stance of Jesus toward the highest ranking religious leaders was seen
by them not as an invitation to their own conversion and a higher form of
justice than that which characterized their lives (5:20) but as a threat that
undermined their authority (which was to have been based on justice). This
made them get their "backs up" and led them to want "to arrest him" (21:46).

Dikaiosynē in the Sermon on the Mount: Matthew's Outline for a Spirituality of Justice

The other five times that *dikaiosynē* appears occur in the most important
of Jesus' five discourses, the Sermon on the Mount. The five uses of *dikaiosynē*
there articulate a spirituality of justice that is unique in the Gospels. While
most scripture scholars do not make such a distinction, I believe the core constituents of spirituality—the inner, the outer, and the contextual elements—
can be found in these five uses.

Mary Ann Hinsdale has noted that "justice" in Matthew "is a concept
which is integral to the *basileia* or kingdom." Aware as I am that not all scripture scholars find such characteristics, I agree with her when she writes: "The
dilemma for interpretation has been whether Matthew intended to focus on
the gift-character of *dikaiosynē* which comes from God's reign or on a first
century Jewish understanding which stressed ethical conduct." With her, I
believe that "the best answer may be to see both Beatitudes (v. 6 and v. 10) as
reflecting the dual character of *dikaiosynē*."[9] Nevertheless, I will also argue
that each of the five seems able to be understood as uniquely (if not only)
exemplified as a gift or demand.

The "inner" or "gift" dimension of spirituality—our experience of God—
grounds Matthew's "justice" insofar as it reflects notions of longing for God.
These can be found in two texts in the Sermon: (1) "Blessed are those who
hunger and thirst for *dikaiosynē*, they shall be satisfied" (5:6) and "But strive
first for the kingdom of God and his *dikaiosynē*, and all these things will be
given to you as well" (6:33). Prayer involves a hunger and thirst for God. Hungering to be grounded in God, one longs to be a part of God's life and household. Searching for that household involves a commitment to enter God's
reign through justice. The "outer" dimension or "ethical demand" of spirituality—our expression of the God-experience in a world often alien to God—
involves a way of justice that exceeds that "justice" as it may be defined and/or
defended by religious leaders (5:20), of Jesus' day, of Matthew's day, or of all

days "to the end of the age" (28:20). Such a commitment to fulfill the law and the prophets through Jesus' kind of justice in a religious system and empire too often characterized by injustice will invite misunderstanding and persecution (5:10). Both the inner and outer dimensions of *dikaiosyne* must take place within a certain group itself, an alternative community committed to justice. In this household defined by *dikaiosyne* the members witness to that commitment through almsgiving, prayer, and fasting (6:1). A Matthean household committed to justice constitutes the new foundation for a transformed kindom; this will be a threat to empire and religious notions of justice that fall short of the rule of God.

Matthew's Households Constituted in Justice (5:6; 6:33)

To achieve the constitutive experience of God's justice in us invites us to hunger and thirst for God's presence and life, power and care, to rule our lives, to ground our being. Since our hearts have been made by and for God, they will never be satisfied until we dwell in God's justice, until we are "right" with God. We are to ask for justice in prayer, seek its power in reflection, and knock until we have opened for us ever-deepening experiences and understandings of this liberating presence of God-with-us. Aware that that God who sees us in need and who cares for us as divine images will also respond to these calls, we experience ourselves being constituted, provided with everything that is good. The "good thing" that we especially experience is the *exousia* of God's Spirit (see 7:11). As our lives become more transformed into images of God, we are increasingly justified or "made right" with God. Blessed in justice, we share in God's life. True to this notion of justice as being "made right," Jack Dean Kingsbury links 5:6 as a hunger for God to set relations right.[10]

In chapter 3 I showed that Matthew, uniquely among the Synoptics, links five notions together: doing good, producing fruit, a rich harvest, justice, and God's will. From this perspective, those who "hunger and thirst for justice" are totally oriented in their hearts (in their thinking, their emotions, and behavior) toward doing what God "requires." What God requires is justice, the fulfilling of God's will. This idea is reinforced when we turn to another passage in the Sermon on the Mount where Matthew's Jesus tells the audience not to "worry about your life, what you will eat or what you will drink," but rather to "strive first for the kingdom of God and his righteousness, and all these things will be given to you as well" (6:25, 33).

I also noted in chapter 3 that, when people of Matthew's day would be considered serving (*douleuein*) objects like eating and drinking, contemporary language would characterize them as being addictive. This means that their thinking, emotions, and actions revolve around ensuring that they will get the food they obsess about and the drink they covet.

People who are wealthy rarely hunger and thirst like the poor. But they can be "given over to" object, process, and relational addictions. It is in this sense that we need to find what "hungering and thirsting" for justice might mean. Furthermore, since an addict is never satisfied until the object of the addiction is realized, it follows that those who hunger and thirst for justice should never be satisfied until justice comes into the world at all levels. When their lives are ordered in this way around justice, Matthew's Jesus promises, they will be honored as *makarioi* in the house churches who share their passion. If this is so, the *skandalon* that keeps this Beatitude from being realized in our lives, individually and communally, collectively and organizationally, is that we don't really care about justice for others as long as we have it for ourselves. Satisfaction with injustice belies authentic spirituality.

Spirituality, Ronald Rolheiser writes, "concerns what we do with desire."[11] Without thirsting, without desire, we too easily settle for a drop instead of a cup of water. We also can blot out our concern for others who hunger and thirst as long as we are nourished. In a similar vein, when we are unsatisfied until we are "made right" with God and God's ordering in our lives, we have gotten a glimpse of what this Beatitude means. As Evelyn Mattern wrote of this Beatitude: "with its emphasis on longing, the inner disposition of the hungerer de-emphasizes behavior not born of deep desire." She also noted: "This beatitude shows us, perhaps more than any, the uncompromising nature of Jesus' view of what humankind both deserves and should desire."[12]

Matthew's Households Living by a Justice That Sets Them Apart (5:10, 20; 6:1)

The way we show our fidelity to the rule of God is authenticated by the way we live under the norms of justice. When this happens the constitutive dimension of justice (God's right relations with us) is translated in the normative dimension of justice (our efforts to achieve right relationships in all levels of our world). This invites us to elaborate on the other two normative uses of *dikaiosynē* (5:20; 6:1). Here the word is used to describe the kind of ethic that should guide the Christian community in its individual members, its groups, and its own institutional life.

The Need for Justice That Surpasses That of the Religious Leaders (5:20)

"For I tell you, unless your righteousness," your *dikaiosynē,* Jesus said, "exceeds that of the scribes and Pharisees, you will never enter the kingdom of God" (5:20). Matthew gives the warning of Jesus to the community after talking about the need to fulfill within its own life everything found in the scriptures (5:17-19).

Throughout his Gospel, Matthew presents Jesus as the one who interprets all law in light of the demands arising from human need. In two key passages—about the standing grain (12:1-8) and the cure of the man with the shriveled hand (12:9-13)—the author of the First Gospel presents Jesus as the one who bends laws to serve justice and people's needs rather than the other way around, the way of the scribes and Pharisees.

Facing Jesus' growing threat to their legitimacy, these authorities "conspired against him" (12:14) for deviating from their interpretations. While Jesus' way of truth addressed the needs of the people (12:15-16), it deviated from the hypocritical prose and practices of the leaders (12:17-21). Noting the authorities' increasingly violent attitudes toward Jesus, Matthew again shows him fulfilling the messianic promises that spoke about persecution for those promoting justice (Isa. 42:1-4):

> Here is my servant, whom I have chosen,
> My beloved, with whom my soul is well pleased.
> I will put my Spirit upon him, and he will proclaim justice to the
> Gentiles.
> He will not wrangle or cry aloud, nor will anyone hear his voice in
> the streets.
> He will not break a bruised reed or quench a smoldering wick
> until he brings justice (*krisis*) to victory.
> And in his name the Gentiles will hope. (Matt. 12:18-21)

The word Matthew uses for justice and judgment that is made victorious is *krisin*. In other places *krisin* (or *krisis*) is translated as "truth." Truth is the foundation for the justice, or *dikaiosynē*, of Jesus. At the same time it unmasks the hypocrisy of the so-called justice of the scribes and Pharisees (5:20). In this sense it is clear that the battle line between Jesus and the leaders of his day was the issue of truth. "I tell you," Jesus said, "on the day of judgment [*krisin*] you will have to give an account for every careless word you utter; for by your words you will be justified, and by your words you will be condemned" (12:36-37).

Even though Matthew's Jesus hardly uses the word, the issue of truth and its violation was central to the whole approach of the scribes and Pharisees. While they paraded as models of holiness and justice, many of the leaders of the Jews (and later the church) were nothing but hypocrites. Jesus saved his most extensive condemnations for such leaders. They were stumbling blocks for the community (23:1-36). Their lifestyles contradicted what they taught. They used their elite status as interpreters of the law to reinforce their own wants, rather than the needs of the people. Their hearts were divided; religiously they were "split." "Interestingly, this split is also called by Matthew, in both cases, *anomia*, 'lawlessness' (7:23; 23:28)." John Meier writes:

In the Septuagint, *anomia* often is used, not for theoretical opposition to Law or particular commandments, but rather for that fundamental rebellion against God's will which marks the truly evil
person.

The fascinating point here is that both the legalistic Pharisees and
the freewheeling charismatic Christians could be equally guilty of
anomia. The "life-styles" may be different. But the rejection of God's
will for the sake of one's own will is the same, and the resultant split
is the same.[13]

The Alternative Way of Justice Lying between 5:20 and 6:1

Although many commentators have written on the six "antitheses" in
Matthew's Gospel, fewer scholars have noted two facts about these alternative
visions of the moral life as offered by Matthew: (1) they are ways that show
how their kind of "*dikaiosynē* exceeds that of the scribes and Pharisees"; and
(2) these alternative ways to the "justice" of the religious leaders are manifestations of the way of perfection that Matthew's Jesus considered "perfect"
(*teleios*) or holy.

This revision of *Spirituality of the Beatitudes* was written in the context of
a second wave of *skandaloi* in the church. In response to this, those operating
from a notion of ecclesiology and spirituality that would reinforce the "justice" of the scribes and Pharisees have argued that the solution to the problem in the church is for the priests, the bishops, and everyone else in "the
church" to be "holy." Somehow this notion of holiness or sanctity is equated
with fidelity, while "fidelity" is equated with an orthodoxy that means submitting to the "church of Matthew 16" with no regard for the "church of
Matthew 18."

Matthew's Jesus has another notion of perfection, holiness, sanctity, and
fidelity, rooted in his understanding of "justice." This justice is manifested not
only in the way we orient ourselves and our resources toward the poor and
marginalized (19:21; 25:31-46) but also in an entirely new moral way of life
that can be found in the six antitheses:

1. A new way of dealing with those from whom we are alienated: reconciliation (5:21-26).
2. A new way of relating sexually to others: nonmanipulative (5:27-30).
3. A new way of honoring the dignity of women: nonexploitative (5:31-
   32).
4. A new code of honor: your word itself (5:33-37).
5. A new way of dealing with abuse and evildoing: disarmament (5:38-
   42).
6. A new model of reciprocity: treating everyone as a member of your
   family (5:43-47).

When we live by this new moral code we not only show the world a new way of "justice" (5:20), but we become "perfect, therefore, as your heavenly Father is perfect" (5:48). We will show in our lives and households that we are under the rule of God. We reveal authentic holiness as well.

Religious Acts and the Promotion of Justice (6:1)

Another time Matthew's Jesus invites his disciples in the house churches to practice a *dikaiosynē* that is greater than the religious leaders' brand of it occurs in his declaration: "Beware of practicing your piety (*dikaiosynē*) before others in order to be seen by them" (6:1). In the triad of justice that follows (6:2-18), it becomes clear that the observance of such justice or "religious duties" stands in stark contrast to the hypocrisy of those who "make a show" of their religion. The former will be blessed; the practice of the latter is shown to be a stumbling block (even though the word *skandalon* is not used).

Because Jesus' teachings about justice via almsgiving, prayer, and fasting have no parallels in the other Gospels, this fact would evidence that they were written to address deviations from justice occurring in the Matthean house churches. Given this, Matthew was challenging any spirituality that stressed prayer or various prayer forms at the expense of a justice that did good (7:21-23). His Jesus railed against a kind of public prayer that is centered on the one who prayed rather than private prayer that evidences a public commitment to make things right (6:5; 23:1ff.). In either case, true justice (another word for piety) demands authenticity in prayer.

Daniel Harrington writes that the words Matthew places on Jesus' lips regarding his contemporaries apply equally to the leaders of Matthew's day. The words apply equally well in our day.

> In their Matthean context these teachings about true and false piety would have been taken as criticisms of the rival Jews who controlled "their synagogues," the "synagogue of the hypocrites." The description of those who practiced this false piety as "hypocrites" (6:2, 3, 16) and the references to "the synagogues" (6:2, 5) make this certain. When read alongside the polemic in Matthew 23, Matt 6:1-18 [on justice as almsgiving, prayer and fasting] functions as part of the attack against the Jewish opponents of the Matthean community.[14]

Religious acts of justice should reflect God's justice. If we live under that normative ethic of justice, then the circle of care can be completed in us as we draw others into its warmth. We draw others into the circle of care by our piety or religious acts.

Justice (6:1) grounds the entirety of Jesus' official prayer (6:9-13). Because it is cultic in its context,[15] justice must be an integral part of our worship and prayer itself. This justice is to pervade all that we are and all that we do. This justice is what makes for authentic piety.

Traditionally, piety was considered a way of showing to others the love one received from God. Thus, almsgiving, prayer, and fasting were common practices of justice. They were recognized as a way to reorder relations with those in need through alms (6:2-4), with God and neighbor through prayer that celebrates forgiveness (6:5-15), and with the oppressed through fasting that enables one to experience the depth of need to respond more easily to the cries of others (6:16-18). Jesus said that each of these three normative dimensions of justice had to be expressed beyond that of the scribes and Pharisees (see 5:20).

Matthew shows how this expression could go beyond that of the leaders in two ways. First of all, he prefaces each religious act by saying, "When you give alms," "When you are praying," and "When you fast." By using the word "when," Matthew seems to be operating from an important "given" about traditional spirituality. If God's justice, order, and life are within us, it should be normative that they are expressed automatically. Matthew simply assumes that a person experiencing God's presence, energy, and power will give alms, pray, and fast. As a consequence, Matthew's Jesus does not say, " *If* you give alms, pray, or fast," as though we have a choice.

Second, our motivation must differ from those who perform these acts of justice for public show. If we give alms, pray, and fast for others to see we "are already repaid" (6:2, 5, 16). But if our deeds of justice reflect an attitude of poverty in spirit, "your Father who sees in secret will repay you" (6:4, 6, 18). A sure test determining if these words will find us judged positively or negatively is to ask ourselves if we continue our acts of piety when no one is around. Authentic spirituality does not give double messages.

The first form of piety which Matthew considers a matter of justice is the giving of alms. This admonition about almsgiving is best understood in light of a consideration found in the Book of Tobit. Tobit was a devout and wealthy Israelite living in captivity among the Ninevites after the fall of the northern kingdom in 721 B.C.E. The angel Raphael showed Tobit that almsgiving was to be more central to his life than prayer or fasting (Tob. 12:7-10).

In the ancient Near Eastern world, a tremendous gap existed between the rich, who had power, possessions, and prestige, and the poor, who were powerless, without many possessions, the "nobodies" of those cultures. The responsibility of the wealthy class toward the poor and needy was described in Hebrew as *tsedāqāh* ("righteousness") and *tsedeq* ("justice"). When prophets and wisdom writers like Tobit spoke of the responsibility of the rich to hear the cry of the poor, they expressed themselves in terms *of tsedāqāh* and *tsedeq* rather than words meaning love. After the exile, these words gradually took on the meaning of almsgiving. Often these words were translated in the Septuagint as *eleēmosynē* (mercy or care) and *dikaiosynē* (justice).

I would like to believe the authenticity of the "approved" apparitions of the Blessed Mother to Catherine Labouré and those at Guadalupe, LaSallette, Lourdes, Pontmain, Fatima, Beauraing, and Banneux, but I have some doubts when she asks people only to "pray" and "fast" instead of the divine triad of prayer, fasting, and almsgiving. It's quite sad, I think, that the accounts of the Blessed Virgin's words do not find her stressing "almsgiving" in her various apparitions and locutions; piety (another word for *dikaiosynē* in some translations) too often is limited to the "safe" areas of prayer and fasting that have little to do with transformation beyond the personal.

Almsgiving is not a matter of feeling. Neither can it be arbitrarily cut off when it happens that the recipient of our alms might not manifest thinking or behavior akin to our own. In the same vein, alms should not be withheld because these may go beyond the individual or interpersonal levels to alleviate that structural injustice that often sustains poverty and brokenness. Evangelical almsgiving cannot be geared only to Band-Aid approaches; it must challenge the economic and political structures of justice as well.

While many North American Christians have been educated to show "charity" toward individuals or even groups, they cannot understand or support the growing involvement of a number of Catholic and Protestant institutions in the ministry of corporate responsibility, a contemporary way of "giving alms." This ministry finds denominations, dioceses, and orders such as our Midwest Capuchin Franciscans using the equities in our portfolios to press for corporate reform. I find it interesting that this kind of advocacy can sometimes result in loss of our benefactors, some of whom can give their alms because they have realized hefty returns from stock in companies that might not be just in their hiring practices, their outsourcing, their tax payments, or their environmental policies. Sometimes, too, we are challenged by church people for such advocacy.

This happened to me in 2000 when I attended the annual meeting of shareholders of the Boeing Company. I went to show my province's concerns regarding its dealings and involvement in the People's Republic of China. Boeing had created one of the most sophisticated lobbying efforts ever seen to bring about Most Favored Nation status for China. Failing to get a hearing for our concerns, we filed a shareholder proposal. We asked Boeing to ensure shareholders that it would respect basic human rights *within its own operations* in China. We knew we would never get any kind of support if we ask the company to promote human rights beyond its own operations. In my remarks at the meeting, I appealed to the golden rule as articulated by Matthew's Jesus. I said something like: "I ask you to imagine yourself working at one of our plants in China. If you knew the shareholders' meeting was taking place today, wouldn't you be hoping the shareholders would vote for this resolution? I ask you to 'do to others as you would have them do to you'" (7:12).

After I spoke at one particular annual meeting in 2000, a Lutheran minister got up and spoke against the resolution. He said that he was a seminary professor in Hong Kong and thought our resolution was the wrong way to address the issue. After the meeting, I asked him how he could have done what he did. He said, "Father, I agree with your ends, but not your means."

Remembering that many said the same thing in the 1960s regarding the marches in Milwaukee for open housing and the boycott of South African-related companies in the 1980s, I said, "We tried everything we could to bring about change with management. The only thing left for us was to bring the issue to the shareholders. Could you please tell me any other nonviolent way we could try to love our neighbor in China as we do ourselves here?" He just smiled and said he disagreed.

The next form of piety that promotes the normative dimension of justice deals with prayer and the attitude we bring to prayer. "Whenever you pray, go to your room, close your door, and pray to your Father in private. Then your Father, who sees what no man sees, will repay you" (6:6). In addition to the Our Father (6:9-13) in this section (6:1-18), Matthew's Jesus presents the proper way to pray in the form of a "do" and a "don't": do not babble (6:7-8) and do forgive (6:14-15).

When we examine much of the prayer offered in our daily lives, in our families and communities as well as in our weekly liturgies, too often I think we have to admit there is a lot of babbling going on. For instance, in some churches and religious houses too many people seem to be performing many forms of piety that reflect a heaping up of "empty phrases" (6:7), such as rosaries, litanies, or other devotions without much social concern. Even worse, at times some of this piety is connected to themes supportive of unfettered capitalism, "free" (but not "fair") enterprise, patriotism, and larger military budgets. If anyone seeks to challenge such ideas, they are rejected as out of place, or "political."

As he affirms a form of prayer that shows itself in justice, Matthew included the "Lord's Prayer" as the model of prayer that does not babble but is committed to social transformation, especially in deliverance from all forms of indebtedness. As we pray these words in our concrete world of people, groups, and institutions, it is good to know that the words invite all levels of the world to change whatever negates the fulfillment of those words on earth as they would be fulfilled in heaven (6:10). If we are not "trying to create a heaven on earth," by applying these words to all people at all levels of our world, we should stop praying Jesus' Prayer. Our actions and lifestyle will show that we do not mean what we pray when we say we want God's reign on earth as it is in heaven. We will have been babbling.

As I showed in *The Prayer that Jesus Taught Us*, Jesus' prayer was written not primarily for our individual practice but for the house churches themselves.[16] Yet, too often, it is used publicly to promote this or that agenda rather than Jesus' agenda of justice. Probably one of the most telling examples of this came in 2001 (before September 11th) when President George W. Bush was not doing well in the polls and had promised to make a decision about the use of stem cells, a decision that might be rejected by many church leaders, including those in the Roman Catholic Church. On the front page of its Sunday edition, the *New York Times* featured a picture of the president and the cabinet at prayer.[17]

The fact that the press had been called into that room to cover the cabinet at prayer was not lost on Arianna Huffington, a one-time conservative columnist. She suggested strongly that the picture was meant to convey something besides prayer. Her column, entitled "Publicly Parading Piety in the Service of Political Expediency," featured the text from Matthew's Gospel we are considering here. This led her to protest: "How dare he turn a private act of spiritual devotion into a public photo opportunity?" She then explained why she considered such "piety" to be hypocritical:

"Beware of practicing your piety before men in order to be seen by them" admonished Jesus in the Sermon on the Mount. "And when you pray, you must not be like the hypocrites; for they love to stand and pray in the synagogues and at the street corners, that they may be seen by men. . . . When your pray, go into your room and shut the door and pray to your Father who is in secret, and your Father who sees in secret will reward you." Jesus didn't leave a lot of wiggle room.

Indeed, the more important prayer is to you, the more offended you should be by the Bush administration's cynical exploitation of it. There is a huge difference between privately sharing a prayer with your fellow public servants and publicly parading your piousness in service of political expedience.

She then concluded her chastisement of the administration facetiously: "What would Jesus do? Certainly not pray and say 'cheese.'"[18]

When we look at the various petitions in the prayer that Jesus taught us, the only one that its author elaborated on involved forgiveness. Thus, at the end of the prayer (6:9-13), Matthew's Jesus says: "for as you forgive others their trespasses, your heavenly Father will also forgive you; but if you do not forgive others, neither will your Father forgive your trespasses" (6:14-15).

Many leaders in the charismatic movement have long known that the obstacles to healing and to deeper experiences of God are very often related to alienation and unforgiveness. People come to prayer meetings seeking healing. They remain broken, only to respond affirmatively when someone asks: Is there anyone here that you are angry with, or about whom you have hard feelings? or Is there anyone in your family, your work, or your past who has hurt you? or Do you still harbor anger and resentments and find it hard to forgive? Brokenness grounded in divisions, resentment, and unforgiveness separates us from union with God. Alienation must always be healed; it can never be rationalized away (see 18:21-22).

The final way justice is to be normative in the community is through fasting (6:16-18). While the bridegroom, Jesus, was on earth, there was no need to fast. A purpose of fasting is to help clear the mind in order to remember someone or something from the past. With the powerful experience of God-with-them in Jesus, the disciples had the living example of Jesus continually motivating them. They did not need to recall his deeds; they witnessed his *exousia*. They experienced Jesus' fast as reordering conditions of need and brokenness (see 9:14-15).

Jesus warned the disciples, "The days will come when the bridegroom is taken away from them, and then they will fast" (9:15). With the commission to go into the whole world (28:18-20), fasting serves two purposes. We fast to remember the bridegroom and his ways. By practicing a kind of violence to our "surface self," our senses, we can be more fully open in our "real selves" to be constituted in religious experience. Second, having set priorities as to what is now truly important in life, we can commit ourselves more fully to the ministry of Jesus. We can more easily give ourselves and our resources in greater solidarity with the poor and those in need of healing.

Fasting makes us more open to experience the transcendent. It also helps shape a vision whereby we can view our world with God's eyes. In the power of that experience, we can call for a reordering of those realities that contradict the reign of God.

Matthew did not elaborate on the concrete form our fast should take. However, because he presented Jesus fulfilling so many texts from Isaiah (especially Second Isaiah), it is safe to suggest the kind of fasting Matthew recommended for his community. Jesus viewed his ministry as fulfilling a fast (see 11:2-5). Following Second Isaiah, our fast, too, should reflect our fidelity to the task of reordering society:

> Is not this the fast that I choose:
> to loose the bonds of injustice, to undo the thongs of the yoke,
> to let the oppressed go free, and to break every yoke?
> Is it not to share your bread with the hungry,
> and bring the homeless poor into your house;
> when you see the naked, to cover them,
> and not to hide yourself from your own kin?
> . . . If you remove the yoke from among you,
> the pointing finger, the speaking of evil,
> if you offer your food to the hungry and satisfy the needs of the
>   afflicted,
> then your light shall rise in the darkness and your gloom be like the
>   noonday.

. . . Your ancient ruins shall be rebuilt;
you shall raise up the foundations of many generations;
you shall be called the repairer of the breach,
the restorer of streets to live in. (Isa. 58:6-7, 9b-10, 12)

We too can be called "repairers of the breach" and "restorers of ruined homesteads" (58:12). If we receive such names, it will be so because we fasted faithfully that the "spirit of the Lord God" constituted us "oaks of righteousness, the planting of the Lord, to display his glory" (Isa. 61:1, 3). Constituted in justice this way, we will be those who "build up the ancient ruins" (Isa. 61:4).

Fasting helps us to be more open to the Spirit of God. In fasting we are inspired to reorder society to reflect God's plan. This is central to beatitudinal living. In a special way fasting is fundamental to the fulfillment of Isaiah 61 and this particular Beatitude: "Blessed are those who *hunger* and *thirst* for justice."

Hunger and thirst are two global realities. Fasting from food and water can make us more aware of how hunger and thirst affect half of the world. By personal fasting we can experience, in a limited, temporary way, the all-pervasive, sustained hunger and thirst experienced by hundreds of millions. Our very resistance to fasting can become an inspiration to resist whatever in our lives, our relationships, and our structures contributes to hunger and thirst in the world.

Often we resist the fasting asked of us (Isa. 58:5; Matt. 6:16-18) because our very lifestyle depends on others' hungers. For instance, though we know that Wal-Mart's huge advantages in buying power and efficiency have forced many local retailers to close, and that the majority of its workers are paid a minimum wage, and that Wal-Mart has become the world's largest company, buying its goods from entities that, in turn, pay their workers the minimum legally demanded,[19] we do not "fast from Wal-Mart." Blind to the justice issues involved, we go because "it's cheaper there."

It is good to fast from such material resources as food and drink. Yet we are also called to "undo the thong of the yoke." This demands that we fast in a way that empowers those in need. We are called to fast from discrimination, exploitation, manipulation, or any other attitudes and actions that create or perpetuate injustice. This manner of fasting will do much to untie the thongs of prejudice's yoke, which keep women, minorities, and Third World peoples oppressed (Isa. 58:6).

Challenging the Lie, the Stumbling Block to Justice

Earlier I noted that the other word for "justice," besides *dikaiosynē*, is *krisis*, which can also mean "truth." In general, inner alienation from God's plan was structurally manifested in the chaos of Matthew's community. Such chaos, sociologically speaking, is also called *anomia. Anomia* reflects the lawlessness and lack of right ordering that result in that kind of "evildoing" (versus "doing good") that keeps us from injustice. The teaching of the scribes and Pharisees was untruthful because it did not promote justice (see 16:5-12). Such hypocrisy was contributing to spiritual as well as sociological *anomie,* disorder and lawlessness within the community.

We have seen that the antitheses (5:21-47) showed a new way of interpreting the law so that its underlying truth would promote the justice that exceeded that of the scribes and Pharisees. Immediately after these antitheses, the community was warned to avoid those forms of piety (*dikaiosynē*) that say one thing externally but internally reflect another dynamic (6:1). Whether the practice be almsgiving (6:2-4), prayer (6:5-15), or fasting (6:16-18), no religious exercise could mislead people; none could be untruthful or hypocritical.

Spirituality cannot be a sham; if it is, it denies God's truth. The word *hypokritēs* means "ungodly" or "unjust" in the Septuagint. It is the opposite of *dikaiosynē,* or godly, which practices what it preaches. Hypocrisy gives mere lip service to God's plan as it follows its own plans.

The need for truth-in-spirituality today is no less urgent than our current need for truth-in-government or truth-in-advertising. We should never be satisfied until we make truth the foundation of our lives, our relationships, and our society.

CHAPTER SEVEN

Blessed Are the Merciful;
They Will Receive Mercy

While scripture scholars differ widely on their interpretation of almost all the Beatitudes, very few find any disagreement with the fifth Beatitude: "Blessed are the merciful, for they will receive mercy" (5:7). Maybe it is because in this Beatitude the last part is the same as the first part: mercy comes to those who are merciful.

Especially in the Septuagint, as I pointed out in the previous chapter, there are strong links between justice and mercy. The great biblicist C. H. Dodd noted that, in the Septuagint, two aspects of justice or *tsedeq* "are polarized into *dikaiosynē* and *eleēmosynē*. In place of the comprehensive virtue of *tsedāqāh*, we have justice on the one hand, mercy on the other."[1] In the Hebrew Scriptures there are 115 occurrences of the noun *tsedeq* (justice), 158 of another noun, *tsedāqāh* (almsgiving), and 208 of the adjective *tsaddiq* (just). The Septuagint translated *tsedeq* as *dikaiosynē* (justice), *tsedāqāh* as *eleēmosynē* or *eleos* (mercy), and *tsaddiq* as *dikaios* (just). Though frequently used in the Septuagint, the Greek word *eleēmōn*, or merciful, occurs only once in the Gospels—here in Matthew's fifth Beatitude (5:7).

In a wonderful commentary on the connection between justice and mercy as evidenced in this Beatitude, Pope John Paul II, in his encyclical letter "Rich in Mercy," asked: "Demonstrating from the very start what the 'human heart' is capable of ('to be merciful'), do not these words from the Sermon on the Mount reveal in the same perspective the deep mystery of God: that inscrutable unity of Father, Son and Holy Spirit, in which love, containing justice, sets in motion mercy, which in its turn reveals the perfection of justice?"[2]

The Greek word for mercy (*eleos*) also corresponds to the Hebrew *hesed*, which means an integrated or holistic state of mind characterized by understanding, compassion, and justice. In a way this stance may be called "solidarity" with those who are in need. Merciful people act out of their own integrity by being open to the needs of those around them.

Jesus, the Merciful One, Offering a Holiness That Is Grounded in Mercy

Not only did Jesus' deeds exemplify mercy at its finest, but his message as well promoted mercy as the way the gospel should be proclaimed and lived. For this reason, Pope John Paul II said that the teaching of Jesus summarized in this Beatitude: "Blessed are the merciful, for they will receive mercy" is "a synthesis of the whole of the good news, of the whole of the 'wonderful exchange' (*admirabile commercium*) contained therein."[3]

According to Eduard Schweizer, "For Matthew, mercy is the focal point of Jesus' message, which shows what it means to fulfill the Law (see the discussion of 5:17-20; 9:13; 12:7; 25:31-46). Mercy has been forgotten by the Pharisees (23:23; unique to Matthew)."[4] Jesus' way of fulfilling the law and the prophets (5:17-20) was the way of justice (3:15); but mercy fulfills justice (9:13; 12:7).

In his "Rich in Mercy," Pope John Paul II noted that, "in Christ and through Christ, God also becomes especially visible in his mercy; that is to say, there is emphasized that attribute of the divinity which the Old Testament, using various concepts and terms, already defined as mercy." Indeed, he stated:

> Christ confers on the whole of the Old Testament tradition about God's mercy a definitive meaning. Not only does he speak of it and explain it by the use of comparisons and parables, but above all he himself makes it incarnate and personifies it. He himself, in a certain sense, is mercy. To the person who sees it in him—and finds it in him—God becomes "visible" in a particular way as the Father "who is rich in mercy." (Eph. 2:4)[5]

With this understanding of Jesus' person as the revelation of mercy, when we discuss the meaning of this fifth Beatitude, its fulfillment will be best evidenced in the way Jesus was merciful and thus himself received the favor of God's mercy (see 17:5). Rather than detailing here these different ways Jesus showed mercy through his teaching, preaching, and healing (which all signified mercy and will be discussed throughout the chapter itself), suffice it to say that Jesus' mercy revealed a central characteristic of God's perfection (5:48; cf. Luke 6:36).

In Leviticus 19:1-2, "the Lord spoke to Moses, saying: Speak to all the congregation of the people of Israel and say to them: You shall be holy, for I the Lord your God am holy." In a sincere effort to be faithful to such a demand, the religious leaders of Israel developed a very detailed taxonomy regarding how the people of Israel would be holy. By the time of Jesus, holiness was virtually equated with purity, purity with cleanness, and cleanness with separation from that which would be defined as "unclean." Thus, "holiness" came to be understood with highly organized structures defined by people's differences rather than by their commonalities and their distinctions, which would result in religious-sanctioned forms of separation.

The phenomenon of Jesus' *euaggelion* revolved around the in-breaking of another notion of holiness: mercy. This involved a radical rethinking of the received dynamics related to holiness. Indeed, according to Marcus Borg, Jesus' words and deeds proclaimed "a radical sociopolitical meaning." He writes: "In his teaching and table fellowship, and in the shape of his movement, the purity system was subverted and an alternative social vision affirmed. The politics of purity was replaced by a politics of compassion."[6] This new approach to the received (and entrenched) ideology of holiness or perfection was upended in the way Matthew presents Jesus' approach to key pillars defining the Jewish religion: the Territory, the Touch, the Temple, the Torah, and the Table.[7]

Holiness That Goes beyond the Territory of Israel to the Boundaries of Another Reign

In the agrarian culture of Matthew, territory defined boundaries, beginning with the constitution of the house. Beyond the household, "belonging" was extended in ever-diminishing circles. Those farthest from one's household represented territory beyond one's own; its inhabitants were "enemies." A key example of how Jesus was a child of his culture and therefore of its "territory" can be found in the story about the Samaritan woman who comes into the space (i.e., "territory") of the male Jew, Jesus, and asks him for "mercy" (*eleos*). On the one hand Jesus is defined by his cultural patterns of restriction; yet, on the other hand, he is able to transcend them because an incessant request for his mercy invites him to show mercy.

The story takes place at the time Jesus left the "land of Gennesaret" (14:34) "and went away to the district of Tyre and Sidon" (15:21). He moves from the safe and secure "land," into enemy territory. There he is confronted by "a Canaanite woman from that region [who] came out and started shouting, 'Have mercy on me, Lord, son of David: my daughter is tormented by a demon'" (15:22).

Elaine M. Wainwright notes that this story of Jesus and the Canaanite woman offers "two very different readings of Jesus and of the reign of God movement within Matthean households."[8] Faithful to the cultural code of holiness that demanded that a Jewish male shun someone "different" (a woman and a Samaritan), "he did not answer her at all" (15:23). Furthermore, declaring his seeming support of holiness-as-separation, Jesus says: "I was sent only to the lost sheep of the house of Israel" (15:24) and even levels at her an ethnic slur used by Judeans against "enemies" such as Canaanites. She is part of "the dogs" (15:26); the equivalent of the "N-word" today.

All these definers of holiness are trumped by her persistent cry for "mercy" (15:22-23). Now Jesus extends the mercy he had said he would limit to Israel's household because of her "great" faith (15:28). Mercy, in Matthew, finds Jesus redefining the holiness codes, which were characterized by separation, to go beyond the boundaries that demanded exclusive control of "God's reign" to be in the hands of the chosen few. It must be inclusive.

Today, deeper than any geographical boundaries are those mental attitudes that create and nurture separation among God's people. Our ideologies make "Canaanites" of women and other ethnic groups, but all sorts of other "outsiders" as well. When I am with young people—who are concerned about "belonging" and not being "put out of the group"—I often tell the story of the Canaanite woman. I draw a circle and ask them to think of all the people we make "our Canaanites." This list of names outside the circle gets quite long very quickly: non-whites, gays, people on welfare, Democrats (or Republicans), the rich (or the poor), persons with AIDS, the disabled, old people, parents, illegal immigrants, and others, depending on the place.

I ask them to form a circle of themselves. Then I write "the reign of God" inside the circle that is on the board. I talk about God's inclusive way and lead them in a guided meditation to help them understand God's presence in their hearts and in the hearts of all those around them. When they sense their connectedness to everyone in the group, I ask them to take the hand of the ones on either side. I talk more about how Jesus envisioned his church as a kind of house where his presence would be ensured, "where two or three are gathered in my name, I am there among them" (18:20).

After this little theological reflection describing the ideal, I do some social analysis—I get real. I ask them to step out of the circle if I point to them and label them with the name of one of the "Contemporary Canaanites" written on the board. I also ask them not to close the circle after the labeled classmate has been put out. It's not long before most everyone from the group is standing alone—both outside and inside the circle. After asking those put outside how they felt when they were labeled and told to leave, I then ask the "insiders" how they feel. It becomes clear that we hurt ourselves, not just the whole body, when mercy fails to characterize our groups.

Holiness That Touches the Untouchables with Healing to Announce God's Reign

Not only in the way he broke down geographical boundaries but especially in the way he reached out to those defined as "unclean" did Jesus practice the *eleos* he preached. In chapter 4 I showed how Jesus' proclamation of

God's reign was linked, from the beginning, with the healing of a triad of people considered "unclean" in varying degrees: the leper, the servant of the centurion, and Peter's mother-in-law. Time after time, Matthew presents Jesus responding to people's needs when they ask him for mercy, especially when they or those dependent on them were suffering from some kind of sickness and, as we have seen in chapter 4, some kind of alienation from society itself. This certainly was the case with the Canaanite woman.

It is fascinating to note how many times people asking Jesus for mercy (*eleēson*) address him as "Son of David" (9:27; 15:22; 20:30, 31). Addressing Jesus with such a royal title makes it clear that they are recognizing in him an authority they have not found elsewhere. Whereas the existing powers, especially in religion, have created patterns in the name of holiness that will restrict them from full participation in community, this "Son of David" will inaugurate a new rule of holiness that invites them to full communion in the name of mercy.

Why would these people asking for mercy of Jesus not call him by his name, since it means the one who "will save his people from their sins" (1:21), especially if sickness was believed to be the result of sins committed or inherited?

First of all, in Matthew's Gospel no one addresses Jesus by his name. But that is not the reason why so many people refer to Jesus as "Son of David"— the foremost title for the earthly Jesus in Matthew's Gospel, as Günther Bornkamm has noted.[9] Whereas Mark and Luke use this title only four times, it is found ten times in Matthew. Invariably, in Matthew the term is connected to the need for healing, both individually and collectively. In a special way, as Jack Dean Kingsbury shows, the fact that Jesus heals the blind and the daughter of the Canaanite woman "correlates with the fact that elsewhere in the Gospel Matthew has Jesus decry Israel as a people that is blind, deaf, and without understanding . . . (13; cf. also 13:14-15)."[10] It is a matter of "their" blindness owing to their restrictive understanding of holiness versus Jesus' inclusive way, which is based on mercy. His is the enlightened vision.

Holiness That Goes beyond the Temple's Boundaries to Include Those Previously Rejected from It—Even on the Sabbath

With the fall of Jerusalem, gradually the synagogues became the predominant locale for word and worship rituals (4:23; 9:35; 10:17; 12:9; 13:54; 23:34). Now, even more than when the temple defined the rituals of the people, rules of exclusion in the name of holiness defined synagogal belonging. In contrast to this way of structuring religion, a key section of Matthew's Gospel shows Jesus promoting a religious system grounded in justice and mercy.

In 12:1-8 Jesus and his hungry disciples are going through a grainfield. The disciples (not Jesus) begin "to pluck heads of grain and to eat" on the Sabbath (12:1). According to the Pharisaic way of "seeing," such behavior put the disciples outside the law (12:2). When the Pharisees challenge Jesus about why they would do this, he counters the querying Pharisees with a riposte of his own. His vision highlights a way of seeing justice that meets people's basic needs in order to fulfill mercy itself. Making it clear that he is "greater than the temple" (12:6) and therefore has a greater power than it or those who serve in it, he shuts down his opponents by saying: "If you had known what this means, 'I desire mercy and not sacrifice,' you would not have condemned the guiltless. For the Son of Man is lord of the Sabbath" (12:7-8).

Immediately after this "he left that place and entered *their* synagogue" (12:9). Here he is met by a man "there with a withered hand" (12:10). Trying to undermine Jesus and find him guilty of violating the law, the synagogue leaders again offer a culturally honorable challenge. They "asked him, 'Is it lawful to cure on the Sabbath?' so that they might accuse him" (12:10). Declaring "it is lawful to do good on the Sabbath" Jesus "restored" the man's withered hand (12:12-13). Again, doing good and showing mercy trump any law. This was enough for the Pharisees to conspire as to how they might destroy Jesus (12:14). To preserve their brand of "holiness" they will be willing to violate the commandment not to kill.

Reinterpreting the Torah to Ensure the Law's True Purpose: Right Relations among All

The law had always been part of the glue that would hold the people of Israel together. However, when the Temple was destroyed along with the rest of Jerusalem in 70 c.e., the highest political body of Judaism—the Sanhedrin—vanished. Fearing the loss of identity for themselves and the people, some Pharisaic scribes went to the imperial city of Jamnia to regroup. There they forged a new identity for the people through a renewed emphasis on the law. The law—and their interpretation of it—would now hold the people together. Through a stringent obedience to the purity codes contained in the law, which defined membership, the Pharisees believed that Israel would be able to maintain its identity by isolating itself from those it defined as "impure" who lived in the empire.

By the time the first Gospel was written, the "law" had likely taken on an even greater force in people's lives than it had at the time of Jesus. Thus, while Territory and Temple had once been key definers of the people, now only Torah and Table would be promoted as the source of meaning for the people. Given the tensions that had arisen between the house churches and the "synagogue down the street," it might be likely that Matthew retro-read into the text the situation experienced by his community as it grew more and more isolated from the synagogues of Israel.

In what has become known as Matthew's diatribe, Jesus launches into a chapter-long harangue of the religious leaders for their hypocritical behavior and faulty interpretation of Torah. In a passage clearly based on the prophecy of Micah, which asked what "God requires" (Mic. 6:8), Matthew's Jesus continues his tongue-lashing of the religious leaders with the words: "Woe to you, scribes and Pharisees, hypocrites! For you tithe mint, dill, and cumin and have neglected the weightier matters of the law: justice and mercy [*eleos*] and faith. It is these you ought to have practiced without neglecting the others. You blind guides! You strain out a gnat but swallow a camel!" (23:23-24).

Later in this chapter I will argue that this passage might be used of the religious leaders today who have used their control of law in the Roman church to revert to the very situation that Jesus here rejects.

Holiness That Welcomes to Table Fellowship Those Systemically Excluded

As noted above, with the loss of Territory and Temple, Torah and Table became stressed as the two poles around which Israel's life would revolve. Now, in a special way, the Jamnian Jews determined that household table fellowship would mirror the social order or structure of justice envisioned for the nation. Aware that Israel's unique union with God had traditionally been expressed in terms of table fellowship (Pss. 23:5; 78:19; Isa. 25:6; Ezek. 39:20), sectarian Pharisees[11] demanded exclusion of non-Jews as a sign of covenantal fidelity. But, for Matthew's Jesus, this was not acceptable.

This is keenly the point when we visit the Matthean Jesus "in the house" after his call of Matthew. By sitting at table (in his own house [*katoikeōn*, 9:1; 8:14; 9:10, 28; 13:1, 36; 17:25; see 4:13]) with those marginated ones[12] called "sinners and tax collectors" (9:11, 12), Jesus challenged the existing social order. He invited it to turn from a model of exclusion to be more open to all. Sharing a meal with others in that ranked society symbolized a kind of equality with them. Inviting the marginated to table not only made them equals; it made Jesus their "friend" (11:19). The Pharisees viewed this behavior as subversive to their conviction of what Israel needed for true social ordering; Jesus saw it as a manifestation of a new way of holiness based on mercy.

Here Matthew uses *eleos* in 9:13 (the meal at Jesus' house), just as in 12:7 (the disciples eating the needed grain on the Sabbath). The word comes from Hosea 6:6: "For I desire steadfast love [*hesed* in Hebrew; *eleos in* Greek] and not sacrifice." In another reference to the desire of God for mercy rather than sacrifice, Matthew's Jesus speaks of how the rituals of the religious leaders were done in a way that overwhelmed the "weightier matters of the law: justice and mercy and faith" (23:23). Here Matthew's Jesus is making a direct reference to the attitudes that God requires when the people gather for the sacrifice, as described in Micah 6:8.

Nearly everyone familiar with the Hebrew Scriptures can quote the famous passage from Micah about what Yahweh requires of us, to "do justice, and to love kindness (i.e., mercy), and to walk humbly with your God" (Mic. 6:8). However, few know that this passage has its setting in the context of the cultic sacrifice. Addressing the prevailing patterns that seemed to put *man*-made laws before those from God, the prophet Micah heard "the Lord" say: "With what shall I come before the Lord, and bow myself before God on high?" Then are named quite a few of these human laws that had been determined were necessary for right ritual: "Shall I come before him with burnt offerings, with calves a year old? Will the Lord be pleased with thousands of rams, with ten thousands of rivers of oil? Shall I give my firstborn for my transgression, the fruit of my body for the sin of my soul?" (Mic. 6:6-7). At that Yahweh says that what is required in God's eyes is something deeper and more constitutive of right order in the assembly: "He has told you, O mortal, what is good; and what does the Lord require of you but to do justice, and to love kindness, and to walk humbly with your God" (Mic. 6:8).

The Human Request for Mercy;
the Divine Response of Compassion

As he presents Jesus and what it means to be part of the reign of God, Matthew makes it clear that healing and restoration constitute God's holiness or reign. At their core, they reveal the way of messianic mercy. However, this mercy is developed further in Matthew. More than the other Synoptic authors, he shows that, if mercy is kissed by justice, it becomes compassion (*splagchnizesthai*). Furthermore, just as we showed a "constitutive" and "normative" dimension of *dikaiosynē*, so *eleēmosynē* contains the inner and the outer dimensions of care as well. As Marcus Borg writes: "An image of the Christian life shaped by this image of Jesus would have the same two focal points: a relationship to the Spirit of God, and the embodiment of compassion in the world of the everyday."[13]

In the five places where the word is used in Matthew's Gospel, *splagchnizesthai* extends beyond selective mercy (to this person or that group) to ever-widening circles of people who are marginated and in need—that is, to "the crowds."

Whenever Matthew uses *splagchnizesthai* ("having a heart that is moved with compassion") we find it strategically placed in the middle of a Matthean triad. The triad begins with the description of some kind of need (being harassed and helpless like sheep without a shepherd [9:36], being sick [14:14] or hungry [15:32], being caught in a huge debt [18:24-25] or being blind [20:30]). These situations of serious need (one of them accompanied by a request for "mercy" [*eleein*, 20:30, 31]) elicit something even greater: *splagchnizesthai*, a movement generated from the core of one's bowels (9:36; 14:14; 15:32; 18:27; 20:34). Finally, the need is not only acknowledged and the heart is not only moved with compassion; something must be done to address the need that has been recognized and which has moved the heart in its depths (10:1; 14:16-21; 15:35-38; 18:27; 20:34). This triad, in my opinion, helps us understand the power of Matthew's mercy Beatitude. In fact it represents the constitutive dimension, the first half, of what Richard Byrne has called "the circle of care."[14] This circle of care becomes Jesus' way of reconstituting everything in creation through compassion.

After Jesus saw the great crowds coming who were harassed and helpless, like sheep without a shepherd, he extended the power to do something about their situation to the twelve disciples when he gave them a share in his *exousia* (10:1). The next two stories extend that same compassion to those who are sick and those who are hungry. However, these stories also include the two accounts of the multiplication of the loaves. At the sight of the crowds who were harassed and helpless, in need of healing and bread, Matthew shows Jesus' heart moved, *splagchnizesthai*.

In the case of those who are hungry, rather than responding to their needs directly; Matthew's Jesus says to the disciples, "you give them something to eat" (14:16). This phrase was not an invitation but an imperative: if they are going to be identified with Jesus, his disciples must follow his pattern of responding to those in need with the resources they have.

Giving food to the hungry (25:35, 42) and to those who asked (see 5:42) was a specific application of Jesus' command. Jesus' command to the disciples to feed the crowd implied that they had the power to do so. This power was given to the apostles earlier (10:1). Thus Matthew's Jesus was not out of order in expecting them to feed the masses, just as had been done in the desert. Joseph A. Grassi notes: "This is an authentic command of Jesus, and was interpreted as such by the early church. The words 'you gave me to eat' in 25:35 are an exact counterpart of Jesus' command. The only difference is the substitution of 'me' for 'them.' In Matthew 25:44, lack of response to the hungry, thirsty, naked, stranger, sick and prisoner is all put together as 'not serving you.'"[15]

As we consider the triad revolving around hearts moved with compassion, we find it to be a summary of the way God has decided to be involved in our world: "the Circle of Care." This involves: (1) a way of seeing that recognizes the need and pain in the world, (2) which moves our hearts in care and compassion (3) in a way that finds us working not just to alleviate these forms of hurt and alienation but making sure those suffering them may never do so again.

While this begins "in the beginning," it is representative of what must be done in every time and place whenever and wherever people are in a mess (i.e., *tohu wabohu* [Gen. 1:2]). In the beginning (which really was the situation of Israel's exile when the Priestly writer tried to give hope to the people in pain), God *saw* chaos and darkness, and God *cared* about it. Chaos was a deviation not only from God's plan but from God's vision, from God's revelation. Therefore God delivered that emptiness from this condition by *calling* it into meaning. Creating *human life* so that all people might image the divine nature, God constituted male and female with the ability to *respond* by *caring* about everything in creation in a way that would advance God's plan for the world. Having fidelity to that plan results in God *seeing* the divine image and activity in the goodness of their deeds. Thus *God*, who made all things good to image the divine reality, is revealed in deeds of care. The Priestly writer showed that the circle of care is essential for human living on earth. Entering the circle of care is the way God is revealed in our experience and the way we express that revelation. It is the constitutive and normative dimensions of the gospel in microcosm. We can chart the circle of care in the following way:

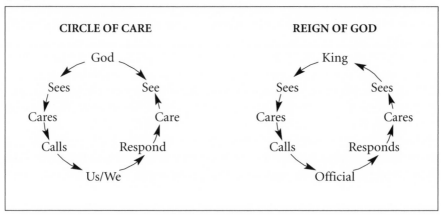

The first half of Matthew's circle of care is found in the Sermon on the Mount. God *sees* all that we need (6:32). Because God *cares* for us more than any earthly parent (7:9-10), God gives "good things to anyone who asks" (7:11; see 6:33). These good things represent all the resources of the earth, which God always sees as good. Above all, these good things are found in *exousia*, God's own power. *Called* by God, we are empowered to bring the circle of care to perfection by extending God's care toward others in need (25:31-40). Under this power, as the last judgment scene demonstrates, we are to complete the second half of the circle of care beginning in the way we *respond* to others in need with our own *care*. When we live by the norm of mercy, we are not only *seen* by God; we are further constituted in mercy itself. Faithful to God's eternal plan for the world, because we have been merciful, we will receive mercy. However, lest our hearts become proud, we must always remember that we were able to be merciful because we already had received mercy itself! When we enter the circle of care in this way we will have faithfully imaged the beatitudinal spirituality of Matthew's Jesus.

Nowhere is this pattern of the "circle of care"—as well as the need to show mercy if we are to receive it—exemplified better than in the fourth of the five times Matthew talks about someone's heart being "moved with compassion" (18:27). The whole passage is not just about a man who owed an unpayable debt in terms of the "daily wage"; it is about a ruler who was willing to bring about Jubilee because his heart had been moved with compassion.

Jesus tells the story in response to Peter's challenging question about forgiveness and reconciliation in the house churches. After Peter asks if the members should be willing to forgive up to seven times (18:21), "Jesus said to him, 'Not seven times, but I tell you, seventy-seven times'" (18:23). Just to be sure that the members of Matthew's audience know how important this way of perfection revealed in forgiveness is for their households, Matthew has Jesus tell a parable unique to the First Gospel. This parable of the kindom of heaven (18:23) is to be realized in every household on the face of the earth, including earthly economies. Needless to say, this approach to accounting begins in a way that would be considered normal economic activity, while it ends with that economy turned upside down in a kind of Jubilee economics.

This parable of "God's reign" begins with the story of a king who began reckoning the unsettled accounts of "his slaves." One "owed him ten thousand talents" (18:24). If a "usual" day's wage was one denarius (20:1-16) and if one thousand denarii equaled one talent, the man owed ten million days' wages. With this man being unable to repay his debt, the king ordered him, his wife, his children, "and all his possessions" (i.e., his whole household) to be sold "and payment to be made" (18:25). Then the king banished him from his sight. Then the slave fell on his knees, asking for patience. He said his debt would be repaid (18:26). At that cry for help, the king began viewing him in another way. This led his heart to be moved with compassion (*splagchnizesthai*). Now, moved with compassion at the sight of the man begging for patience and mercy, the king does two things: he releases him and forgives him the debt (18:27). In other words the man who was once full of debt is released of debt and is now full of "debt forgiveness" because of the way the king showed compassion. He was thus *empowered* in forgiveness, restored to himself and his household. He had experienced the first half of the circle of care (see p. 128). But the mercy experienced must be expressed.

Now we are ready for the way he will show to others what has happened to him. Ideally the normative dimension of mercy will express his constitution in mercy and compassion. As the story develops, however, it becomes clear that this will not happen. He will not reveal to others the compassion shown him via release and forgiveness of his debts. When he sees a fellow slave who owes him but one hundred days' wages, he seizes him by the throat and demands: "Pay what you owe" (18:28). When this other slave goes through the same pattern he had previously performed toward the king demanding payment of him, the first slave refuses and throws the debtor into prison until he could "pay the debt" (18:29-30). When "his fellow slaves saw what had happened," they were greatly distressed and reported to the king what the slave had done to his fellow slave (18:31). When summoned by the king, he is called "wicked"; he has not done good. The king declares: "I forgave you all that debt because you pleaded with me. Should you not have had mercy on your fellow slave, as I had mercy on you?" (18:32-33).

In this parable we find exemplified the finest example of the fifth Beatitude: "Blessed are the merciful, for they will receive mercy." Now the moral of the story is made clear for audiences of all times. It comes from the storyteller himself: "So my heavenly Father will also do to everyone of you, if you do not forgive your brother or sister from your heart" (18:35).

Forgiveness from the heart not only should characterize a key way we manifest mercy; it invites us to enter the circle of care. When we forgive from the heart, we recognize (see) the various forms of personal and institutional deprivation and helplessness around us and allow our hearts to be moved with compassion. This compassion is not something that moves our hearts without some kind of action on behalf of justice. Instead we feel compelled to release those in need from their debts, whether these are personal and communal or economic as well (see also 6:12, 14-15). Matthew's households at every level are called to "forgive debts" of all kinds. For some individuals this demands reconciliation; for some groups it demands conflict resolution; for some nations it demands cancellation of debts that prevent other nations from being free. Whatever the debt forgiveness, Matthew's households were to witness to an *oikonomia* of Jubilee (see 11:2-5). This lifestyle proclaims the year of God's favor and care to the world (see Isa. 61:2).

Abraham Heschel wrote that mercy and care reveal God's pathos. The Jewish philosopher wrote that pathos means that God is never neutral, never beyond good and evil: "God is always partial to justice. The divine pathos is the unity of the eternal and the temporal, of meaning and mystery, of the metaphysical and the historical. It is the real basis of the relation between God and humankind, of the correlation of Creator and creation, of the dialogue between the Holy One of Israel and His people."[16] Since God's holiness reveals itself in mercy, evangelically grounded spirituality—which has perfection as its goal (see 5:48; 19:21-23)—can never be separated from mercy toward those in need. To be *a-pathos,* or without mercy, is to be outside God's reign. We are not constituted in pathos or care if we refuse to live by the norm of God's mercy in our sympathy and empathy toward others. If we do not care, we do not image God; if we do not image God, we ourselves are now "outside" God's holiness, God's reign, and God's justice.

We do not care when we are apathetic about the hurts and pains of others. We do not care when we remain uninvolved or apathetic in the face of the systemic ways nations and races keep others in debt through fear and control. Since pathos defines God's revelation or presence in the universe, not to care is to cut ourselves off from God's revelation and sight. There can no longer be any excuses for uninvolvement, even including a lack of information or the need for neutrality. In a complex society we will never have all the information on any subject. As part of the network of injustice we are always involved in one way or another, for all life is interconnected. We must choose to care as our own way of faithfully continuing the mercy and forgiveness of God in history.

At this point, when we realize how far we are from entering the circle of care, Matthew's Jesus tells his audience one more story that is meant to serve as a springboard for grounding their discipleship in the circle of care and compassion. This final story involving *splagchnizesthai* narrates the situation of two blind men sitting by the roadside as Jesus leaves Jericho on the way to Jerusalem. "When they heard that Jesus was passing by, they shouted, 'Lord, have mercy on us, Son of David!'" (20:30). After the crowd tries to quiet these "outsiders," they repeat their plea for mercy "even more loudly" (20:31). When Jesus calls them and asks "What do you want me to do for you?" they "said to him, 'Lord, let our eyes be opened.' Moved with compassion, Jesus touched their eyes" (20:32-34a). In touching their eyes, Jesus performs a deed that would ostracize anyone else from the temple: you can't touch the untouchables. "Immediately," however, Matthew tells us, "they *regained* their sight." However, the story does not end here. Matthew adds three words that are meant to translate Jesus' action of compassion fifty years into the future into the lifestyle of his house churches: "[they] followed him" (20:34b). In other words, now able to see again, they follow Jesus in the way they are called to put his teachings into practice. Constituted in mercy, they must be its ministers.

In this story we are told initially that the two men by the roadside are blind. What becomes the moral of the story becomes clear at its end. They were not just blind; somewhere along the path they went blind. Something happened that made them go blind. They encountered some kind of stumbling block that led to their lack of vision, that kept them from seeing.

When we try to follow Jesus by entering the circle of care, it is important to ask ourselves three things that may be our stumbling blocks. First, since the circle of care begins with how we "see," we need to ask ourselves: What keeps us from seeing? As I examine my conscience I find many things that can blind me: self-, group- and collective-centeredness, bias and prejudice, lack of information, fear, narcissism, and ideological controls are just a few. These need to be faced if we will regain the way of seeing that will lead to compassion. However, if we do begin to truly "see," the second question we need to address revolves around what might keep our hearts from being moved with compassion. Again I find quite a few possibilities. Because we can get so saturated with sights of poor people and violence in so many places and in so many different forms, we can become numb. This psychic numbing can keep us from caring. Or, to use a contemporary phrase, we can suffer from "compassion fatigue." Or again, it may be fear that keeps us from caring. Why? Because we know that if we really care we may have to move to the third step on our journey of compassion: feeling called to do something about the situation. Here again we can find stumbling blocks: issues around human respect can keep us from action, fear of failure or being rejected, a mistaken idea that one person can't make a difference, or just an unwillingness to reach out and touch those in need with the hope of restoration.

Social anthropologist Marshall Sahlins has shown that, in a traditional society, compassion was required of people in the household or the village inasmuch as kinsfolk were expected to show mercy in the face of needs. But, he adds, "the quality of mercy is strained in peripheral sectors, strained by kinship distance, so is less likely" in the case of those beyond one's *oikia* or village.[17] For Matthew's Jesus, the house churches were to be filled with people showing compassion (18:27). However, this compassion was not to be limited to the members of the house church or the gathering; it was to be universally ordered to the *oikoumēnē,* to the crowds. It was to be universal.

Mercy Expressed in Release, Forgiveness, and Reconciliation

Many commentators characterize the twofold way of mercy expressed in the fifth Beatitude (5:7) with the dynamics of forgiveness that must be practiced in the house churches. This is quite true if we consider chapter 18, which includes the story of the merciless official who shows compassion to a member of his household, a model of that compassion which is expressed in release and forgiveness. As I have shown elsewhere, the patterns outlined herein by Matthew's Jesus, structure a new kind of *Haustafel,* or house ordering, that will bring about a Jubilee community.[18] It represents a new way of forgiveness that involves personal, relational, and economic restoration of those who are burdened by debt.

Mercy is related to the forgiveness of failings, hurts, and sins. It reflects God's forgiveness of us and the way we forgive others (6:12). It is covenantal. It signifies, in its very manifestation, God's eschatological entry into whatever condition and situation may need reordering. As we show mercy, God becomes present. The more merciful we are and the more perfect we become, the more God's forgiving presence becomes a dynamic that transforms households at every level of the world.

Forgiving "from the heart" demands not only compassion but the release of people from the bonds that have enslaved them and forgiveness of the debts that keep them under the control of others. This includes the "isms," the unequal power arrangements that stand as stumbling blocks to right house order (see 18:6-7), whether it be in the empire or in the *ekklēsia*.

Following the pattern of Jesus, who responded to others in need by showing mercy (9:10-13, 27; 15:22; 17:17; 20:30, 31), "the merciful" (5:7) are healers, people who seek to put right that which has gone wrong not only for their own selves and/or group but even for outsiders (9:10-13; 15:21-28). Mark Allan Powell shows that this includes their effort to remove "everything that prevents life from being as God intends [such as] poverty, ostracism, hunger, disease, demons, debt."[19] In Jesus' world such stumbling blocks became a pretext for ostracism rather than an invitation to compassion. In contrast, Matthew demands that an alternative community of mercy will be blessed in the way its members work to remove such stumbling blocks from people's lives. In the process of showing mercy, mercy will be theirs.

In *Jesus, Liberation, and the Biblical Jubilee: Images for Ethics and Christology,* Sharon H. Ringe also stresses the notion that, at the heart of any community trying to structure its way of living on the principles of Jubilee, forgiveness is essential to this new way of ordering households of disciples. Noting that the parable about the king who showed compassion to the man with the huge debt followed upon Peter's concerns about "how many times" forgiveness should take place in the house churches, she writes that "the saying itself envisions a new reign or order in which receiving the message of 'release' or 'forgiveness' as both a gift and an obligation is a condition of one's participation in this community." As a gift, the mercy that is expressed in forgiveness becomes the constitutive dimension of the circle of care; as an obligation, it becomes its normative dimension. Continuing her comments on the parable as an example of the Jubilee-defined household, Ringe concludes that the parable fleshes out Jesus' understanding of forgiveness by placing it

> in the context of God's reign, the onset of which is marked by forgiveness and release from the patterns of debt and obligation by which the old order is maintained. Human resistance to living with the consequences of that cancellation of old patterns is not an unforgivable sin. Rather it constitutes a self-exclusion from God's reign and from the life characterized by mercy and liberation that is its hallmark.[20]

Mercy: The Foundation for Word and Worship

Mercy is the foundation of both law and cult, Torah and worship. Consequently, all sacrifices, be they liturgical rituals or the ministry of our lives, should express mercy, forgiveness, care, compassion, sympathy, and empathy toward those in need. Otherwise they will fall short of the rule of God's pathos, care, and mercy.

Jerome Murphy-O'Connor reminds us, in discussing house churches and the Eucharist, that private houses were the first centers for church life: "Christianity in the first century A.D. and for long afterwards, did not have the status of recognized religion, so there was no question of a public meeting place, such as Jewish synagogues. Hence, use had to be made of the only facilities available, namely, the dwellings of families that had become Christian."[21] The early community was divided in its interpretation of the law. Such tensions would naturally arise in the households when the members came to celebrate Eucharist. This was counter to mercy.

When we consider our contemporary celebrations of the Eucharist in the Roman rite, it is clear that mercy must characterize the dynamics of the community as it gathers together. Indeed, mercy must define our communion or coming together. Having gathered together in the name of the trinitarian reality that defines all membership in the church, the first thing the priest does is to acknowledge the "real presence" of Christ in the gathered members of the church. His greeting generates their recognition of the "real presence" in the priest.

In this simple greeting and response following the opening doxology or invocation of the trinity, the church recognizes two of the four forms of the real presence of the glorified Christ. Thus, in the old as well as new ritual outlined for the "General Structure of the Mass" we read:

> At Mass or the Lord's Supper, the people of God are called together, with a priest presiding and acting in the person of Christ, to celebrate the memorial of the Lord or Eucharistic sacrifice. For this reason Christ's promise applies supremely to such a local gathering together of the Church: "where two or three come together in my name, there am I in their midst" (Mt 18:20). For at the celebration of Mass, which perpetuates the sacrifice of the cross, Christ is really present to the assembly gathered in his name; he is present in the person of the minister, in his own word, and indeed substantially and permanently under the Eucharistic elements.[22]

Unfortunately, many people, including myself, have found in the revised norms for the celebration of the Eucharist a regression to the notions of "holiness" that defined the ways of the original scribes and Pharisees, which

Jesus rejected in the name of a more inclusive form of table fellowship grounded in mercy and compassion. Indeed, it seems the stress is more on how the priest is to be separated from the people, isolated in the sanctuary, rather than with the people acknowledging the real presence in them and with their reciprocating in a way that opens them both to the other two forms of the real presence: in word and worship.

When it comes to how we are to recognize the real presence in the word, Matthew helps us understand more fully why mercy must ground our assemblies, especially in the two accounts of the multiplication of the loaves (14:13-21; 15:32-38). While I have discussed these passages above, it is important to remember their context: the situation that precipitated the ritual of taking, blessing, breaking, and giving the loaves (14:19; cf. 15:36) was the reality of human need.

Both 14:14 and 15:29-31 show a merciful Jesus responding to the suffering of others by healing their brokenness. This signified part of the messianic fulfillment of the covenant. The other part of this covenant would follow immediately in the ritual sharing of bread. This meal would further illustrate Jesus' mercy (14:15-21; 15:32-38): "Jesus called his disciples to him and said: 'My heart is moved with pity for the crowd. By now they have been with me three days, and have had nothing to eat. I do not wish to send them away hungry, for fear they may collapse on the way'" (15:32). Jesus did not wish that the crowds—a symbol for humanity in need—should ever be left with those needs unmet. By extending to the community his power to heal broken humanity (9:8; 10:1, 8; 28:18-20), Jesus' power to feed a hungry world now has been given to us: "Jesus said to them (us): 'There is no need for them to disperse. Give them something to eat yourselves'" (14:16).

Hearing that they were to use their own resources for those in need, the disciples gave the same response we are tempted to give once we realize we too are called to minister healing in our world of suffering and poverty: "We have nothing here" (14:17). We have limited resources and weaker faith. But Jesus' power can transform even that smallness into a miracle of care for the world.

This is the first lesson we learn from the two accounts of the multiplication of the loaves. The other reveals the absolute radicality and countercultural dynamics that the Eucharist entails if it will be grounded in the dynamics noted in the pattern of taking, blessing, breaking, and giving. In both accounts, whether of the five thousand in chapter 14 or the four thousand in chapter 15, we are told that "all of them ate and were filled" (14:20; 15:37). Then we find out that those "who counted" in the eyes of Jesus were everyone. That the writer still cannot grasp the way the Eucharist discounts all forms of discrimination is revealed in his words: "those who ate were about five (or four) thousand men, besides women and children" (14:21; 15:38). In a patriarchal culture, the Jewish Jesus creates an alternative form of table fellowship. Not only will all eat and be filled, but all persons, including women and children, will get the same resource of bread.

Thus, even though Matthew has just portrayed Jesus as reluctant to show mercy while he is at table because of bias (15:22-27), everything changes when we come to the ritual of taking, blessing, breaking, and giving. Already this action is so identified with the real presence of the one who will be risen from all forms of death and division that, in this ritual itself, all boundaries of discrimination are broken. As such, this fourfold ritual prefigures the inclusive kind of discipleship that comes with the resurrection and the Great Commission (28:18-20). Now in the community of Jesus, symbolized in the eucharistic gathering, resources should be used to respond to the people's needs for healing and sharing. There should be no discrimination. None should have more than they need, for this is a sign of alienation from the covenant and of the sin of the world that perpetuates suffering and poverty.

When Matthew discusses the need for reconciliation in the eucharistic assembly, he does so by inviting his audience in the house churches to make sure they are in communion relationally before they participate in the communion ritually. In a passage that is unique to Matthew, the members of the house churches are told that, if they are divided, they must "leave your gift there before the altar and go; first be reconciled to your brother or sister" before coming to offer their gift (5:24). Any division in the community demands reconciliation before the ritual can continue.

This is one of the most radical and revolutionary approaches to reconciliation in all the scriptures. I know this from experience in my own life when I have had to "make up" with someone I know is opposed to me when we are participating in the Eucharist. It is also one of the most difficult things I can ask people to do when they themselves assemble together.

Once I met a couple who were very involved in their parish. However, another couple was bitterly opposed to them. Their opposition was so strong that they refused to give the "kiss of peace" to their neighbors at the daily Mass they attended. One time the man spontaneously reached out his hand at the kiss of peace to the woman who did not like him. Either taken off guard or distracted, she extended her hand. Yet, the minute they shook hands, the woman withdrew her hand in a gesture of great physical pain. It was not long after they came home that morning that the first couple got a call from the woman's lawyer: she was considering a lawsuit alleging abuse on the part of the man who had shaken her hand.

It was in this context that I gave a mission at their parish. On the last night, in which I reflected on the four forms of the real presence and then celebrated the Eucharist, they were discovered taping my reflections. It seems this was a pattern. If they felt someone was unorthodox that person would be taped and the tape would be sent the proper authorities. Now discovered, they were told by the pastor to cease their taping.

At this same Mass, to show our common need for reconciliation, especially with those who have anything against us, I suggested that we advance the kiss of peace to conclude the word service. At that point I read the passage from Matthew about how they were to be reconciled before they would bring their gifts to the altar. When I approached the wife of the man who had shaken the hand of the woman who threatened to sue, she said: "Father, you've just asked me to do one of the hardest things I've ever had to do in my life."

Afterward I found out that, when she had approached the woman who had threatened to sue her husband, she said, "I know that you have something against me and Frank and I want you to know that I want to be reconciled to you," as she reached out her hand.

The woman refused. Yet she "went to communion."

Having moved from the real presence that is found in God's word, the fourth level celebrates that form of the real presence that can be found "indeed substantially and permanently under the eucharistic elements." Again, even at this critical point, mercy is asked throughout the eucharistic prayers; forgiveness is sought at the recitation of the prayer that Jesus taught us; and, finally, three times we ask for that mercy from the Lamb of God that will characterize ours as a community of peace, free of the sin of our world.

Through the sharing of the bread and wine, we celebrate the sign of what authentic spirituality should proclaim. Experiencing Jesus' mercy with us as we share in the one bread, we become a mercy-filled community respecting the dignity of all our tablemates. The way this bread is shared in the sacrament is the way life's resources are to be shared.

Mercy is central to the way the eucharistic meal is shared among tablemates. It contradicts the intolerance, lack of forgiveness, and prejudice that otherwise create barriers to God's covenantal plan. Thus, to celebrate the ritual of the Eucharist appropriately, it is of primary importance that we first examine ourselves to determine if we are bringing to the Eucharist an attitude of separatism, rejection, or exclusivism. Such negative attitudes stand as the main obstacle to the mercy that is central to Matthew's spirituality and understanding of the Eucharist.

The Lack of Mercy, Anger, and the Quality of Care

As we saw in the last chapter, Matthew's Gospel reserves Jesus' greatest anger for uncaring leaders of the Jews and the church whenever they frustrated justice by professing one thing and practicing another. He called such a lifestyle "hypocrisy," or a lie. Truth and the lie were the issues at stake when Jesus and the leaders argued with each other over the breaking of laws. The uncaring leaders were misusing their power by not responding to the real needs of the people; they used their authority to keep the people bound up and indebted in one form or another (23:4ff.). Jesus invited the leaders to manifest a deeper form of authority, namely, the quality of mercy, which would unbind the yoke by serving the people's needs (20:25-27).

As *eleos* was uniquely used by Matthew in 9:13 and 12:7, so, in 23:23 this word for "mercy" appears also in the context of a dispute between Jesus and the intolerant leaders. An examination of Matthew's unique use of mercy here should throw yet more light on our understanding of the fifth Beatitude: blessed are the ones who show mercy because mercy will be shown them (5:7). Jesus' anger, reflecting God's anger, was directed in the spirit of Micah at the leaders precisely because they did not show covenantal mercy: "Woe to you scribes and Pharisees, you hypocrites! For you tithe mint, dill, and cumin, and have neglected the weightier matters of the law: justice [*krisis*] and mercy [*eleos*] and good faith [*pistis*]. It is these you ought to have practiced without neglecting the others" (23:23). Justice, mercy, and fidelity must ground all law.

Matthew's whole spirituality concretely spells out what is good and what is required of the community for all time. Doing what is good and right fulfills the law and the prophets not only for Jesus but for each of us. Thus, David Hill explains, the need for justice, mercy, and faith (23:23) is essential to the spiritual life:

> This triad is the third expression in Matthew's gospel of Jesus' understanding of the essentials of the law (and therefore of obedience), the other two being the formulation of the Golden Rule (vii.12) and the twofold love-commandment (xxii.40). It is perhaps by this kind of emphasis that Matthew attempts to give content to the "righteousness" that surpasses that of the scribes and Pharisees, and that is demanded of disciples for entrance into the kingdom of heaven (v.20). Three times in controversy with the Pharisees, Matthew has Jesus point to the neglect or absence of *eleos;* it is part of the evangelist's redactional intent to affirm that *eleos*—the constant love for God that issues in deeds of compassion—is at the heart of the better righteousness that is essential for admission to the kingdom.[23]

Fidelity to the covenant means doing good through justice, mercy, and faith. Whoever does good enters the circle of care and walks with God as disciples of Jesus. We walk with God and experience divine mercy to the degree that we express to others the mercy that has constituted us in God's favor. Such mercy is shown not just by fasting one or three hours from food or water before the Eucharist (although it can help set a reflective mood in us); the fasting that God requires of us is to abstain from forms of rejection and prejudice. We are to fast by working to undo the thong of the yoke that comes from discrimination and alienation in our world (see Isa. 58:3-7).

Specifically, Matthew's Jesus also warns us that mercy means avoidance of anger and the need to seek forgiveness (5:22-26). As we approach the altar where we celebrate God's mercy, mercy toward our tablemates must accompany us. Jesus' words about seeking mercy imply that the spirit of negative anger is diametrically opposed to the quality of mercy and the circle of care.

Jesus showed that God's anger is the divine reaction to *our own* lack of justice and mercy. Once we realize that only the lack of these justifies anger, we might also realize how seldom our anger reflects the divine justification for anger.

Not too many years ago I was very angry—at individuals and groups, at white people, at the corporations, at the United States, at the pope—and, I discovered, at myself especially. Many reacted to my anger with their own.

But, by grace, one day I woke up and asked myself: Who do you think you are, thinking all these should change to your ways? You are convinced you are right. Don't they think they are right and that you should change? Furthermore, do you even care about what they think? Do they feel your care for them? How can you justify your anger at all these when you really don't care for them?

Once I realized that my anger was based in a lack of pathos, I discovered that care, mercy, and genuine understanding must be at the heart of evangelization that invites people, groups, and institutions to conversion. Care or mercy must be the basis for any invitation to change; otherwise people hearing our call for conversion will "get their backs up." If we do not care, we have no right to ask anyone to change. If we lack mercy, we have no right to get angry when people do not change. Only God has the right to get angry whenever we do not change, because only God always cares. Our anger will be justified only when it reflects God's righteous wrath. God's anger is shown only when people refuse mercy and covenantal fidelity.

In the days when I had more than my share of negative anger, many people kept me at arm's length. Once I started honestly caring about others, especially the brothers in the province, it seemed that they started to change and show more care as well. Perhaps it was just a case of the plank being removed from my own eye (see 7:5). At any rate, a feeling of mutual care gradually replaced former expressions of anger and defensiveness. For me, this conversion reached an apogee during our 1978 Provincial Chapter. The candidates for provincial shared their reflections about our Midwest Province and how we would serve as provincial if elected.

When I spoke, I talked about my former anger and the resulting defensiveness of so many. "But I'm not angry anymore and neither are you," I said to the brothers that night. "I've changed and you've changed. We have all been growing in care; we're giving up the need to control. In the process we are working together more effectively. And, as we continue to work together, we will be a dynamic force for good in this country and the world." It was an evening I won't forget; it proved that mercy is greater than anger; compassion trumps control every time. The brothers even elected me to provincial leadership!

CHAPTER EIGHT

Blessed Are the Pure of Heart;
They Will See God

So far, no satisfactory understanding for this Beatitude has been put forward by scripture scholars. The "purity of heart" described in the Beatitude seems to characterize a kind of interior lack of duplicity, a guilelessness and a wholeheartedness. Likewise, "seeing God" does not mean some kind of physical "sighting" of God or the beatific vision as we would understand it today. "Seeing God's face" depends on a purity of heart that represents a person's total commitment to God's plan. This inner dedication is manifested by doing good, by showing care.

The closest scriptural foundation for this Beatitude can be found in Psalm 24. Here the psalmist links the experience of seeing God's face with purity of heart and righteous deeds:

> Who can ascend the hill of the Lord?
> And who shall stand in his holy place?
> Those who have clean hands and pure hearts,
> who do not lift up their souls to what is false,
> and do not swear deceitfully.
> They will receive blessing from the Lord,
> and vindication from the God of their salvation.
> Such is the company of those who seek him
> who seek the face of the God of Jacob. (Ps. 24:3-6)

The question on the psalmist's lips at the beginning of this psalm asks what kind of person can "ascend the hill of the Lord." Traditionally, what the NRSV calls the "hill" has been called a "mountain."

Being from Wisconsin, I have never had the experience of climbing a mountain, since our state has none. However, from those who make a practice of climbing mountains I have learned three principles. First, it's important that we load ourselves only with what is important for the climb. Second, if we will get to the top of the mountain we need to move further and further away from the surface. Finally, as we get closer and closer to the top we not only become increasingly aware of our breathing, but we find we have less and less to say. These three principles can guide us as we make our climb up the mountain of contemplation, when we seek to be centered in God's embrace.

Jesus, the Pure of Heart,
Living in the Vision of God

Jesus fulfilled this psalm in his own beatitudinal living. Because he was faithful to his call (3:15; 11:2ff.), Jesus experienced the blessedness of God's favor on the Mount of Transfiguration. Here his external appearance evidenced the interior transforming light of God's presence with him. What happened momentarily at the transfiguration was indicative of Jesus' relationship with God at the depth of his being. The favor of God's presence was constitutive of his experience (17:1-5) because Jesus' works showed that he had lived according to God's ethical plan for the world (Isa. 61; 11:4-5, 27). Because he was just, he lived in God's beatitude.

This Beatitude is not the only reference connecting the "heart" with "seeing." In the phrase immediately following the treasure verse (6:22-23) indicating where one's heart will be (6:21), Matthew's Jesus speaks of the eye being good, sound, or single (*haplous*) rather than evil (the "evil eye"), unsound, or divided (*ponēros*). While *haplous* has traditionally been translated as "simple," "whole" and "single-minded," it has an ethical connotation meaning "to be generous" or ready to sacrifice for another.[1] In the same way, *ponēros* has been translated not only as an individual, group, or collective who is evil or does wrong (as in "evil empire" or the "axis of evil"); it also has its own ethical meaning indicating covetousness or avarice.[2]

Matthew consistently stresses that the righteous or the just ones are those who respond to God's word with their works. The just ones are those wholehearted people who are poor in spirit, who listen to God's word, and obey God's will (6:33; cf. 5:17-20; 25:31-46). Matthew contrasts the just ones with the unrighteous ones. Unlike politicians and pundits today, who easily talk about this person and that nation being "evil," Matthew uses the word "evil" (*ponēros*) to describe those who do not obey God's will by their works. They are double-minded in obeying God's will (5:37; 6:23f.; cf. 7:15-20; 12:33-37; 18:23-35; 25:14-30).

Given the social dimension of the Gospel and Matthew's Beatitudes, it would seem that purity of heart can be determined negatively as the absence of stinginess or greed and positively as the presence of generosity and openness to others, especially those in need. Whether the members of Matthew's house churches will "see God" will be contingent on whether their economic ordering of the house is based not on self-interest, group-interest, or collective self-interest but on alleviating the needs of others.

This meaning for purity of heart becomes clearer when one realizes that, immediately after distinguishing between the eye that is *haplous* or *ponēros,* Matthew's Jesus says, "No one can serve two masters; for either he will hate the one and love the other, or he will be devoted to the one and despise the other. You cannot serve God and mammon" (6:24). Mammon represented the peak of idolatry; it was the essence of greed and stinginess (i.e., *ponēros*). Those with hearts centered on themselves and their mammon serve (are "given over" to) avarice and covetousness. Conversely, people whose hearts are centered on God reflect openness and generosity in the way they relate to each other.

Matthew made the conventional association between "seeing" and "heart" not only in this Beatitude, and in the section from the Sermon on "treasure," but also, in that patriarchal world, when he noted Jesus saying that all those who *looked* lustfully at a woman coveted her and thereby committed adultery in their *hearts* (5:28).[3] Equally, from the original connection between the ninth and tenth commandments, as well as the context of this pericope from Matthew's Gospel, it becomes clear that those who looked upon their neighbor's possessions covetously possessed divided hearts; they could not see God.[4]

In contrast, those experiencing God's presence (i.e., "seeing God") would manifest the authenticity of that experience in their generosity toward those in need. Meeting the needs of others reveals integrity of heart. In the final judgment, those who have demonstrated this kind of integrity—which is justice toward those in need—will see God (25:31-46).

For Matthew's Jesus, one's external actions indicate interior preoccupations. To determine where the heart or inner life is based, one should consider words and behavior: "For where your treasure is, there your heart will be also" (6:21); in other words: find out what is most important to you and your group, your "bottom line," and you will know what will preoccupy your thinking, feelings (especially your fears about losing it), and actions.

The First Step in "Seeing God": The "Looks" That Keep Us from "Seeing"

In the previous chapter, I talked about the "circle of care" as bringing us into God's reign in the way we "see," "care," and feel "called" to do something about the needs of the world around us. I noted that this circle has a constitutive dimension (seeing, caring, being called) and a normative dimension flowing from the empowering that comes from the constitutive dimension. This normative expression involves the way we "respond" to our call of care in a way that witnesses that "care" to others. When we care in this way, we reveal ourselves as God's images; in this way we will be "seen" by God.

In this chapter I will show how the dynamics of this circle of care can represent the ways we "climb the mountain" of contemplation. If we go through the steps of becoming "clean of hands" and "pure of heart" we will have climbed the mount to that point where we can live contemplatively in a way that opens us more fully to the blessed experience of "seeing" God.

However, before we experience this blessedness, we must make it our practice to avoid the stumbling blocks that get in our way of such "seeing." This demands that we be aware of the "looks" that are the stumbling blocks to "seeing." We will begin to understand what these stumbling blocks to God's reign may be (6:33) when we examine the preoccupations of our hearts, for where our "treasures" are, so will be our heart (6:19-34).

Immediately after saying we'll know the preoccupation of our heart by determining what is most important (our "treasure") in our lives, Matthew's Jesus moves us to a further examination of the obstacles to "seeing" God when he says: "The eye is the lamp of the body. So, if your eye is healthy [*haplous*], your whole body will be full of light; but if your eye is unhealthy [*ponēros*], your whole body will be full of darkness. If then the light in you is darkness, how great is the darkness!" (6:22-23).

Today our understanding of biology identifies the eye as that part of the body that lets in light that we might see. However, people living in the Mediterranean world of Jesus believed that the eye was a mini-sun; it let *out* the light that came from a fire within the heart, the center of the body. If the eye was well focused, it would be sound. However, if the light within the body was unsound, the eye would naturally reflect "evil"; thus the evil eye. Furthermore, as the Sermon on the Mount makes clear, the lesson is reinforced that if the eye is pure or simple, so will be the heart (*kardia*). If one is absorbed in the experience of God's reign, one's whole person will be endowed with light's perfection (see 5:48).

True to the biology of his time, Matthew's Jesus argued that the surface expressions (which I will call "looks") originate in internal dispositions in the heart. *Kardia* is Greek for heart—the center of our thinking, feeling, and acting. Thus, again moving from the outer extremities of the body to the inner, he declared: "Do you not see that whatever goes into the mouth enters the stomach and goes out into the sewer? But what comes out of the mouth proceeds *from the heart*. . . . For out of the heart [*kardia*] come evil [*ponēros*] intentions" (15:17-19). The heart's thoughts and emotions will be revealed in the looks. These looks or ways of "seeing" will be *haplous* (healthy) or *ponēros*.

Our surface or external "looks" are expressed in attitudes and actions, words, and works. If these surface "looks" take authority over our hearts, they will be the source of worry, tension, and anxiety instead of rest, restoration, and peace. To the degree that the "cares of the world" are part of the surface-self, or the "looks" we manifest, we will be kept from experiencing God's living word and reign in the ground of our being (13:18-22).

Given this background we can ask: What forms or ways of negative seeing do the looks identified as of *ponēroi* take? How can their control keep us from developing a contemplative stance in life; how can they be the stumbling blocks to our experience of God, that is, "seeing" God? I think we can get a good understanding from the late Richard Byrne's powerful thesis, "Living the Contemplative Dimension of Everyday Life."[5]

In the last chapter we considered his "circle of care." Now I will develop this "circle" and suggest that it offers a way to "see" God. However, to "see" the Divine One means that we examine our "looks" insofar as these may be stumbling blocks or obstacles to seeing God contemplatively. While "seeing God" in this Beatitude cannot be equated exactly with our notion of contemplation, it approximates an experience of the divine. Byrne's "looks" represent dynamics that can be considered Matthean impurity of heart. If we can be free from these looks we can be open to the divine gaze and vision; we can be seen by God and open to see God. While we will always have some obstacles to "seeing God," to the degree we remain in the control of these "looks" we cannot see God.

1. The curious look. The first stumbling block we encounter on our climb up the mountain of care is the curious look. This occurs when cares and anxieties become the preoccupation of our hearts (6:25, 31). Jesus described a person controlled by this look as "the one who hears the word, but the cares of the world and the lure of wealth choke the word" in such a way that "it yields nothing" (13:22). As the Latin word "*cura-ositas*" implies, the curious look makes one "full of cares."

While there is nothing wrong with normal curiosity, the parent of invention, people controlled by the curious look are outside the possibility of experiencing the word, especially the word of God's rule; they are not rooted in *themselves* either. They are rootless, superficial, ungrounded. They reflect a kind of chaos, a separation, an alienation within themselves. When we experience someone giving us the "curious look," we feel they don't "care." When you are given the "curious look" you don't forget it.

I still recall how I got this "look" shortly after I received my doctorate in theology at Berkeley. The Catholic Theological Society was going to be meeting across the Bay in San Francisco. However, I didn't "feel" like I was a "doctor." Even more, I didn't feel that my former professors would act toward me as one of their peers. So, when I saw someone I thought was a friend, I tried getting close to him. Every time I did he was "schmoozing" with somebody and looked away. When I finally could engage him, he kept looking over my shoulder. I felt I didn't "count." He gave me the curious look; I felt he didn't "care."

Years later when I was able to talk with him about it, he was very honest. "Mike, at that time in my life, you were about twentieth on my pecking order of who was important to connect with." I didn't know I was that low on the totem pole, but at that convention I knew I wasn't near the top!

Jesus was aware of the power of the curious look. To counter its influence over us, he offered a new way of seeing that would help us go beyond our surface cares and anxieties to experience and trust in God as the source of our life and living (Matt. 6:25):

> Look at the birds of the air; they neither sow nor reap nor gather into barns, and yet your heavenly Father feeds them. Are you not of more value than they? And can any of you by worrying add a single hour to your span of life? And why do you worry about clothing? Consider the lilies of the field, how they grow; they neither toil nor spin, yet I tell you, even Solomon in all his glory was not clothed like one of these. But if God so clothes the grass of the field, which is alive today and tomorrow is thrown into the oven, will he not much more clothe you—you of little faith? Therefore do not worry, saying, "What will we eat?" or "What will we drink?" or "What will we wear?" For it is the Gentiles who strive for all these things. (6:26-32)

"Gentiles" in Matthew's world represented those who did not believe in the God of the Jews. Today we have many such "gentiles" inviting us to serve their gods. One of the most significant of these gods is the one promoted by the advertisers and marketers to keep the engines of our economic system humming. They help us be concerned about what we will eat and about the clothes we should be putting on our bodies in order to be accepted. When we are controlled by the curious look, our needs remain at the surface level of life. Our identity is found in what others tell us we "should" be wearing this season.

When, in the seminary, we were first allowed the use of small amounts of money, a classmate said, "I'm going to go downtown to see what I need." When our true self (our "I am") is controlled by the surface self and its cares and anxieties, we are not grounded in our souls, where God's power should have full authority; other powers like the media have authority over us. The normal attitude of curiosity found in each of us is manipulated by the media through advertising. It exploits our curiosity and fears. It plays on our identity and security needs. We too often seem quite happy to be led into its temptations. Yet, for Jesus, the greatest are those whose security rests in finding their identity in him (see 11:28; 18:1-4).

2. The lustful look. The next stumbling block to seeing God is the lustful look. This is the "eye of pleasure" that keeps us from the good: "out of the heart come evil [*poneros*] intentions, murder, adultery, fornication, theft, false witness, slander." Such ways of thinking, feeling, and acting are the things that make us defiled or impure, Matthew's Jesus insisted (15:19-20). While most of us are not making a habit of the kind of activities Jesus elaborated, today these forms of *ponēroi* are manifested in other ways. They find a home in many of our attitudes and actions. This is especially so in the way the eye of pleasure controls us in our dealings with people, events, and things.

When we are controlled by the lustful look, we seek instant gratification at the level of our bodily concerns (see 6:25). We instinctively avoid any pain. The Alka-Seltzer ideology plays on the lustful look. Instant relief. To the degree that we remain controlled by this approach to life, we will find it difficult to find our meaning, identity, and pleasure in abandoning ourselves to the way of seeing that finds us living in God's reign. This avoidance of pain may also keep us from being concerned about others' bodily forms of poverty when we know our involvement might result in some form of personal pain or rejection by others in society (see 10:16f.).

James and John, along with their mother, were overly influenced by the lustful look. They were attracted to Jesus partly because they sensed that he would meet their power needs (20:20-28). The rich young man was attracted to the person of Jesus. Yet he was kept from conversion by his surface self, by the eye of pleasure. He could not reorder his wealth on behalf of the poor (19:21-22) to become truly free. He went away "grieving"; he was depressed.

Reinforced by social norms that keep us at a surface level, our very depressions often indicate our inability to relate to God at the level of our real selves. Therefore, when we are defined by our surface cares, we meet its empty desires by seeking immediate pleasure as we try to avoid pain at all costs. Pornographers, marketers, and image makers know how to appeal to this dynamic better than most. Often we who listen to people's confessions hear that the cause of their lustful actions is grounded in an experience of depression, as in "I was depressed and so I . . . ."

In the late 1970s I was giving conferences to a religious order. I saw one of the nuns walking toward me in a great-looking outfit. "Gee, that outfit looks handsome on you," I said.

"You really like it?" came the response with evident happiness at the fact that I had noticed. "I was depressed one day. So I decided to buy this. It cost me only fifty dollars."

Some people at that time might be concerned about the expenditure of fifty dollars. What I heard, however, was the fact that this person did not seem able to use her personal pain to discover ultimate value in a relationship of fidelity to the living God (26:36f.). When identity becomes so locked into a commodified self that we can be bought and sold, our victim status keeps us at the surface level.

We also can approach prayer from the lustful look. Unconsciously we seek God for the pleasure we desire from this religious experience. It seems this is why Matthew's Jesus railed against some of the wandering charismatics and their prophecies, exorcisms, and miracles (7:22). Moving to another form of prayer, it seems that the lustful look keeps us from contemplation itself, despite our protestations to the contrary. It takes too long; there are no results; it is too much effort. Some of us go to prayer to get some kind of pleasurable "high" there. Others of us desire to recapture the original experience of the Spirit's release in us every time we pray. When we experience "nothing," we quit; however, this very "nothing" is precisely all we can bring to prayer of ourselves. Nothing is all we have before God, but it doesn't satisfy.

3. *The ideal look.* A key characteristic of the "ideal self" is that people under its control are preoccupied with comparing themselves and others in terms of power, possessions, and prestige. Usually this comparison takes the forms of "more or less," "better or worse." One's stimulation, identity, and security come from meeting this "ideal look." Since we never seem to attain that ideal image, very often depression, a negative self-image, and fear can become our heart's preoccupations.

If we sought just to be "good enough" or even "very good," that would be perfect, for this is the way God wants us to be (Gen. 1:31). However, we seek not only to be good but to be better (than others), even perfect. The more we are controlled by this ideal of being better or having more, the more we will be dominated by notions of "should/should not," "ought/ought not," and "must/must not." Not content to be dominated by our own personal "shoulds," we try to control others with them as well. If others are to be "good," they also should, ought, or must do as we say and/or do (see 20:25; 23:2).

Unable to accept our true selves, we find it difficult to accept others for just being "good enough." We really don't care about ourselves or them; we are under the control of the "ideal look." Unable to care about or love ourselves, we cannot love or care about others. Frustrated at never meeting our goal of perfection, we often relate to others with anger and harsh judgments. Jesus warned that such a way of "seeing" has to be dramatically eliminated from our lives if we are going to "see" properly. Immediately after telling his followers to seek God's way in their lives rather than being preoccupied and worried about life's daily concerns (6:33-34) he says:

> Do not judge, so that you may not be judged. For with the judgment you make you will be judged, and the measure you give will be the measure you get. Why do you see the speck in your neighbor's eye, but do not notice the log in your own eye? Or how can you say to your neighbor, "Let me take the speck out of your eye," while the log is in your own eye? You hypocrite, first take the log out of your own eye, and then you will see clearly to take the speck out of your neighbor's eye. (7:1-5)

Evelyn Underhill, one of the great mystical writers of this century, stated that authentic contemplative experience demands a suspension of critical attitudes so that no surface entity separates us from God. She spoke about the need to have one's attitude or heart correspond perfectly with "the essence of things."[6] This is another phrase for being integrated, finding our center, and being in communion with all things.

4. The resentful look. The final look that stands as a surface obstacle to seeing God is resentment or unforgiveness. Not only does it keep us from "seeing God"; it destroys our very souls. Holding on to our resentments, we learn in the Twelve Step program, is self-destructive. It does violence to the soul.

Murder was viewed by Matthew's Jesus as stemming from that evil the scriptures call *ponēros*. While we may not be killers as such, we can be destructive in our anger, criticism, envy, gossip, and, especially, unforgiveness. Always seeking to unmask the inner attitudes that indicated alienation from God, Matthew's Jesus was unwilling to live by a law that only rejected murder; he wanted to eradicate all attitudes of the heart that could lead to such violence:

> You have heard that it was said to those of ancient times, "You shall not murder"; and "whoever murders shall be liable to judgment." But I say to you that if you are angry with a brother or sister, you will be liable to judgment; and if you insult a brother or sister, you will be liable to the council; and if you say, "You fool," you will be liable to the hell of fire. (5:21-22)

A good friend of mine was abused by his parents in almost every way except sexually. When he talked about the violence his parents perpetrated on him, you could feel his anger and resentment. However, he knew that these forms of murder, in the sense of Matthew's Gospel, were killing *him*. He knew he had to forgive his parents. So he "worked the rooms" available in his city, literally day and night. His whole goal in life was to be free of his parents' sins; to be free of their control. For years it went this way until one day I got a call from him. You could hear the relief that had come to him. "Mike," he said, "I'm free. I know in my heart I am free of my resentments and anger against them."

In a *Time* essay spurred by Pope John Paul II's trip to the prison in Rome to visit the man who had tried to assassinate him, Lance Morrow found an "example of forgiveness for a troubled world." In arguing the "psychological case for forgiveness," he wrote:

> Not to forgive is to be imprisoned by the past, by old grievances that do not permit life to proceed with new business. Not to forgive is to yield oneself to another's control. If one does not forgive, then one is controlled by the other's initiatives and is locked into a sequence of

act and response, of outrage and revenge, tit for tat, escalating always. The present is endlessly overwhelmed and devoured by the past. Forgiveness frees the forgiver. It extracts the forgiver from someone else's nightmare. "Unless there is a breach with the evil past," says Donald Shriver, "all we get is this stuttering repetition of evil."[7]

Lack of forgiveness is connected with that evil (*ponēros*) from which all of us need deliverance (6:12-13). Hence we must pray and work, as my friend did, that we not succumb to the temptation promised by the "resentful look" that it is better to remain in anger and resentment than to rest in the peace that comes to us when we forgive. In my own life, I know that, only if I "forgive from my heart" will I be able to be free; only then will I have come under the reign of God (18:35, 23).

As we conclude our examination of the various "looks" that are obstacles to experiencing the fullness of this Beatitude, we discover that these forms of *ponēros* or evil/impurity of our heart (*kardia*), are easily exploited ideologically by the institutions that control the infrastructure. Advertisers play on our tendency for greed. Politicians exploit our fears. Racists and (hetero)sexists demean their enemies. Clerics threaten the laity. Producers demean consumers. As a result, these arrangements within our culture can so dominate our attitudes that we remain addicted by their power. We are kept from entering the circle of God's care.

To the degree that we come under the control of these looks, we cannot see. Because we cannot "see," our hearts remain unconverted. With our hearts unconverted we not only are kept from being "pure in heart," but our hearts become dull (*epachynthē*). Thus Matthew's Jesus would grieve that the "people's heart has grown dull, and their ears are hard of hearing, and they have shut their eyes; so that they might not look with their eyes, and listen with their ears, and understand with their heart and turn—and I would heal them" (13:15). In contrast, Jesus blesses his followers who have moved beyond the surface cares when he declares: "But blessed are your eyes, for they see, and your ears, for they hear" (13:16).

This realization of being freed of the obstacles to seeing now makes us open to enter the circle of care more fully.

The Second Step in Entering the Circle of Care: Knowing We Are Seen in Need by God

Explaining why his disciples did not need to be coming under the control of the looks, Matthew's Jesus told them that those who do not believe strive after all "these things." Rather, the disciples were to realize that "your heavenly Father knows" what is really needed (see 6:32). Therefore they were to strive first to come under the rule of that God (6:33). Not many verses later, the disciples will be told:

> Ask, and it will be given you; search, and you will find; knock, and the door will be opened for you. For everyone who asks receives, and everyone who searches finds, and for everyone who knocks, the door will be opened. Is there anyone among you who, if your child asks for bread, will give a stone? Or if the child asks for a fish, will give a snake? If you then, who are *ponēroi,* know how to give good gifts to your children, how much more will your Father in heaven give good things to those who ask him! (7:7-11)

As we try to pray, it is important to realize that "seeing God" is never anything we can attain by our own efforts. Therefore we need to know that this is a matter of grace. Consequently, as we work to be freed of the *ponēroi* that can be stumbling blocks that keep our hearts dull, we also need to ask God for the grace of "seeing."

Those of us who are very self-motivated and independent can often find this step in the circle of care very difficult. We find it hard to ask *anyone* for help. But this is precisely what we must do at this point if we are to proceed into a deeper way of contemplation, if not contemplation itself. I learned this the hard way.

I was increasingly frustrated with my prayer life. While I tried to pray at least one-half hour a day, "nothing" was happening. It was because of being overly controlled by the surface looks and, I knew, by distractions and daydreaming. I was not making it a real "practice" (see 6:20) to seek first God's reign. So I brought my issue to John Baldovin, S.J., my spiritual director at that time. He recalled for me the recommendation of St. Ignatius that we should ask for what we desire as we begin to pray, the "fruit" of the grace we seek.

Throughout his *Spiritual Exercises,* Ignatius begins each of the Four Weeks with the need for a "preparatory prayer" in which we are to "ask God our Lord for the grace" we desire; "to ask for what I desire"; "to ask for grace. . . ."[8]

The next morning when I tried this, I found I could not do it. Why? I discovered that I did not want to stand before God as a beggar, despite all my knowledge about prayer. In practice, I did not want to be "needy" before God. No matter how we run from being humble, we need to balance being poor in spirit with being pure of heart so that we not only recognize our need but are willing to ask of our Father in heaven, who will "give good things to those who ask." After all, praying, by its very wording, involves asking.

Knowing God's love for us, we acknowledge our dependence on God by asking for what we need. This makes us more open to be grateful for God's revelation of care that moves us deeper into the circle of God's reign.

The Third Step: Becoming Grounded in Care

The process of coming to purity of heart demands that we move beyond our surface cares to be grounded in authentic care. This invites us to begin "looking" in a new way at ourselves, at others, and at God. The "call" to go beyond our surface cares comes to us in one of three main ways: (1) by the experience of God's unconditional care for us, (2) when we come to love ourselves free of the looks, or (3) when we experience others' caring about us free of the "looks" themselves. In whatever way we experience these forms of care, they invite us to go beyond the surface looks to be grounded in care itself.

Some people have such an experience of God's care that it moves them forever from being controlled by surface cares. Examples of this divine intervention range from Paul of Tarsus on his way to Damascus to Bill W. sitting in his kitchen. Sometimes "the Lord" will lead us to this experience through our embrace of the "lepers" of our day, as it happened to Francis of Assisi and Mother Teresa. All of these unsolicited experiences of God's care contain a call that moves us from our former preoccupations to be grounded in care itself.

Another way we can move beyond the surface level may be by our own insight (realizing God's grace is never separated from this). Growing in union with God enables us to come to a greater awareness of what keeps us from deepening that union. It makes us come to a deeper form of personal wisdom. Wisdom is the gift that helps us understand what is truly important. With wisdom, we can independently see how our surface reactions of defensiveness, curiosity, pleasure-seeking, anger, envy, and resentment seek to control us. Realizing how easily we are being controlled by these attitudes at prayer better enables us to recognize our need to be free of their domination.

While coming to purity of heart can result from divine intervention or our own wisdom, we usually are invited to move beyond our surface selves when other people look at us in a new way, the way of care. Such people themselves must be quite free of the "looks" if they are going to view us through the lens of care. Thus, when they respond to us free of these looks, it can become an invitation to freedom. Often this happens when we are "caught" in some embarrassing situation that may or may not be sinful. When someone treats us with care rather than their "ideal look," that is, reinforcing the "shoulds," we don't easily forget such a manifestation of care. When it happens, it becomes revelatory of God. In this care, we are enabled to look at others from the perspective of genuine care that we have experienced ourselves.

Once we experience being called from our surface needs by the experience of genuine care, we can move from our surface cares. At the same time, we can be open to the next step of achieving purity of heart. We can enter Peter's ritual of care in the way we dedicate ourselves to leaving all things for the sake of God's reign (see 19:27).

The Fourth Step: The Call to Respond
in the "Ritual of Care"

At this point in our effort to live contemplatively in a way that will lead us to contemplation of the experience of God's abiding care in us, we can give in to discouragement. When we consider our own lives and the life of our society, we can easily see how little genuine care they often reflect and we can become quite depressed. So often, we discover, we live at the surface level of life. And then, when we begin to move from its control, we still can find ourselves far removed from any experience of care, whether from God or others. Yet precisely at this time, Richard Byrne suggests, there is a way to respond to the call of care. This comes with an invitation to enter the ritual of care. He suggests that we ask: Do I really care? Who or what do I care about? And when I see my lack of care—my lack of humanity—I can begin taking the first faltering steps toward a life of care. I can make my own the words of T. S. Eliot:

> Blessed sister, holy mother, spirit of the fountain,
> spirit of the garden,
> Suffer us not to mock ourselves with falsehood.
> Teach us to care and not to care.
> Teach us to sit still.[9]

Purification of heart is achieved by learning to care and not to care, as well as by taking time and making space to be still. Learning to care and learning not to care are forms of mortification and detachment; these traditionally have been considered by spiritual writers as "purgation." On the other hand, the process of becoming quiet and still has been termed "recollection." Purgation and recollection are the next steps that we must take as we climb the mountain to purity of heart. Living under their influence, we become more open to the grace of God's presence; we become more disposed to "see" God.

In traditional spirituality, purgation has two dimensions: detachment and mortification. Detachment is the process of not caring; mortification is the process of caring about what God cares about in such a way that we choose the "good" in ways that leave other things behind.

Detachment is the process of giving up comforts for rest (see 26:42-45). It is the process of seeking and finding, selling and buying (13:44-46). It is the process of surface-self-stripping to discover the true self in whose ground God's presence reigns with us.

I never agreed with my novice director who urged us, "Die to yourself." I always thought that phrase reflected some kind of masochistic spirituality. I thought that people would be unwilling to die to anything *unless* it was on behalf of something they could live for more fully. Consequently, I would ask him: "Why don't we ever hear about experiencing God more fully so we'll want to die to certain things?" I never got a satisfactory response.

While the call to detachment can come from outside us, it is better if detachment is freely cultivated. One of my strongest memories of being invited to detachment and to not care came to me when I realized all my art-work had been destroyed. I considered myself to be a halfway decent artist. Throughout my college and theology years I had built up quite a portfolio of my work. In 1966, I worked at the Franciscan Communications Center in Los Angeles. While there, I became acquainted with Corita Kent, then a nun at Immaculate Heart of Mary College. At that time, she was gaining international renown for her art work. After I left Los Angeles, I would periodically send Corita my latest endeavor and she would send me something of hers. Soon I had many of her seriographs in my art folder. To say the least, they had become part of my "treasure-house."

One time I left the folder on a cart in the kitchen instead of bringing it to my room. A few weeks later I noticed that the folder no longer was on the cart. So I asked one of my fellow Capuchins (who happened to be a compulsive cleaner), "I left a blue folder on the cart a while ago. Do you know where it is?"

"You mean that blue thing with some pictures in it?" he responded. "Oh, I threw that out a week ago. Because it was just lying around, it didn't seem important."

Thud! Part of my life on the garbage heap! The reality of the moment offered me an immediate choice. I could be controlled by surface looks, especially the "ideal look" that would have said "You should have . . ." both to my brother, the Capuchin cleaner, and to myself. My "critical look" could have controlled me by an outburst of anger. Or I could respond by moving into the ritual of care. I could leave *all* of my things behind, including this very deep part of my life.

In just about the time it took to go through these reflections, I was able to experience detachment from this important expression of my life. Even though I wished I still had my art, I merely said to him something like, "Oh, I see. . . ." But what that "seeing" implied! Without alluding to the fact, I had entered more deeply into the experience of the sixth Beatitude. I could be free from the baggage of life in order to climb the mountain to see God's face.

The next form of purgation, after not caring, or detachment, is to begin to care for what truly matters. This is mortification. In many ways, detachment is easier than mortification. Once my art was lost, it was gone. "Out of sight, out of mind." Mortification, however, is the attitude we bring to bear on the choices we make toward people, possessions, and our various privileges. It is easier for me to live in a small Capuchin fraternity where we decide not to have certain foods than to live in a large friary where the various kinds of food and drink are always available. In such a situation, I must make a free choice not to take the second salad or go to the liquor cabinet. My choice will be based on my own attitudes toward my self, my God, and my brothers and sisters throughout the world.

Mortification is the discipline we bring to bear on the choices we make regarding the two central projects of life—the reign of God's will or society's way of running after all things (6:24, 33). It is the process of discovering what is truly important in our lives. Mortification is part of the gift of discernment. It is based on our experience of God's justice in us, which in turn finds our lifestyle reflecting our solidarity with others, especially in their need. We experience solidarity with others in need, because we know God has come to us in our need.

Following Eliot, having learned the way of care and non-care, we now find ourselves ready to "sit still." Through recollection we begin to "sit still," instead of running after all these things. Whereas our surface self can be controlled by illusions and ideologies, recollection is the process of slowing ourselves down, entering into silence and space to experience solitude and the truth of God's revelation to and in us (11:27-28). We not only try to "sit still," but we see the value in "being still."

Being "still" invites us to another way of listening; this listening invites us to begin by quieting ourselves. We take time and make space to quiet our surface selves and our inner voices so that we are able not only to hear but to understand. This quieting of our surface selves leads to silence. Next, silence enables us to become still. The more still we become, the more our silence takes us beyond the surface to the still point of solitude. At this place, it is much like being in a quiet room by ourselves only to sense that we are in another's presence. Silence is surface stillness with ourselves; solitude becomes solidarity with God, who is present at the heart of the world. We discover ourselves there, in our heart, with God, but there we also discover ourselves in solidarity with the universe itself.

In solitude we sense God in the spaces between the words and prayers that no longer seem important. As we grow in our ability to listen to ourselves, we discover in this growing solitude that we are filled with a Presence who cares and listens. At the same time we discover that our listening to the way God enters into our lives is in proportion to the way we listen to and care about all those voices and all those cares of the universe (see 25:31-46) that are part of God's concern. Because we have brought our solidarity with humanity to our solitude, we begin to experience ourselves now as part of the very revelation of God. We discover that everything has already been said in one word, Jesus.

Many times, in solitude, we merely sit. And we wait. Unlike people waiting in bread lines and in welfare offices, who despairingly rely on human whims, we wait in hope because of the everlasting promise made by our God. In this experience of waiting, however, we cannot escape acknowledging our

absolute need for God to see us in need (6:32). This very awareness of our
need and our powerlessness, in itself, should inspire us to greater solidarity
with all others in their need and powerlessness; in addition, fully expecting to
be heard, we ask to receive, seek to find, and knock to have opened to us the
experience of God's presence with us (7:7). And then we wait, in need. What
has helped me during this time of waiting is an easy-going, slow recitation of
a little phrase or mantra. A quiet repetition of a little saying gradually merges
surface distractions and preoccupations into a deeper part of our being. To
aid this process, the Eastern spiritual writers often centered their asking, seeking, and knocking on the repetition of a prayer called the Jesus Prayer: "Lord,
Jesus Christ, Son of the Living God, have mercy on me a sinner."

I first learned about the Jesus Prayer in 1963 when I read J. D. Salinger's
Franny and Zooey. For a while I tried to repeat these words whenever I was
distracted in prayer; yet I never seemed able to make this mantra part of my
reality. I did recognize, though, that something like the Jesus Prayer could be
a great aid to prayer, especially when I realized that my prayer was limited to
waiting on God. Invariably, God seemed to want me to experience nothing
but void.

My frustration in not being able to feel "at home" with the Jesus Prayer
led me to ask: How can I have a mantra, or something like the Jesus Prayer,
suited to myself? A book I once read said, quite simply, that I could create a
mantra suited to myself by reflecting on my reality. By considering what I
desired for my life in terms of union with God and all that is of God, I should
then try to summarize my desire in six to eight syllables. The more I would
give voice to this summary statement of my spirituality, the more disposed I
might be to become what I prayed.

Since then I have found that my mantras change, depending on "where
I'm at." More and more I find that they have something to do with God's
spirit breathing in me. This, of course, is aided by the way I breathe at my surface level and try to move this into an awareness of God's breath or spirit or
life-force in me and the universe around me.

Despite saying mantras and all the other ways I try to achieve purity of
heart, so often it seems that emptiness defines my prayer. I wait. Nothing
seems to happen. I can call on God all I want and I can "ask" but I seldom
sense I've received. Yet I have learned to continue to sit there until God
decides to grace me with an experience of the divine presence that I know by
faith is always in my depths. In faith, I know the Spirit who gave flesh to God's
word in the depths of Mary (1:20) is praying with my spirit, even though I do
not experience this reality.

Whether I know it or not, fidelity to the prayer of faith is bound to have
some effect on my surface self, my preoccupations and vocal prayers. Even
though "nothing" seems to happen when we pray with purity of heart, without realizing it, our hearts are growing in conversion (see 13:15). I discovered

this deepening process at work in a member of our Capuchin fraternity when I returned home from Europe in late 1978. While I was away, Perry McDonald, one of our brothers, had made an eight-day directed retreat at our retreat center in Marathon, Wisconsin.

One day we were having our fraternity's weekly review of life. Perry had mentioned the fact that he had made a retreat commitment to get up early so he could spend more time in prayer. He was beginning to backslide, he said, "because nothing ever seems to happen."

"That's interesting," I responded. "I have noticed since I've been back that your spontaneous prayers at Mass and common prayer seem so much deeper than when I left. Maybe you experienced nothing, but your externals show that God must be at work in the depths of your life where the Spirit is praying with your spirit." He found my reflection consoling.

The Fifth Step: The Blessedness of Seeing God

In the Old Testament, to "see God" meant to experience God's favor, to be in God's presence. At the transfiguration, the surface of Jesus' exterior reflected a deeper reality. Jesus evidenced God's favor because his eye had been sound; he had been faithful to God's plan (17:5). Because his eye was sound, his body was filled with light (6:22; 17:2). The transfiguration became the breakthrough in his body of that fire that resided in his heart. Here Jesus was transformed into God's light because he was pure in heart. His transformation became the basis for the religious experience of light for those who accompanied him. No wonder they wanted to remain there! Who wouldn't! Who wouldn't!

Few of us will ever have such an experience of transfiguration; yet we are promised that, if we become pure of heart we will "see God." Does this have to wait until we "go to heaven?" I don't think so. Recalling from the second chapter that heaven is really where God dwells, we must move from a geographic notion of the "kingdom of heaven" and the "reign of God" to the reality of God. If, as we have seen, God is love, and if we love God and our neighbor as ourselves we are not far from that reign, then love is how we "see God." Such love invites us to live in this kindom now.

Once in awhile we get a glimpse of that "heaven." Something happens in the depth of our being that is totally unexpected. We are overwhelmed with a sense of God's presence bringing us to union. At the very same time we get a sense of being in solidarity with everyone and everything in the universe. We are brought into God's compassion and, in this compassion, we see the world from the eyes of God. We have experienced contemplation; we have "seen" God.

Giving ourselves over to union with God enables us to have access in the one Spirit of Jesus to God; it is to become a living sacrifice of praise. We have climbed the mountain through our effort to be free from *porneia* and surface looks. We have struggled up the heights by our purgation and recollection. We are ready to face the divine presence and to experience its blessed light (Ps. 24:3-6). In our solitude we have come to rest in the peace of God's presence-with-us.

In this presence we experience that we are part of the revelation; we have experienced the liberating and life-giving yoke of Jesus. In the Spirit of Jesus' care for each of us, we too can proclaim in our own way, with hearts full of gratitude:

> I thank you, Father, Lord of heaven and earth, because you have hidden these things from the wise and the intelligent and have revealed them to infants; yes, Father, for such was your gracious will. All things have been handed over to me by my Father; and no one knows the son except the Father, and no one knows the Father except the Son and anyone to whom the Son chooses to reveal him.
>
> Come to me, all you that are weary and are carrying heavy burdens, and I will give you rest. Take my yoke upon you, and learn from me; for I am gentle and humble in heart, and you will find rest for your souls. For my yoke is easy, and my burden is light. (11:25-30)

In the experience of God-with-us, we discover that we are with God. There we dwell in power, *exousia.* Here we discover that all the words of our lives are being summarized in the one word we have received as gift from God in the depths of our hearts: Jesus-Emmanuel. Wanting only to remain in this divine rest, we can praise God with Jesus' Spirit and ours. In this experience of power we discover that we too are being transfigured into the very image of God. We experience our whole bodies becoming light, because we are seeing that God who is recognizing the pattern of Jesus' life in the care of our lives. Now, on us, God's favor rests. We discover ourselves entering into the blessedness of God's reign (25:34).

From this perspective we can best understand Paul's Second Letter to the Corinthians, wherein he talks about the Israelites who were unable to "see God" but says that, in the Spirit of Christ within us, that way of seeing is offered to us. In 2 Corinthians 3:12-4:6 Paul summarizes all that we have said in this chapter. Going beyond surface needs, we are led to the experience of seeing God. We enter that experience of God with our ministry of justice in an alien world of *ponēroi.* Recognizing the image, the pattern, of Jesus' life in us, we are received into the divine presence by God. Because we have tried to live in purity of heart, we now can see God. Because we have lived in the norm of care, we are constituted in care; because we are constituted in care, our ministry of care extends to everyone and everything in the universe. The darkness has become light. In this light we live in awe-filled hope in God's world and our broken world.

In the beginning, "when darkness covered the face of the deep," the God of the universe proclaimed: "Let there be light" (Gen. 1:1-2). That "beginning" occurs every time we go through the circle of care into the compassion of God. Now, grounded in care because we have been ministers of care and being able to express the normative dimension of care because we have been constituted in care, we see that the God of the universe shines in our hearts, and we, in turn, can make known to our world the glory of God that shines on the face of Christ. In this way we ourselves become the light to the world that has transformed the ground of our being. As Paul writes: "For it is the God who said, 'Let light shine out of darkness,' who has shone in our hearts to give the light of the knowledge of the glory of God in the face of Christ" (2 Cor. 4:6).

Paul continues by saying we hold "this treasure" in earthen vessels, but this is so in order that "it may be made clear that this extraordinary power" at work in our hearts (2 Cor. 4:7), freed from the surface level, will never find us losing heart. "Even though our outer nature is wasting away, he reminds us: "our inner nature is being renewed day by day. For this slight momentary affliction is preparing us for an eternity of glory beyond all measure, because we look not at what can be seen but at what cannot be seen; for what can be seen is temporary, but what cannot be seen is eternal" (2 Cor. 4:16-18).

Truly, how blessed are such ones who have climbed the mountain and have "pure hearts." Indeed they will see God.

CHAPTER NINE

Blessed Are the Peacemakers; They Will Be Called Children of God

In empowering his disciples (10:1) to go into the various towns and villages proclaiming *his* gospel (which stood in direct contradiction to the "*euaggelion*" of Caesar's world), Matthew's Jesus told them that, as they entered the various households, they should greet the people with peace (10:12-13). In Jesus' day "spreading peace" meant subjecting other peoples to Roman dominion, the *Pax Romana*. Such an understanding of "peace" arose from the proud conviction that Rome had been "vested with the mission of imposing [its] laws and way of life on the rest of the world."[1]

While Jesus' peace was nothing like the *Pax Romana*, neither was it a passive peace that accepted disorder. Rather it resulted only when it would be "made" or created from the disorder. This demanded a new kind of justice that would bring about that reign of God wherein justice and peace would meet (Ps. 85:11). Such was the vision of a world ruled by the Christ.

In the scriptures, justice is the basis for peace. In the Old Testament, both *shālôm* and *mishpāt* involve a justice that needs to exist if there will be peace. Since this peace must be the work of justice, as Pope Paul VI's motto had it, biblically grounded peace is not just the "tranquility of order"; it commits its advocates to the work of justice. Like any creative "work," peace must be "made."

The term "peacemakers" (*eirēnopoioi*) is not used elsewhere in the NT, but it appears in Greco-Roman writing. Here it refers to rulers who establish security and socioeconomic welfare (justice). A somewhat broader paradigm identifies peacemakers as those who seek reconciliation with the world at large.[2] Peacemakers are instruments of God who actively work to create *shālôm*, a new world order enhancing the integrity of creation itself.

"The meaning of 'peace' [*šālôm*]," H. Benedict Green writes, had gone through "a process of domestication" after the fall of Jerusalem. "While it continued to be thought of as a gift of God, and as a condition that would characterize the restored Davidic kingdom of current messianic expectation, its emphasis had shifted from the total well-being of Israel to good social relationships and an absence of strife within the Jewish nation."[3]

Blessed Are the Peacemakers . . .

Matthew's Jesus highlights the task of the honored ones in his households when he declares in the seventh Beatitude: Blessed are the peacemakers. Indeed, peacemaking is the task of all homemakers. The fact that peace must be "made" by the members of the households at the various levels of life (*oikia, oikonomia, oikoumenē,* and *oikologia*) should not be easily overlooked. The result is the promise of being called children of the head of that household: the Father in heaven. This makes peacemakers brothers and sisters.

Within Our Own Oikia

When I give workshops on this Beatitude I ask the participants to think about someone they know—in their family of origin, among their co-workers, parishioners or members of their various communities—whom they would say has "made peace" with him or herself. I ask them to reflect on what they think made it possible for these persons to come to make peace with themselves in this way. What are a couple of the "ingredients" for making peace in one's life? What should one do? What should one avoid doing?

When they have noted these, I ask them to share their "recipe" with their tablemates. Then I ask: "Are you finding any common ingredients?" "Are there any things that should never be put into the mix?" Then I ask them to write these down. When all the groups have finished, they summarize their small group's recipe for making peace in our individual lives.

In the more than twenty years that I have been doing this, the recipe has always remained the same. Two ingredients always stand apart from all the other options. One might be considered the "stumbling block" that must be avoided at all costs. This is translated as: "I give up the need to control." The other ingredient is the only positive ingredient needed to make peace possible within our hearts: "I accept myself for who I am."

When we consider the obstacle to peace, we need look no further than Matthew's well-known words of Jesus. He invites the audience, which seems to have been conflicted about leaving dynamics of control behind, to come to him and find their rest, to dwell in his peace (11:28).

As we saw in chapter 4, weariness, heaviness, and the feeling of being burdened all reflect dynamics of "control." When we give up the need to control, we are freeing ourselves from the key stumbling block to personal peace. Then, when we place ourselves under the "yoke" of Jesus we "will find rest for our souls" (11:29). We accept ourselves, in the depth of our being, as the "very good" people whom God has made in the divine image.

When we are free of the need to control and accept ourselves for who we are, we have discovered the recipe for making peace. At the same time, we share this recipe with others in the way we refuse to try to control them and accept them for who *they* are. By following this recipe, we put in the mix the household dynamics that create *shālôm*.

In the Oikoumenē: *Overcoming the* Skandala *in the Institutions and "Isms"*

If we are going to "make peace" among the various institutions and "isms" that define our infrastructure, we must be aware of the stumbling blocks in our attitudes that can lead to war.

Ralph K. White has shown that every war has underlying and precipitating causes. Without six underlying causes, he discovered, there could be no war. We can consider these six causes in terms of the Vietnam War.

1. The first step in any conflict is to perceive the opponent in terms of the *diabolical enemy image.* The other is seen as diametrically opposed to what one represents. The enemy Vietnamese were "the gooks"; they could never be trusted. Even their eyes showed how slanted and shifty they were! The enemy Americans were "the running-dog imperialists"; their soldiers were the lackeys of the capitalists who were trying to take over the world. To stop such a diabolical enemy, strong steps had to be taken.

2. The *"virile" self-image* provides the weapons. Whether these armaments be words or silence, missiles or guns, each side believes it has the physical resources to win. The Vietnamese were guerrillas; just as they outlasted the Japanese and French with guerrilla warfare, they would also beat the United States. The United States was the strongest nation on earth; it had never lost a war. It could bomb the Vietnamese into submission. Furthermore, if it lost Vietnam, all the other nations would fall like dominoes. To capitulate would be humiliation. Commitments had to be honored.

3. Buttressed by the *moral self-image,* both sides view themselves as peace loving, rational, orderly and just. For U.S. citizens, God was the protector of democratic values. The nation was challenged to protect its values for future generations. The Vietnamese saw themselves as protecting their own interests; their struggle was an internal matter. The foreign aggressor should be taught not to interfere. U.S. citizens saw themselves safeguarding democracy and freedom. With Cardinal Spellman blessing the troops and Billy Graham blessing the Commander-in-Chief, God had to be on the American side!

4. *Selective inattention* focuses only on the extremes; mitigating circumstances and significant historical background are glossed over. The Vietnamese refused to consider that their internal problems had created a

situation that resulted in many people calling for outside aid. U.S. patriots refused to remember the fact that, like Vietnam, the United States was a nation conceived in a revolutionary war. The founders did not like it when the Prussians helped the British colonizers in their effort to squelch the nation's independence movement.

5. The *lack of empathy* means that both sides are unable to see matters from the other's view. Bluntly, neither side cares. The Vietnamese were so controlled by their fear of the "Americans," seeing them as the personification of evil, that they could not understand their belief in democracy. The Americans, controlled by an ideology reflecting the white experience, never understood the Asian mind. What resulted from this insensitivity, combined with the previous attitudes, was the final step.

6. Each side developed an overconfidence reflecting an overall *irrational interpretation of reality*. Both sides were so controlled by their ideologies and subjective interpretations that it was simply impossible for them to think otherwise. Each side viewed itself as correct and justified in its position. Anyone within those nations who questioned that "party line" was considered disloyal. Thus Catholics in North Vietnam who wanted some of their rights were considered subversive. Those in the United States who questioned the morality of the war were probably pink, if not out-and-out communists.

When such ways of thinking are reinforced and cultivated by the media and the educational system, people develop a stance toward the other (the "enemy" as "evil") and themselves ("right" and "just"); these become the justifications for war when a "last straw" is placed on the ideological haystack. This is the precipitating cause. Now convinced of no alternative but "going to war" (or, invoking the "strike" or "getting the divorce"), it is all justified.

In the Oikonomia *of Our Households*

If an understanding of this ideology or these background attitudes can be applied to the "isms," or the social arrangements of the infrastructure, how much more, I discovered, can an understanding of their influence help bring this seventh Beatitude to bear on potential conflicts within our families, between wives and husbands, parents and children, as well as within organizations and communities. Failing to understand how subtly these attitudes can infect perceptions among members of these groups can leave the members open to the many forms of war that rule too many households. The Third Street Capuchin Community in Milwaukee going to "war" is a case in point.

After the war had begun, I realized I was one of the combatants. Though it happened a long time ago, I have not found the dynamics that led us to war replicated since. While I would like to give a more current example of going to war, I have no such "war stories" because this experience taught me that it's better to avoid such stumbling blocks and to make a "holding environment" that will be conducive to peace. So to my original "war story."

Four of us Capuchins were living in a rented house in Milwaukee. I was the only solemnly professed member of the community. The simply professed Capuchins were Mark Ramion, Larry Webber, and Bill Erickson.

Larry and I were too much alike. We both had a deep desire to discipline ourselves into a form of gospel living; we both had a kind of obsession with perfection. To use a term from the previous chapter, we both suffered from the "ideal look" with its shoulds, oughts, and musts. Our problem resulted from the different ways we expressed these goals, how we perceived each other in the process, and how we tried to influence each other with our "shoulds."

Creating the Stumbling Blocks

At various times and with various degrees of emotion, we tried to discuss our differences and thoughts about each other. As each of us justified our positions, we gradually came to a standoff. Larry did not think he could do much of anything right in my eyes, and the feeling was mutual. Unconsciously each of us was starting to build up our defenses as we attacked each other's positions. We were legitimizing our defensive positions around the six steps that lead to war. We just needed one precipitating incident to "go to war."

When the "incident" occurred that found us in conflict it happened because Larry and I had never dealt with our growing alienation. Now, these underlying attitudes came to legitimize what we had done with our verbal barrage. Furthermore, each of us justified why, at this time, we should not lay down our arms.

How did each of us regard the other from the six underlying causes that lead to war? How did our attitude toward each other parallel the way the United States and Vietnam justified their hostilities?

1. Both of us needed to view the other from the perspective of the *diabolical enemy image*. Each of us saw the other as diametrically opposed to the truth we each tried to represent. The enemy Larry was so self-righteous; his piety turned me off. The enemy Michael was so conceited; his so-called spirituality was really dangerous. To stop each other, a stand would have to be taken. This brought us to the next step.

2. We both thought of ourselves as having the weapons necessary to conquer the other. This was our *"virile" self-image*. Larry had to change. It was my responsibility to use my role as a solemnly professed to make him change if he wanted to stay around. If I did not do it, who would? On the other hand, anyone could see through Michael to uncover what made him tick. Only

Larry would have the guts to stand up and not be cowed by him. Whether he was on the Provincial Council or not, Larry could cut through Mike's defenses. After all, if Larry did not do it, who would?

3. With our common obsession for perfection, both of us would justify our stance with *a moral self-image*. Because Larry had such a crazy notion of spirituality it was in his best interest that I keep pressing and not give in. On the other side, Michael was really a phony. With his judgmental attitude and pride, how could God be blessing him? If Larry would not expose such an approach, who would? After all, if his housemates kept quiet, who in the province would have the guts to stand up to Michael Crosby?

4. To legitimize our positions we both needed to focus on each other's extremes by *selective inattention*. I was unable to see all the good that Larry did in his jail ministry and with those in need. And, I suppose, there were things about me that Larry would not want to consider. If either of us would have attended to those and other factors, we would have found less reason to remain at war. We needed to be blind to them to continue our hostilities.

5. We both *lacked empathy*. We said we cared, but because we were both overly defined by the "shoulds," the "oughts," and the "musts" of the ideal look, we were more into the need to control than to actualize our stated desire that said we cared. Even though I was like Larry when I was his age, I could show no weakness and give in. Larry had to learn; so did Mike, from Larry's viewpoint. Our professed "care" was eclipsed by our control.

6. Reinforced with such attitudes both of us could be confident that we were justified in attacking each other. We would have cause not to lay down our arms because of our *irrational interpretation of reality*. Even though meekness means a rational interpretation of reality, our pride had to defend our positions, irrational as they might be. Both of us had strained mercy. The whole conflict was crazy, irrational.

The morning after Larry and I had the final incident that led to our "war," Larry, Mark, and I came together for the liturgy; Bill was not with us. We could have applied the steps of community conscientization conversion noted in chapter 3 in a eucharistic setting.[4] But we—like so many before us— celebrated the ritual without the reality of mercy and reconciliation.

After beginning in the name of the God who promised to be with us in *community* if we two or three gathered in the name of Jesus, we came to the reconciliation rite, which initiates the *conscientization* process (see pp. 56-57). Reading our reality would have shown us enslaving each other by our anger and resentment. We could have also known that God's power could have helped us *convert*. But, despite the reconciliation service, our anger justified continuing in our warlike positions. We had no problem saying, "Lord, have mercy. Christ, have mercy. Lord, have mercy."

The next part of the Eucharist brings us, with our enslavements and empowerments, to hear the Word of God to deepen our *conversion*. Into that battlefield, which had moved from the kitchen the night before to the living room that morning, the day's first reading began with a selection from First Corinthians. "I will show you a still more excellent way," it began. "If I speak," it continued, and, at that point I realized the words that would follow. Panic hit me as I said to myself, "Oh, shit!"

> If I speak in the tongues of mortals and of angels, but do not have love, I am a noisy gong or a clanging cymbal. And if I have prophetic powers, and understand all mysteries and all knowledge, and if I have all faith, so as to remove mountains, but do not have love, I am nothing. If I give away all my possessions, and if I hand over my body so that I may boast, but do not have love, I gain nothing. (1 Cor. 12:31b-13:3)

At this point of the reading I thought, "If it ends here, I think I can get by." But the Word of God addressing the world of Michael Crosby with a call to conversion continued: "Love is patient; love is kind. . . ." At that point I remembered what a retreat director had once suggested: we should insert our name instead of the word "love." God's Word judging my life-reality was saying: Michael is patient; he is kind. Michael is not envious or boastful or arrogant or rude. He does not insist on his own way; he is not irritable or resentful [from dishes the night before]; he does not rejoice in wrongdoing, but rejoices in the truth. Michael's love bears all things, believes all things, hopes all things, endures all things."

And then there was the clincher: "Michael's love never fails" (1 Cor. 13:4-8a).

Now, thirteen hours after the battle had begun between Larry and Michael, what were we going to do about our World-at-War, having heard God's Word? Would we respond "Thanks be to God" and make it a sign of conversion? Or would "Thanks be to God" be another empty cliché? Would the idolatrous worship continue in the face of the reality of irreconciliation? Although not another round had been fired since the night before, both of us definitely knew we were at war. With that realization of our sin, I looked at Larry as he was looking at me and said, "I'm sorry, Larry." And he simply replied in kind, "I'm sorry, too, Mike."

How could this have happened to two people both honestly seeking God's will? We discovered we had not *structured* a way to ensure that we would not be controlled by underlying attitudes that could easily lead to various forms of rejection. Never dealing with such attitudes as they built up, it was only a matter of time before war would be declared.

Once we came to share the one bread in the eucharistic service, we discovered each other's brokenness in a whole new way. We could now say "Amen" to this bread of life. Because we had finally opened our eyes to recognize the real presence in the bread we found each other there as its members. Now we could say "Amen" to each other. Since "Amen" means "Let it be," I was now saying, "Let Larry be, Mike." Larry also was saying to himself about me: "Just let him be, Larry." No longer could we continue trying to remake each other into our own images—if the recipe for peace would rule our house.

Making peace does not end at the point of avoiding the *skandala* that may lead to war. Awareness and avoidance of these underlying causes leading to war are just the first step in making peace. Larry and I would come to understand the next steps that must be made when we found ourselves living together again in another house a few months later.

Putting in the Right Ingredients to Make Peace

Our move from Third Street was precipitated by various factors. Bill had decided to leave the Order; Mark would be away for his deaconate experience; Larry had to move because formation policy dictated that simply professed friars change communities every two years. Since no friars wanted to move from their local fraternities to Third Street, we decided to close it down. In looking around for the best possible fraternity (given various considerations), I decided on our Capuchin Prenovitiate at 31ˢᵗ Street. This fraternity was composed of Perry McDonald, Steve Wettstein, Mike Merkt, and Larry Webber.

At our first monthly day of reflection, Perry asked us to consider four questions without a hitch: (1) What gifts was I bringing to the fraternity? (2) What were my personal goals for this year? (3) What did I envision for the fraternity this year? (4) How did I see this vision being realized?

Returning from our private reflection, we breezed through the first two questions quite rapidly. Then we addressed the third and fourth questions. After hearing what the others envisioned for the community, I said something like: "You know, we tried something at Third Street to help us make peace and it didn't work. But I think the reason why it failed was that we didn't structure a form to make it happen. This would have made sure we did what we had promised to do.

"I still dream of the time in our fraternities when all the members will be able to just live according to one ground rule," I continued. "It would go something like this: Say, for instance, the five of us would be able to affirm each other. I could affirm you and you could support me. But, building on this affirmation, we'd also let each other know what was bugging us. So I could correct you and you could confront me. Do you think," I concluded, "that we could do something like this during the year?"

While I do not have the exact words of their responses, they all agreed. When it came to Larry, he looked at me and the rest and said, "Well, you know we tried something like this at Third Street and it didn't work. But I still believe it's the way communities should be living. I realize it may be rough at times and we have to work off some of our tensions, but I want it. I want it badly."

We started calling the way we could make peace in our house the "ground rule." Then I said, "You know, I think the word of God is telling us that what we're about to do in community is just what Jesus wants." We went to the eighteenth chapter of Matthew. There, in Jesus' advice to a community in transition that experienced alienation and division, we discovered the way the brothers and sisters could structure their coming together to create peace.[5]

. . . They Will Be Called Children of God: Matthew's New *Haustafel*

Throughout this book we have seen that Matthew was writing not so much to individuals as to households. These *oikonomiai* were constituted by the persons and resources that brought them together. Their social ordering of the core constituents of a household (husband/wife, parents/children, owner/slave) was defined by certain norms or patterns which the Germans called *Haustafeln*. These household codes defined the social ordering that was expected to take place. In the New Testament we find *Haustafeln* expressed in two main structurings. The first form has two components. One deals with relationships among various household members, and the other addresses the allocation of resources, especially the art of making money (1 Tim. 6:6-10, 17-19).[6] The second style of *Haustafel* also had two parts: one dealing with how the members of the household relate to the civil authorities, and the second, how submission should take place among wives to husbands, children to parents, and slaves to masters (1 Pet. 2:18-3:7; Col. 3:18-4:6; 1 Tim. 2:1-8; and Tit. 2:1-10).

According to Leland White, Matthew's approach to settling conflicts within the house church indicates the lack of a formal, hierarchical/ patriarchal power structure and the prohibition against recognizing rank or achievement within the community. The Matthean peace procedures, he writes, "reflect a pattern of organization that places minimal reliance on formally distinguished roles. *When we ask who governs Matthew's community, who enforces its norms, we find no evidence that such functions have been assigned to any individual or group.* The community apparently functions in the ad hoc fashion of an extended family."[7]

This extended family is no longer one reflecting a patriarchal order of domination but a collegial model of greater egalitarianism. In such a community all are to be brothers and sisters under a common Father. This seems evident in the last part of the seventh Beatitude. Thus White notes that we are now talking about a dynamic that "transforms the community of disciples. No longer a mere voluntary group, it has become a quasi-family, a fictional or legal family, whose father is God. This status means that *responsibility for the members' individual well-being is now vested in God as father; his honor rests on their well-being.*"[8] Under this Father, a new kindom was to be created.

In Matthew 17:24-18:35 we find an example of the second kind of *Haustafel.* The two parts of one kind of *Haustafel* are divided between how a household will relate to the world "outside" and how its members will relate to each other "inside." Without realizing it, we had embraced the ordering of our house vis-à-vis our wider world (i.e., the "civil authorities") by deciding to live as simply as we could (see 17:24-29). This would be our way of setting ourselves apart from the *makarioi* of the culture around us. It would be our way of not giving *skandalon* (17:27). However, the dynamics of our "inside" household code would be quite powerfully experienced.

Avoiding the Skandala *(8:1-9)*

Community, for Matthew, begins with the realization of the dignity of each member. Each person is considered by the others to be precious in the eyes of God. Thus, in response to the disciples' question regarding who was the greatest (18:1), Matthew's Jesus "called a child, whom he put among them, and said, 'Truly I tell you, unless you change and become like children, you will never enter the kingdom of heaven'" (18:2-3).

At the time of Jesus, children were denied, by their age as well as by law, the rights of persons or access to needed resources. Now whoever would be greatest would reflect a childlike abandonment, wanting to fulfill the ideal of God's reign. Such people would orient their rights and resources to God's rule: "Whoever becomes humble like this child is the greatest in the kingdom of heaven" (18:4). In any community where everyone defers to the other out of reverence for each other's rights and need for resources, the image of Jesus is recognized in the one who is in need. Furthermore, the image of Jesus is revealed in the one who may be responding to the one most in need (see 10:40-42; 25:31-46) as well: "Whoever welcomes one such child in my name welcomes me" (18:5). Welcoming the least makes me a member of the kindom.

Moving directly to address the *skandala* that could tear the house churches apart besides the power-plays around who would be "greatest," Matthew's Jesus spends some time talking about their debilitating effect in general:

If any one of you put a stumbling block before one of these little ones who believes in me, it would be better for you if a great millstone were fastened around your neck and you were drowned in the depth of the sea. Woe to the world because of stumbling blocks! Occasions for stumbling are bound to come, but woe to the one by whom the stumbling block comes! (18:6-7)

Having addressed the undermining power of the stumbling blocks in the house churches, Matthew addresses two in particular: those coming from the "hand" or "foot" (18:8), that is, the way people would give "the back of their hand" or "the foot" to others in ways that would be dominating, and those coming from the "eye" in the way they would give each other the "evil eye" (18:9). If they use their power in such a destructive way, such activities would not just be stumbling blocks to healthy community life, they would lead the perpetrator(s) into "the hell of fire."

Following any good recipe for "making peace," we would avoid the stumbling blocks that might get in the way of healthy relationships among us. Following Matthew's model, we would not allow ourselves to be defined by dynamics of control. These would especially revolve around attitudes defined by dynamics related to the "ideal look" as it might be expressed in our house. Thus we would seek to become humble "like children" rather than be defined by who would be "the greatest" or whose ways would be "best" (18:1-5). Next we would not "put a stumbling block before" any of the members of the community (18:6-7) by any way of acting or "seeing" that would cause another brother to stumble (18:8-10). In other words we would "cut out" any thinking or behavior that would reflect dynamics of control.

Creating the Makarios *Way of Making Peace (18:10-20)*

Having made sure we avoided the stumbling blocks to peace, we were now ready for the second part: creating right relationships. This demands the right ingredients. These involved committing ourselves to dynamics that would result in mutual affirmation and mutual correction. As I read "Matthew's Advice to His Divided Community," the commitment to affirmation can be found in 18:10-14, while the effort to be made around communal correction and challenge involves the passages in 18:15-20.

Having established the need for all people in community to make sure they are not leading a life that hinders the faith of any brother or sister, Matthew's Jesus goes on to outline the next three steps that will bring about the blessedness of a community that has made peace among its members. In contemporary language this involves dynamics of what Donald W. Winnecott calls the "holding environment" or the "envelope of care"[9]; mutual affirmation and correction done in a way that finds the members wanting to remain committed to each other.

In a rightly ordered household, the processes of the whole community itself should revolve around the affirmation of each member as significant; none can be lost. The community exists to ensure that each, including the "littlest" one, is never lost. It cannot be the other way around—that we exist for the community in a way that undermines our God-given uniqueness. As Jesus showed clearly, community exists for each of its members. In Matthew's community, all the members are to be committed to making sure that none strays from the group. In this communal style, the give-and-take of affirmation creates a synergy that makes the members want to stick around rather than stray. Consequently, each member must "take care that" he or she does nothing to undermine the goodness of the least member.

Developing this notion of the need for affirmation, Jesus asks: "What do you think? If a shepherd has a hundred sheep, and one of them has gone astray, does he not leave the ninety-nine on the mountain and go in search of the one that went astray. And if he finds it, truly I tell you, he rejoices over it more than over the ninety-nine that never went astray" (18:10-13).

If we lived within an environment of affirmation (affirming and being affirmed), we would be much better able to sense if something was hurting anyone in the house. We could more easily stop business as usual, go to that housemate (in our friary, for instance), and try to meet his needs. We could see him in need, care about him as well as his need and do something to make him feel he belongs. In this care and affirmation he could respond to others in need by caring more for them than for his own problems. "So it is not the will of your Father in heaven that one of these little ones should be lost" (18:14). If this heavenly Father is the head of the household, we all are brothers in our friary; in this sense our fraternity must live in the circle of care.

After we had made the "ground rule," I returned home after being on the road just a few days. "Am I glad to see you," Perry said, giving me a big bear hug. "Welcome home again!" I looked quite stunned at his spontaneous sign of affirmation and affection. Then I realized I had come to expect nothing from anyone in the way of recognition, much less such a show of care. But Perry saw me in a new light, from the "ground rule." He wanted me to know how he felt. It was a little gesture, but it meant a lot. Sharing this sign of affection and care, he would be for me an angel of God's care. In his show of care, he would be inviting me to become more sensitive by affirming others. I could say more positive things to these others—from the way they looked, to the prayer they led, to their insights, to the simple joy of having them around.

The second step in making peace in our households or creating the "envelope of care" involves the way we mutually correct and challenge one another. We soon discovered that the other half of our ground rule flowed from the affirming touch of care for each other. If we could build each other up, that would be the trusting environment within which we could correct each other. Thus, at this point in Matthew's *Haustafel*, we hear Jesus say: "If another member of the church sins against you, go and point out the fault when the two of you are alone. If the member listens to you, you have regained that one" (18:15).

In confrontation, the initial step should be a private sharing of what might bother us, even the petty things. This should precede any communal "laundering." Thus, a week after we made the "ground rule," I was packing for a trip. Larry came knocking on my door. When he came in, he said: "I feel a little funny coming like this, Mike, but 'Remember the ground rule'?" (We had agreed that "remember the ground rule" would become the symbolic phrase that would get our "care system" in gear.)

I said, "Sure, I remember. What's the matter?"

After he told me his concern and I indicated that I had not meant to question him, Larry said: "Wow, isn't the ground rule great!"

Some might say you can get too petty about correcting and confronting each other. Immature people will get petty. So the ground rule is not practicable with immature people. But, assuming a family, group, or community is composed of basically healthy people, it can also be said that the petty things are usually those little things that can build up and lead to war.

Larry had been faithful to the initial step of correction. He had come to me (18:15). If he hadn't gotten anywhere with me that night, he could have moved to Matthew's next step: "But if you are not listened to, take one or two others along with you, so that every word may be confirmed by the evidence of two or three witnesses" (18:16). If Larry and I had not been able to work out our problem, Larry could have discussed it with Perry, Steve, or Mike. They could have offered another perspective, because either of us might be blinded by our past hurts, anger, or inability to be as objective as we ought.

Sometimes people use this second step instead of the first step—going to the person himself or herself. While it should be done for Matthean reasons, often this process takes the form of talking behind the other's back. If each of us in the fraternity is conscious of this when it happens, then we can ask, "Did you share your problem with Mike?" This, in turn, might be a reminder to meet with the one who has inflicted the perceived hurt.

If the first two steps in the correction process prove unworkable in making peace (making peace is work!), Jesus said that we should "tell" the matter "to the church" (18:17). This group gathered in Jesus' name, even if only two or three, would be promised the abiding presence of Jesus. This would enable the community to bind and loose the erring member in the way that would receive heaven's assurity.

We decided that our weekly Review of Life and monthly Day of Reflection would serve this purpose. As part of the ritual of each subsequent meeting, the leader would ask, "Does anyone have anything they want to bring up about the ground rule?" Soon we had disciplined ourselves to such a point in practicing the first two steps that we rarely had to invoke that ritual. Yet it was always good to recall the phrase about the ground rule as part of structuring peace.

The Friday after we initiated the ground rule was the first and only time Larry saw fit to invoke it with me. We both tried to respect each other and build up our relationship in care. As a result, within a few months, we were able to come to full reconciliation not only in our heads but in our hearts as well.

This occurred as I came back earlier than expected from some speaking engagements. When he saw me, Larry wrapped his arms around me exclaiming, "Mike, we didn't expect you until next week!" That hug meant an awful lot. As we both realized a few days later, at that moment we both *felt* like we meant it, that we were happy to be with each other again.

When we reflected on this third positive step for a reconciled community, following affirmation and correction, we realized how powerful all other dimensions of our community life could be. This would bring new meaning to prayer itself as well as all other forms of communication. With such a ground rule, someone mentioned, we could finally understand what Francis meant in our Rule when he wrote, "Wherever the friars meet one another, they should show they are members of the same family. And they should have *no hesitation* in making known their needs to one another."[10] Without such a ground rule, soundly articulated, the fear of possible rejection always remains. With the structure for making peace, we can approach each other in confidence, without hesitation. We can *confidently* make known our needs so the circle of care can begin.

We ended up making Matthew 18 our Word Service that Saturday afternoon. Then we articulated the ground rule in specific words as our way of realizing this new vision as a covenant with each other. We signed our names to it and made this covenant of fidelity our sacrifice of offertory praise to God. Making peace makes us God's children—and kin to each other.

Trying to avoid any tensions and working to affirm and confront each other in care, a community that senses itself gathered in the name of Jesus would do well to try to make various scripture passages more evident in its lifestyle and relationship. As part of that community's faith experience, each person could ask the others in equal care how a specific statement was fulfilled in her or his individual life. The community could ask the same of its corporate expression.

Matthew's Jesus indicated that the extended family constituting the house churches themselves had the very power of heaven to bind and to loose that had been given Peter (16:19). Would that we would stress this passage in the Roman Catholic Church as much as we have the text on Peter's power to bind and loose! But here the local church is assured: "Truly I tell you, whatever you bind on earth will be bound in heaven, and whatever you loose on earth will be loosed in heaven" (18:18). The goal of reconciliation and peace demands that opposing factions come to agreement. Thus, where Peter may have received the assurance of the "keys," in being granted the power to bind and loose, Matthew's Jesus promised such a group of people committed to forgiveness and reconciliation his abiding presence for all time: "Again, truly I tell you, if two of you agree on earth about anything you ask, it will be done for you by my Father in heaven. For where two or three are gathered in my name, I am there among them" (18:19-20).

Being Children of God Makes Us Brothers and Sisters in God's Household

Larry and I had not only become "gathered in" the name of Jesus, the one who would save us from our stumbling blocks. Because we took the steps to make peace, we found ourselves not only "God's sons" but brothers under that God who is the head of every household.

Matthew's Jesus twice was called "son" by a voice from the heavens. The first was Jesus' inaugural experience of baptism, when he committed himself to the way of justice (3:15). The second came with his transfiguration, when Jesus' experience of the reign of God's *dikaiosynē*, or presence within him, was revealed to others (17:1-8). In both these experiences the voice proclaimed of Jesus: "This is my Son, the Beloved, with whom I am well pleased" (3:17; cf. 17:5).

In Matthew, the favor of God's blessing is identified with messianic restoration. This is *shālôm*. In spirituality circles, it is also called the unitive way. However, any coming to peace with ourselves and each other also demands that God's unity and peace be witnessed to others. The gift of God's power and peace, which the disciples received (10:1, 7), was to be given as a gift to every household: "Whatever town or village you enter, find out who in it is worthy, and stay there until you leave. As you enter the house, greet it. If the house is worthy, let your peace [*eirēnē*] come upon it; but if it is not worthy, let your peace [*eirēnē*] return to you" (10:11-14). The initial activity of the first evangelizers was to extend the blessing of peace not just to the members of their own house churches but to towns and villages beyond them.

The good news of God's rule is to be realized in *eirēnē*, peace. Just as the disciples were told at the Mount of Transfiguration to listen to Jesus (17:5), so the world that will not listen to the disciples' proclamation of God's way of peace and be evangelized (see 10:40-41) will lose the peace once offered it (10:13). Assured of God's presence of peace with them (10:20), Jesus also warned his first followers that not all would be receptive to this "gospel." They would prefer the gospel that proclaimed a *Pax Romana* or other such forms of "good news." If they and/or their message would not be welcomed, they were told to "shake off the dust from your feet as you leave that house or town. Truly I tell you, it will be more tolerable for the land of Sodom and Gomorrah on the day of judgment than for that town" (10:14-15).

Why would people reject those who proclaimed the *euaggelion* of *eirēnē*? Why would such a "gospel" itself fall on deaf ears and hardened hearts? For the same reason Sodom and Gomorrah rejected the good news that was proclaimed in it: the *euaggelion* that would usher in God's reign of *shalôm* must be grounded in justice.[11] When a society rejects justice and the right way of ordering relationships among persons and resources within its various households—which leads to peace—that society will not be "honored" by Jesus; it will receive his reproach (see 11:20-24; 23:33-39).

Because he tried to make peace through truth and justice, Jesus was constituted God's son. In Jesus' transfiguration, the disciples experienced the transformation in peace that can come to anyone who tries to live this Beatitude. Experiencing God's power and favor within us, we too can be transfigured before the world's eyes as was Jesus. On the mountain "he was transfigured before them, and his face shone like the sun, and his clothes became dazzling white" (17:2).

Our liturgy on the Feast of the Transfiguration every August 6 recalls the splendor of a moment long ago when the divine favor in all its effulgence glorified Jesus for his fidelity to the process of making peace. On that day we, along with Peter, James, and John, are told to "listen to him!" (17:5). That listening will find us taking up that cross imposed on us by a society that will not accept our gospel of peace (16:24-28). But as we celebrate, we cannot forget that on another August 6 another kind of light was released in the universe. This light emanating from the power within Jesus glowed with the brilliance of the sun. Whereas the light coming from Jesus brought peace and hope into the world, the light coming from the atom bomb over Hiroshima that August 6, 1945, brought death to at least 65,000 people and ongoing fear to millions as it inaugurated the nuclear era. Now, rather than working for the justice that results in peace, being prepared for war would become the new name for making peace, a direct contradiction to this Beatitude.

Instead of leading people to the power and peace that could be found in Jesus, another power was unleashed in the name of "peace." It has since brought nations to the edge of the precipice. It has been the forerunner to "weapons of mass destruction." Surviving under this new power has become a way of life. The resource once intended by Einstein to promote peace has become, in military and other kinds of technology, a source of heightened fear and mistrust, greed and hate, division and insecurity. This violence-laden reality now threatens the *oikologia* itself.

Jack Dean Kingsbury says that the kind of peacemaking we discovered to be needed for our newly ordered household on 31st Street in Milwaukee must be expressed beyond our own walls to the whole world. This demands that we who work for peace among ourselves also "work for the wholeness and well-being that God wills for a broken world."[12] Such a peace, if grounded in justice, mercy, and compassion for the crowds, especially for the oppressed, will be cosmic. As Warren Carter notes of such "cosmic peace," it demands the work of bringing all things into right relationship with God and all that is in the universe. Such peace, he writes, "consists not of exploitation but of all things cosmically in right relation to God." At the same time, with its grounding in right relations or justice with all, it also demands that we work not to bring about "the empire's will but God's merciful reign, toward this wholeness and well-being and against any power that hinders or resists it."[13]

Such is the only way we can understand Jesus' other saying in the missionary discourse: "Do not think that I have come to bring peace to the earth; I have not come to bring peace, but a sword. For I have come to set a man against his father, and a daughter against her mother, and a daughter-in-law against her mother-in-law; and one's foes will be members of one's own household" (10:34-36). If a household does not find its members united around those right relations that reveal it as just, it will never have peace. Thus, Matthew's Jesus makes it clear that he did not come to bring peace but justice. However, this "justice" will bring about divisions when people decide not to accept this *euaggelion*. However, to those in the households who do accept this message and this model for peace, "truly I tell you, none of these will lose their reward" (10:42).

CHAPTER TEN

Blessed Are Those Persecuted for Justice' Sake; The Reign of Heaven Is Theirs

Matthew's last Beatitude is a twofold *makarism*. The first blessing, following the pattern of the previous seven Beatitudes, comes to "*those* who are persecuted" for justice' (*dikaiosynē*) sake (5:10); the last one (actually a ninth Beatitude) blesses "*you* when men revile you and persecute you and utter all kinds of evil against you falsely on my account" (5:11). They are written in the two different voices (those/you) to show that *those* disciples who faithfully witness to justice will be persecuted but, if such disciples remain faithful, they can be encouraged that "they" will be "themselves," the readers of Matthew's Gospel—hence the change from the third person (*they*) to the second person (*you*). With this in mind we read the final two-part makarism:

> Blessed are those who are persecuted for justice' (*dikaiosynē*) sake, for theirs is the kingdom of heaven.
>
> Blessed are you when people revile you and persecute you and utter all kinds of evil against you falsely on my account. Rejoice and be glad, for your reward is great in heaven, for in the same way they persecuted the prophets who were before you. (5:10-12)

Since the Beatitudes are part of the Sermon on the Mount, which ends by calling "wise" the one who "hears these words of mine and acts on them" (7:24), the "you" refers to those in Matthew's households who are trying to live the Beatitudes in their daily lives and thus were feeling opposition if not outright persecution from the "world."

The earlier persecution of the Christians came in the form of their expulsion from the house synagogues. But now it seems not to have come from elements only within the Jewish religion; it also seems to have come from the wider society. Matthew changed the person described from "them" to "you" to address the concrete reality of persecution being realized in his community. As Jesus, the just one (27:43), was persecuted for justice' sake and was blessed in the resurrection, so the members of the Matthean house churches could feel honored if they should be persecuted in the cause of justice.

For many years scholars have noted the images related to tensions and persecution in the First Gospel. Both Christian and non-Christian sources indicate that, at the time of its composition, various forms of persecution were used against religious enemies: death, floggings, imprisonment, exclusion from the synagogues, as well as social and economic reprisals such as boycotts of goods, the imposition of fines, and refusal to hire those professing other beliefs.[1] Matthew's terminology for the last Beatitude reflects such an environment of persecution. The lines were being drawn. An "out-group" and an "in-group" were defining their distinct identities.

If one sociologically examines a community that is experiencing alienation from a more powerful group, words referring to the distance between "us" and "them" become noticeable. W. D. Davies, one of the best authorities on Matthew's Sermon on the Mount and the Beatitudes, has noted that the frequent use of words referring to "you" and "they" manifests the attitude of a persecuted and alienated group within a wider, alien culture.[2] We've already seen this in the way Matthew refers to "their" synagogues and the way Jesus "went on from there to teach and proclaim his message in *their* towns" (11:1). Evidence such as this suggests that the church was already outside "their towns." Quite possibly it was settled in such non-Jewish areas as Antioch in Syria (see 4:11).

Douglas Hare and Robert Gundry have shown that the Jewish persecution of Christians underlies many of the passages in Matthew's Gospel (10:16-33; 22:6; 23:29-39), including this Beatitude (5:10-12). Hare lists the following as causes for the persecution: Christians lived in a manner that reflected justice (5:10); they were advocating the cause of Jesus (5:11); and they were living the lifestyle of the prophet (5:12).[3] However, even though the pain of past harsh rejection remained, Hare may be making too much of any persecution of the Matthean households, since any former persecution had generally subsided by the time of the final redaction of the First Gospel in the 80s and 90s. While definitely alluding to this persecution, Matthew does not limit his narrative to the past or even the present; rather he speaks to the way of life that will generate *any* persecution that results from living the normative dimension of justice.

Persecution for the Promotion of Justice

Matthew tells the community that its experience of persecution results from its fidelity in promoting *dikaiosynē*, or God's justice. The community's fidelity to its call is equally a sacrament. It signifies the disciples' experience of another reality, namely, that the reign of God is theirs who live by this justice (5:10).

The eighth Beatitude contains the only other expression outside the first Beatitude that, as the result of a specific activity or attitude, the reward of

God's reign can be immediately expected. Since God's reign is constitutively linked with justice, the disciples' ministry for justice automatically deepens within each disciple the experience of God's reign, which is justice. The inevitable sign that the disciples are being faithful to this ministry of justice is evidenced in the experience of misunderstanding and persecution from various elements within their world. This includes martyrdom.

Matthew's community was conflicted from within and without. This Beatitude told the community that rejection from within the community was to be expected. Even members of the disciples' own families might not be willing to convert to a gospel message that called into question some of the gods that, like the unbelievers, they were running after (6:32):

> Do not think that I have come to bring peace to the earth; I have not come to bring peace, but a sword. For I have come to set a man against his father, and a daughter against her mother, and a daughter-in-law against her mother-in-law; and one's foes will be members of one's own household. Whoever loves father or mother more than me is not worthy of me; and whoever loves son or daughter more than me is not worthy of me; and whoever does not take up the cross and follow me is not worthy of me. Those who find their life will lose it, and those who lose their life for my sake will find it. (10:34-39)

We live in a society today wherein affluence has choked off God's word in such a way that Jesus' promise of having foes within "one's own household" seems all too evident. We find this occurring when religious apologists for some of the excesses in our political economy publicly attack those who address such patterns that threaten people and the planet. When someone in the church does speak out about some injustice in the *oikonomia*, as did the U.S. bishops in their pastoral letter, "Economic Justice for All,"[4] rejection will not be far behind. I learned this in my own case when an ordained pastor in the Christian Reformed Church in North America wrote an article in *Plastics News* describing his attendance at the 2003 ExxonMobil shareholders meeting. There some of us had presented shareholder resolutions on behalf of our religious orders and other individuals and groups asking the company to make more concrete efforts concerning global warming and the development of renewable energy sources.

When I and others placed our resolutions, members of the Acton Institute spoke against them. That same day the *New York Times* carried an article about ExxonMobil's backing of groups who challenged efforts such as ours.[5] In 2002, the company gave the Institute $30,000.

In the article in *Plastics News*, Gerald Zandstra (one of the Acton speakers at the meeting), wrote: "There is nothing wrong with religious leaders having and voicing opinions on matters of public import; by doing so they can fulfill a vital and prophetic role in society." However, he noted, he "spoke against" me and Sister Patricia Daly because we "have been captured and are being used by radical environmental, leftist organizations to which they lend moral legitimacy."[6] We were not blessed but were dupes for justice.

Many people who promote the ExxonMobils of this world as *makarioi* (especially when such might benefit them) will not be open to their *skandala*. As a result, some will not easily understand when the word of God starts being addressed to the institutional powers and principalities that promote and reinforce unjust aspects of that society. Some will not easily hear the scriptural call for the promotion of those dynamics that advance the dignity of every person and that help all people share more fully in the earth's resources. As a result, many Christians themselves will not be readily open to the questioning of an ideology that heretofore had reinforced their share in society's power, possessions, and prestige in ways that benefited them.

Second, persecution and misunderstanding are not to be expected only from members of one's own family and former friends. It can be anticipated from society itself: "I am sending you out like sheep into the midst of wolves; so be wise as serpents and innocent as doves. Beware of them, for they will hand you over to councils and flog you in their synagogues; and you will be dragged before governors and kings because of me, as a testimony to them and the Gentiles" (10:16-18).

Assured that this very persecution will be the inevitable sign of God's presence and reign with them, the disciples have no need to worry how they should respond to such powers and principalities. They will be under another *exousia* (10:1): "When they hand you over, do not worry about how you are to speak or what you are to say; for what you are to say will be given to you at that time; for it is not you who speak, but the Spirit of your Father speaking through you" (10:19-20).

Although I try not to be fundamentalistic in the way I apply the scriptures to my life, this passage can be very assuring when I write to the Roman Curia about things I consider unjust regarding women or sexual minorities or go to shareholder meetings to challenge the practices of the global corporations on issues ranging from the environment to sweatshops. I may not be handed over to councils and flogged in the synagogues; but it can seem that way when you are called a "heretic" for applying to the institutional church its own teachings on justice. It also can be consoling to know that, even though I am not being "dragged" before the leaders of our political economy, when I go to shareholders' meetings to bear witness, I can believe that "the Spirit of your Father" will be speaking when I speak there.

Those representatives of the Jews' and Romans' infrastructures did not kill Jesus because he went up a mountain, sat down, gathered his disciples around him, and concretized in *exousia* his teachings of wisdom. Jesus was put to death because he put his preaching into practice. In this light,

Matthew's Gospel was letting his community members know that they were suffering the same fate as Jesus. They too had not been content with just mouthing the Beatitudes. They too had tried to concretize them in their hearts, shared faith, celebrations, and ministry. Now they were experiencing how scandalous an unjust world considers them to be.

Matthew was trying to let them know that those who hunger and thirst to experience justice and to manifest it in a just lifestyle within a seriously unjust society must be open to the very real possibility of rejection and persecution. Controlled by the rationalizations and ideology of the infrastructure, society will not understand what is being stated by such a witness. Much less will society be open to the conversion that is being requested by this witness. It is little wonder, then, that suffering at the hands of "them" is the only earthly promise made for fidelity and commitment to God's plan. The world's reaction to Jesus and his faithful commitment to live the Beatitudes will be the same response his disciples can expect for their fidelity (10:24-27, 32-33).

What society considers normative is reversed by the lifestyle of Jesus and his faithful community. What Jesus calls *makarios* stands as a *skandalon* to what society considers *makarios* (11:6). Only the poor in spirit, who experience the authority of this new reign of God in their depths, can be equipped to withstand society's persecution. The disciples' persecution stands as a sign of society's refusal to be converted from those ideological reinforcements and structural patterns that deny the dignity of every person and perpetuate inequity in the way the earth's goods are distributed.

Fidelity to a life of the Beatitudes means continual resistance and readiness to reverse those norms in society that do not reinforce God's plan.

Justice and the Prophetic Call

Continually Jesus declared that fidelity to God's plan demands a spirituality that goes beyond pietism and angelism, authoritarianism and legalism, as well as separatism and nationalism. Realizing that the implications of this spirituality challenged their vested interests, the leaders rejected not only Jesus' message, but Jesus as messenger: "When the chief priests and the Pharisees heard his parables, they realized that he was speaking about them. They wanted to arrest him, but they feared the crowds, because they regarded him as a prophet" (21:45-46).

Matthew presents Jesus in the role of a prophet rejected by the leaders because his words and deeds threatened their position of power and prestige. The placement of this Beatitude in the Sermon on the Mount, as well as the comments about persecution in the next discourse, the Apostolic Sermon, make it clear that similar societal rejection could be expected by all those in the church who would manifest a similar prophetic charism and mission.

Whoever would witness to the power of the Beatitudes in their call for conversion in a world marked by the grave sin of social injustice could expect to suffer a prophet's rejection from that world.

Many times the most severe stumbling blocks, resistance, and persecution would come from the religious leaders of the very institutions supposedly existing to help people "enter" God's reign:

> Therefore I send you prophets, sages, and scribes, some of whom you will kill and crucify, and some you will flog in your synagogues and pursue from town to town, so that upon you may come all the *dikaios* blood shed on earth, from the blood of *dikaios* Abel to the blood of Zechariah son of Barachiah, whom you murdered between the sanctuary and the altar. Truly I tell you, all this will come upon this generation. (23:34-36)

Jesus' society's rejection of him is replicated in every generation's rejection of those disciples who, at any point in history, lead the prophetic lifestyles of the Beatitudes. Rejection can be expected by anyone preaching Jesus' word to a world that refuses to change its ideology and be converted. As Matthew showed in the thirteenth chapter, a society that has legitimated its accumulation of "more," even at the expense of "what little" others have (13:12), will refuse to convert to a new ethic that promotes "just enough" in order to *be* more. The reaction of the infrastructure of Jesus' day and Matthew's day would be the same as in Isaiah's day. Thus Matthew's Jesus would say that he spoke to "them" in parables because:

> "seeing they do not perceive, and hearing they do not listen, nor do they understand." With them indeed is fulfilled the prophecy of Isaiah that says:
>
> > "You will indeed listen, but never understand, and you will
> >   indeed look, but never perceive.
> > For this people's heart has grown dull,
> >   and their ears are hard of hearing, and they have shut their eyes;
> > so that they might not look with their eyes, and listen with their
> >   ears,
> > and understand with their heart and turn—
> > and I would heal them."

But blessed are your eyes, for they see, and your ears, for they hear. Truly I tell you, many prophets and *dikaioi* longed to see what you see, but did not see it, and to hear what you hear, but did not hear it. (13:13-17; cf. Isa. 6:9-10)

It is significant that, in explaining the hardness of society's heart to conversion's call, Matthew here has Jesus quoting another "fulfillment" text (Isa. 6:9-10). Paradoxically, this text was written by Isaiah to his community in the context of its feeling of persecution, that is, the exile. Here, as Matthew applied it, persecution represented the reaction of a hardened society to the example of a life lived according to the teachings of Jesus. Society's hardened reaction to the prophet's call for conversion (Isa. 6:9-13) is a consequence of fidelity to the prophetic call itself (Isa. 6:1-8). Isaiah's prophetic theology would be, for Matthew, Jesus' spirituality. In turn, Matthew's christology would be his ecclesiology. Finally, Matthew's ecclesiology should be our spirituality. As many of us find ourselves in a kind of internal exile within our own *oikonomia* as well as our *ekklēsia*, a reflection on the steps involved in Isaiah's call to prophecy (Isa. 6:1-8) might encourage us in fidelity to our own call to be prophets for our generation. To this reflection I now move.

Isaiah's Call as Prototype

Probably no better articulation of the key components of the mystical/prophetic call can be found than in chapter 6 of First Isaiah (chapters 1-39). This occurred in 742 B.C.E., the year King Uzziah of Judah died. Using powerful, almost apocalyptic images, First Isaiah describes what happened to him when the mystical/prophetic call invaded his life:

> In the year that King Uzziah died, I saw the Lord sitting on a throne, high and lofty; and the hem of his robe filled the temple. Seraphs were in attendance above him; each had six wings: with two they covered their faces, and with two they covered their feet, and with two they flew. And one called to another and said:
>
> > "Holy, holy, holy is the Lord of hosts;
> > the whole earth is full of his glory."
>
> The pivots on the thresholds shook at the voices of those who called, and the house filled with smoke. And I said: "Woe is me! I am lost, for I am a man of unclean lips, and I live among a people of unclean lips; yet my eyes have seen the King, the Lord of hosts!"
> Then one of the seraphs flew to me, holding a live coal that had been taken from the altar with a pair of tongs. The seraph touched my mouth with it and said: "Now that this has touched your lips, your guilt has departed and your sin is blotted out." Then I heard the voice of the Lord saying, "Whom shall I send, and who will go for us?" (Isa. 6:1-8a)

Until now, according to First Isaiah, everything about his mystical call appeared to be wonderful and awesome. Even at the point where he "heard the voice of the Lord saying, 'Whom shall I send; who will go for us?'" the observer might feel inspired to begin singing the words of the contemporary song: "Here I am Lord. Is it I Lord? I have heard you calling in the night. I will go Lord, if you lead me. I will hold your people in my heart."[7]

The passage makes it clear that Isaiah's vision presented him with an entirely new consciousness of God's holiness. His confrontation with the divine glory evoked in him a deep sense of his own unholiness, of how far short he fell from that glory. Immediately it also made him conscious, seemingly for the first time, of the sinfulness about him; what in his society profaned the holiness of God. Overwhelmed with God's holiness, he came to new understanding of what was truly "unclean." Having become critically conscious of what constitutes authentic holiness, he finds himself grounded in and operating from a new moral sensitivity. Aware that his coreligionists will insist on their traditional meaning of what it means to be holy, he assures himself that he has been touched by God's true holiness. Empowered in God's word, he feels compelled to go to his own people and call them to take up a life that reflects what true holiness must be about. But they are ideologically convinced of their own righteousness. They are sustained by a culture that blinds them from seeing its injustice, deafens them to the cry of the poor, and ritually sanctions sin and abuse in the name of religion. Given their cultural captivity, the voice tells him that his preaching will fall on closed eyes and deaf ears; the people have developed hardened hearts. Hardened hearts is a biblical word for sociological apathy or anomie. Thus he heard the voice say:

> Go and say to this people:
> "Keep listening, but do not comprehend;
> keep looking, but do not understand.
> Make the mind of this people dull, and stop their ears, and shut their
>   eyes,
> so that they may not look with their eyes, and listen with their ears,
> and comprehend with the minds, and turn and be healed."
>
> (Isa. 6:9-10)

When Isaiah asked "How long, O Lord?" God answered that his prophetic vocation would not be concluded until cities would lie in waste without inhabitants and the land would be "utterly desolate" with everyone being sent "far away." Only one ray of hope would be allowed to break through: when the only thing left standing would be the stump of an oak, a holy seed would be the stump (Isa. 6:11-13). New life would come forth from the death of the old. A remnant would come forth; a refounding community would rise up and take the place of the unrepentant priests and their institution.

Evelyn Underhill notes that the elements contained in Isaiah's experience of God's holiness constitute the heart of every prophetic/mystical vocation.[8] While this call is to be witnessed in a special way by those in the consecrated life in the Catholic Church,[9] baptism itself makes this call part of everyone's universal call to holiness. As such, we need to examine its dimensions and how they apply to all of us today.

1. The call occurs within concrete historical exigencies: In the year "Our King Uzziah" died (Isa. 6:1a). Isaiah tells us his call came to him while he was in a house. The fact that his vocation came to him in a "house" is significant because, as we have seen throughout this book, the Greek word for house is *oikia* or *oikos*. In the Mediterranean world that gave rise to his writing, "house" or *oikia* did not mean so much a building as a whole "world" or network of interconnected relationships at every level of life, the *oikia, oikonomia, oikoumenē,* and *oikologia.*

Unlike those who want religion to be divorced from reality or a church removed from the culture, Isaiah's vision makes it clear that all authentic spirituality must be lived in the world as it is. This world, above all, is interconnected at every level and within everything. This is a world not of the past or future but of the now. Accordingly, our own mystical/prophetic vocation to be faithful to our call cannot be divorced from this reality, which demands an entirely new way of "seeing" how everything in the universe must be in relationship for the common good; how everything in the universe is meant to be at the service of the holy.[10] This places our call within the political dynamics of a growing imperial presidency, of an economy built on insidious greed, and of a church whose clerics—especially those at the highest levels—have arrogantly abused their power and undermined the people's trust. This dominant culture constitutes the only milieu in which we can hear our call and respond to it spiritually.

2. This call imprints on our consciousness the reality of God's own holiness (Isa. 6:1b-4). Isaiah writes that he "saw the Lord sitting on a throne, high and lofty" (6:1b). Such language reinforces for many the primitive anthropology of God being located in some geographic place called "heaven," which exists beyond the dome of the "heavens" that covered the earth. However his choice of words merely expresses in human language the ineffable and indescribable experience Isaiah had of being transported into the vision of God's ultimate transcendence; his "seeing" was his experiencing.

Once we experience the reign, the realm, the reality, and, indeed, the rush of God's presence and power breaking into our lives, all else becomes relativized; indeed, it becomes illusion as well as illusory. The experience of God that we express in our world at all its levels through our participation in community is what I call spirituality. This spirituality represents the way we feel called to reflect the holiness of God; it becomes our way of being holy in the contemporary world. However, while such spirituality demands that we *express* this holiness in an unholy world, its foundation is in our *experience* of the holy that makes us look at the world in an entirely new way. This experience is another name for contemplation. Without contemplation, the experience of the holy, there can be little or no authentic prophetic utterance.

"Holy, holy, holy is the Lord of hosts; the whole earth is full of his glory," Isaiah heard one of the seraphs call to another (6:3). The Hebrew Scriptures outline three related ways one could be holy: the *wisdom* writers highlighted the need for individual integrity in the sight of God; the *prophets* stressed the need to make a connection between worship, social justice, and conversion; and the *Priestly school* of the exile insisted on observable separation for cult along with the practice of the "holiness code" in order to fulfill the scriptural imperative: "You shall be holy, for I the Lord your God am holy" (Lev. 19:2).

Since the turn of the new millennium, it has become quite clear that the priestly viewpoint has eclipsed the prophetic and wisdom approaches to holiness. Rather than the care, mercy, and compassion that would find the house churches who followed such a way of holiness honored and blessed (as I showed in chapter 7), the notion of holiness as separation of the priests from the people was stressed more and more. In the view of the prophet, this would have to be considered scandalous and sinful. Thus the next element in Isaiah's call.

3. Experiencing God's holiness gives us an enlightened consciousness of sin in its individual and social manifestations (Isa. 6:5). In response to his experience of what truly represented holiness, Isaiah, the priest once committed to a certain kind of "holiness," could only respond: "Woe is me! I am lost, for I am a man of unclean lips." At the same time, his own awareness of how he personally was falling short of God's glory made him deeply conscious of sin all around him. Thus he added: "and I live among a people of unclean lips." Experiencing God's holiness, Isaiah was brought to a new moral consciousness. At the same time, given the conviction of his fellow clerics that their way was God's way and was, therefore, not only moral but holy as well, Isaiah realized they would never grasp what he now knew: their way of "grace" was not only deeply flawed; it was sinful. But only one who experienced what now was truly holy would be able to understand: "Yet my eyes have seen the King, the Lord of hosts!" His contemplative experience now centered him on the periphery; his newly discovered vision forced him to "see" in a way that marginated him from his social institutions and their ideologies.

Until this experience of God's holiness, Isaiah seems to have been quite comfortable in the world of meaning that had been mediated to him through the dominant consciousness of his culture. Herein the injustice of the political economy was sanctioned as just by the religious leadership of his day. With his experience of *God's* holiness, all of that changed. His mystical experience generated in him a gut-wrenching stirring of conscience. His mystical insight became a moral imperative. What before his conscience had considered "moral" was now failed, profane, and sinful.

Conscious that his contemporaries would consider his vision bogus because it did not correspond to their "royal consciousness," he reminded himself that his new experience must now ground all of life. He assured himself: "My eyes have seen the King, the Lord of hosts" (Isa. 6:5b). The truth of what he experienced revealed the lie that sustained the political, economic, and religious worldview or ideology that heretofore had mediated meaning. Never again could he look at these forces with the same eyes, hear their message with the same ears, or accept their ways with the same heart.

4. The recognition of sin in our lives opens us to be healed and empowered by a force beyond us: the Word of God (Isa. 6:6-7). If we can't acknowledge that we are sinners, we will never convert. Refusing to see the need for conversion, we remain the same. If we stay the same, we will remain in our sins. Righteous in our sins, we can easily convince ourselves that we are holy. Unable to see how far we are from measuring up to God's trinitarian holiness, we will never be empowered to live holy lives if what profanes our lives controls our thinking about them. I know the seduction of this "royal" and "papal" consciousness from my own experience.

The experience of my own sinfulness gave me a fresh understanding of how Isaiah, only after he recognized his own sin and could admit it publicly, could be open to be healed of its influence and hold over his life. Only then, he writes, "one of the seraphs flew to me, holding a live coal that had been taken from the altar with a pair of tongs. The seraph touched my mouth with it and said: 'Now that this has touched your lips, your guilt has departed and your sin is blotted out'" (Isa. 6:6).

Not only did the coal—which most take to represent God's word—heal Isaiah of his own sinfulness; it empowered him to live from its force. Now, in the power of this word grounding him in God's holiness, he could be commissioned to proclaim authentic holiness to a sinful nation. For us, anything falling short of this holiness, this revelation, this trinitarian reality, is, to that degree, unholy or profane. The experience of God's healing word in us invites us to live reordered lives. It also serves as a mandate to spend our lives challenging whatever in our world—be it the culture itself or our religious system—stands outside the reign of God's trinitarian holiness (Isa. 6:7).

5. Empowered in this word, we accept the invitation to go into the world as God's ambassadors (Isa. 6:8). Isaiah's experience of being empowered by the burning coal made him realize that his life was not just freed of his past sins; God's word had fired him to proclaim its message in his world. At the heart of every mystical/prophetic call is the concomitant demand that one's religious experience of God be accompanied by a commission to be present in the world in an entirely new way: as one who has been empowered to proclaim the rule of God's sovereign presence and power in the midst of contrary imperial pretensions and infallible proclamations.

According to Abraham Heschel, traditional religious experience tends to be "a private affair in which a person becomes alive to what transpires between God and himself, not to what transpires between God and someone else; contact between God and man comes about, it is believed, for the benefit of the particular man. In contrast," he says, "prophetic inspiration is for the sake, for the benefit, of a third party. It is not a private affair between prophet and God; its purpose is the illumination of the people rather than the illumination of the prophet."[11]

"Whom shall I send, who will go for us?" God asks. This is a question everyone called to the prophetic vocation must be open to hearing; reluctant as they may be, they must also be willing to act upon the invitation. In effect, the prophet is the ambassador of God, the one whose words are divinely authorized. Divinely inspired prophets speak with power because they have been empowered in the word to proclaim, whether that proclamation be one of words or works, gesture or symbol.

6. Preaching God's holiness and society's sinfulness promises rejection by those made apathetic by its imperial/infallible consciousness (Isa. 6:9-13a). Upon accepting his divine mission, Isaiah was told that nobody would listen; he'd be a failure. The force that had enfleshed God's word in him said:

Go and say to this people:
"Keep listening, but do not comprehend; keep looking, but do not
   understand.'
Make the mind of this people dull, and stop their ears, and shut
   their eyes,
so that they may not look with their eyes, and listen with their ears,
and comprehend with the minds and turn and be healed."

(Isa. 6:9-10)

This passage about the people seeing but not perceiving and hearing but not listening, lest they understand in their hearts and turn and be converted, is the only one in the whole Hebrew Bible quoted in all four accounts of Jesus' life. All refer to the resistance Jesus would receive from his religious leaders. This fact reminds us that the insensitivity and hardness of heart Jesus encountered might happen to us as well—if we faithfully translate his message into our world. As Isaiah's vocation prefigured that of Jesus, so his prophetic call must echo in our hearts, both individual and corporate. Such a vocation can be exercised only in the midst of the hardness of heart that is found in the dominant culture of our political economy of corporate capitalism and of the dominating dynamics of our clericalized church.

The fact that we will be resisted by the "true believers" and that their resistance will be justified by their sense of being righteous, does not mean they are evil people. It should not be surprising that they will call us unpatriotic, anticapitalist or disloyal to the pope when we dissent from the dominant consciousness. Such charges will come because they think that the ideologies that keep their systems going represent incontrovertible truths. While we see these as forms of idolatry that profane the holiness of God, they honestly believe them to be divinely blessed. They also believe they have the right to sanction anyone who deviated from their vision. And they are ready to do so.

7. Despite rejection, an alternative community will serve as the seed for implementing the new vision of God's holiness (Isa. 6:13b). Although Yahweh promised Judah's annihilation to such a degree that, even "if a tenth part remain in it, it will be burned again, like a terebinth or an oak whose stump remains standing when it is felled" (Isa. 6:13a), this same God also promised that, despite this annihilation, there would be a new, enlivened community that would arise from its decimation: "The holy seed is its stump" (6:13b). This seed will be the new family that constitutes an alternative household in the face of the demise of that which formerly held people's allegiance in the *oikonomia* and *ekklēsia*. This family will constitute the new kindom.

According to Warren Carter, "allegiance to Jesus means being a 'voluntary marginal,' living a liminal existence in alternative households."[12] All this makes clear the need for alternative communities formed by alternative consciousness to enable the members of these communities to support one another as they critique the dominant culture and its consciousness. Being in solidarity with people who are poor in society and marginated in the church, these members will allow their experience of oppression to move them to even deeper forms of compassion. This will find them promoting justice for those who are oppressed and conversion for those who do the oppressing so that Jesus' vision of God's reign might bring good news to the poor. In such gatherings, women and men gather together in the spirit of other alienated people: they find themselves liminal in relation to the surrounding world.

The Need to Be Part of Communities
That "Honor" the Prophetic Stance

To be true prophets we cannot just speak the word of justice; such a word must be the echo of our experience of God's just word within us. This *experience* of God's word that is expressed is what makes a prophet authentic and prophecy true. Sonya Quitslund explains: "That their words reveal a deeper knowledge *of* God rather than new knowledge *about* God distinguishes them from the other religious teachers of Israel. Their encounter with the Word of God meant a totally new way of life, total dependence on the Lord, the loss of all normal social and economic securities." She continues:

> Of the 241 times the expression "the word of the Lord" occurs in the Bible, 221 or 92% relate to a prophetic oracle. When "the word of the Lord" came to a person, it was truly a mystical experience, setting that person in a new historical situation, in a new relationship to God. It was always *the* Word that came, never *a* word, indicating the completeness of the Word addressed to a particular situation. This word made the recipient an authoritative teacher of Israel. However, what happened as the prophet faced his contemporaries and was faced by God, or what was actually experienced when "the hand of the Lord came upon" him, defies the imagination.[13]

Given our membership in that part of the world that contributes significantly to the grave sin of social injustice, the possibility that many of us have muted this call within us might have to be seriously faced. As Moses said: "Would that all the Lord's people were prophets, and that the Lord would put his spirit on them!" (Num. 11:29).

Today, in the face of the almost unquestioned power of the twenty-first-century kings, priests, and false prophets, people inside and outside the church are increasingly demoralized; they are perishing for want of prophecy (Prov. 29:18). Consequently, there is more reason than ever (especially for religious, whose life is meant to sacramentalize the prophetic dimension of discipleship) to ask seriously if one might not have this gift and to seek the kind of environment within a caring community that will nurture it.

As noted in chapter 3, in response to society's cultural addictions, those who radically commit themselves to God become a remnant community. As such disciples desire to be free from the alienation at the heart of the infrastructure, they need support. They no longer want to be caught in its network of domination, oppression, and abuses, which stifle people's freedom and keep the greater part of humanity from sharing more equitably in the world's resources. As a result, like-minded disciples come together, with their own cultural addictions, to be poor in spirit. They form *community.* Regularly gathering together with their gifts in the name of Jesus (18:19-20), they commit themselves in a common spirit to Jesus and to one another. Reflecting on their cultural addictions in light of the Twelve Steps, these disciples *conscientize* themselves. They look at the reality of their world, in light of the history that has been formed by God's word. Such disciples recognize their enslavements and powerlessness. They seek empowerment; they seek to be freed.

Seeking to discover a power stronger than their addictions, the community comes to experience *exousia* at work among its members. The Spirit of God comes with anointing. With this power at work in the continually conscientized community, a sign of *conversion* is given. This is outlined on p. 56.

Within a church whose leaders too often refuse to look at the stumbling blocks to justice manifest in their own way of operating,[14] such support groups are especially needed. Too often, it seems we have come to stress loyalty to the magisterium of the institutional church more than obedience to God's justice. While Matthew offers a spirituality that honors both dimensions, he never questioned that both were vital to the church. Why can't we do the same.

Too often, in contemporary spirituality, it seems we have suffered from excessive stress on one part of one pole of discipleship. In many ways, clerical domination has effectively redefined spirituality in terms of prayer and ministry from the perspective of clerical leadership. When this occurs, prophecy, which once was considered essential as a corrective to priestly excess and clerical control, is effectively muffled. Sonya A. Quitslund has noted:

Unfortunately, because of abuses of or difficulty in recognizing true prophetic words in the early Church, attempts to control teaching apparently stifled or silenced the prophetic voice. For centuries prophetic figures have been rare, acceptance and recognition in their own lifetimes even rarer. A certain ecclesiastical skepticism has greeted any departure from the established norm, having decided the prophetic or teaching office to be embodied in the office of bishop. Perhaps greater familiarity with the prophets will enable us to be more attentive to and receptive of their voices in our world today.[15]

As a Capuchin Franciscan, I am the inheritor of the charism of a prophetic figure whose original inspiration for the Order was based on a vision of the institutional church (signified by St. John Lateran) falling into ruins. The church of that day was clerically controlled. It used that social arrangement to link the religious, economic, and political institutions into an infrastructure that also controlled the ideology. Deviations could be met with excommunication. Yet into that world, God's word was incarnated in the words and deeds of St. Francis of Assisi. This prophetic figure called for a renewed gospel spirituality to the very leaders who no longer thought it could be accomplished. Unfortunately, today any mention that the institutional church may have problems, much less be falling into ruins, is often considered disloyal and even heretical, possibly demanding dismissal.

The Hebrew Scriptures showed the need for a healthy tension between priest, prophet, and king. Franciscan literature speaks of the prophet Francis inviting both pope and emperor to conversion. Yet many modern Franciscans are repelled at the thought of contemporizing the expression of Francis's charism. They reject the fact that one can question the pope or lobby the president, or Congress, or file a shareholder resolution! Such an attitude indicates how we have come to live in a church dominated by a clerical ideology that no longer reinforces the traditional tension among roles in the community. Rather, it shows we have come so far as to equate unquestioning submission to church leaders' fiats as obedience and loyalty to the reign of God itself. In this light, there is more reason than ever to return to Matthew's spirituality. For Matthew was also responding to this false use of authority in church leadership almost two thousand years ago!

This realization makes it all the more imperative to follow Paul's advice to his house churches at Corinth: we should seek after the gift of prophecy (1 Cor. 14:1). In our eagerness to bring the normative dimension of God's justice into our world, and particularly into our own church, we can easily be guided by motives of anger, guilt, resentment, retaliation, and manipulation instead of genuine, Spirit-filled care. Thus, we have a special need to be constituted in the reign of God's word of justice. This will help us discern correctly what kind of prophecy is needed within and without the church.

Conclusion: Our Commission
to Be Prophets in an Unjust World

If Matthew had ended the Beatitudes with the eighth, promising that those who would practice *dikaiosynē* would be persecuted but also blessed, it would have been one thing. However, when he goes on to change the addressees from "them" to "you" and states that the way of perfection demands a way of life that will result in this kind of rejection and persecution, it can be quite unsettling. Indeed, Mark Allan Powell writes:

> When the beatitudes are read from this perspective, the sudden shift to the second person in 5:11 assaults Matthew's readers in the world outside the story as surely as it does the disciples within the story. Until now, the readers have been learning, along with the disciples, that the coming of God's kingdom brings blessings. Then suddenly, the disciples are told that their commitment to Jesus means that they will be numbered among the suffering virtuous ones and thus, in some sense, among the unfortunate ones as well.[16]

Because his community was experiencing societal rejection for practicing a beatitudinal spirituality, Matthew added this last Beatitude. He wanted to offer a rationale to explain why Jesus' disciples would experience persecution. However, while this element about realized eschatology (or the "future made present") may be true, it also seems there is a strong possibility that Matthew placed this Beatitude last, and at this precise position, to indicate something much more powerful.

According to M. Jack Suggs, it might well be that this special redaction of Matthew's Gospel serves as more than a conclusion of the Beatitudes.[17] Indeed, rather than ending the Beatitudes, I believe it serves as a kind of launching, empowering and commissioning disciples of all time to enter their particular worlds with the teachings of Jesus in a way that will be salt for the earth and will bring light into the world.

To evidence this direction, Matthew employs one of his unique triads. Some triads have one element in each member (such as the three temptations [4:1-11], almsgiving, prayer, and fasting as exemplifications of *dikaiosynē* [6:1-18], or Father, Son, and Holy Spirit [28:19]), while others are dyadic (asking and receiving, seeking and finding, knocking and having the door opened [7:7-8], or the narrow gate versus the wide gate, the good fruit versus the bad fruit, and the house built on rock versus the house built on sand [7:13-27]). However, here we have a structural triad. Its structuring revolves around three elements: (1) the giving of authority or reception of a blessing, (2) the giving or listing of names, and (3) some commission.

Other similarly structured triads with which we are familiar can be found in the Great Commission. Here Jesus gives (1) authority (*exousia*) to the eleven disciples, (2) to baptize *in the name* of the trinitarian God, along with (3) a commission to have the baptized "obey everything that I have commanded you" (28:18-20). Earlier Jesus had given the twelve disciples (1) authority (*exousia*) to preach and to heal. (2) Then they were named (10:2-4). (3) Finally, they were commissioned to "Go nowhere among the Gentiles, and enter no town of the Samaritans, but go rather to the lost sheep of the house of Israel" (10:5-6).

Nowhere is the threefold connection among the blessing or authority, the bestowal of a name, and the commission to minister in the world clearer than in Matthew 16:17-19. This section, which established Peter's role in the church, has many parallels to the wise and foolish ways of building a house, which Matthew describes at the conclusion of the Sermon on the Mount (7:24-27). Peter's call and commission in the new house of Israel (which is being battered through internal and external persecution) consists of three parts. The first begins with the pronouncement of an empowering blessing to Peter in response to his acknowledgment of Jesus as "the Messiah, the Son of the Living God" (16:16): "Blessed are you, Simon son of Jonah! For flesh and blood has not revealed this to you, but my Father in heaven" (16:17). Next he is given a new name "I tell you, you are Peter, and on this rock I will build my church and the gates of Hades will not prevail against it" (16:18). Finally, the commission to manifest this power concretely in society is given: "I will give you the keys of the kingdom of heaven, and whatever you bind on earth will be bound in heaven, and whatever you loose on earth will be loosed in heaven" (16:19).

Suggs links the loosing and binding of 16:19 with the functions of the scribe (23:13). He also says that the passage "every scribe who has been trained for the kingdom of heaven is like the master of a household who brings out of his treasure what is new and what is old" (13:52) serves as a conclusion to that part of Matthew's Gospel that has often been called the Book of Wisdom (11:2-13:53). Then he links the last *Beatitude* (which empowers us with God's own reign of *exousia*) with the *naming* of the disciples in the house as "salt of the earth" and "light to the world" in such a way that they are *commissioned* to be faithful to their call.[18]

Matthew begins the last Beatitude by assuring the community that it will receive the blessing of the reign of God for its fidelity to the ministry of justice, even as it experiences persecution from a world that calls this blessing a scandal (5:10). Then he presents Jesus giving another blessing: "Blessed are you when people revile you and persecute you and utter all kinds of evil (*ponēros*) against you falsely on my account. Rejoice and be glad, for your reward is great in heaven, for in the same way they persecuted the prophets who were before you" (5:11-12).

If we honestly live the Beatitudes we both experience the blessing of God's justice and call for this blessing of justice concretely in society. Having been thus empowered in this blessing, we are given not just a new name but two names that express our beatitude—as well as a caution not to let the blessed name become a stumbling block; it must make its name known in the world for good:

> You are the salt of the earth; but if salt has lost its taste, how can its saltiness be restored? It is no longer good for anything, but is thrown out and trampled under foot.
>
> You are the light of the world. A city built on a hill cannot be hid. No one after lighting a lamp puts it under the bushel basket, but on the lampstand, and it gives light to all in the *oikia*. (5:13-15)

The disciples, blessed with God's power and given two names are now commissioned to be salt of the earth and light to the world in a special way.

This light, however, cannot be limited to the community alone. Whoever is blessed by God's Spirit and is called in light is *commissioned* to illuminate the whole world as well: "In the same way, let your light shine before others, so that they may see your good works [*kala erga*] and give glory to your Father in heaven" (5:16). "At this point," Suggs writes about the third dimension of commissioning:

[I]t becomes apparent that Matthew has in view some group of opponents. Whether it is the Pharisaic scribes who "preach but do not practice" (23:3) or Christian false prophets who cry "Lord, Lord," but are evildoers (7:15-23), or both, is not for the moment of importance. In any case, the Christian scribe is told that unless he performs "good works" . . . he has put his light under a bushel, made his salt insipid. The commission is, not merely to teach the law but to do it to the glory of God.[19]

The commission to go into the whole world (28:19-20) demands that we become its salt and light. But even more, as a blessing for the world, we are to show every age and every nation, for all time, that the Beatitudes are at the heart of gospel spirituality.

Living the Beatitudes may bring down society's yoke of revilement and rejection. We may be called evil or *ponēroi*. Yet, unlike the rich young man who could not follow Jesus in the way of perfection which demanded a reordering of his life on behalf of the poor (19:21), we will be like the woman who is committed to doing good (*kalon ergon*). In this way we will continue God's very work of making everything on this earth and in this world "very good." Submitting to this way of wisdom deepens in everyone going through transition a sense of peace and rest. Living the beatitudinal life on this limited planet will ultimately bring us wisdom's reward: "Come, you that are blessed by my Father, inherit the kingdom prepared for you from the foundation of the world" (25:34).

Notes

Preface

1. Among others, see Warren Carter, *What Are They Saying about Matthew's Sermon on the Mount?* (New York/Mahwah, N.J.: Paulist, 1994), 115f.; William Spohn, *What Are They Saying about Scripture and Ethics?* (New York/Mahwah, N.J.: Paulist, 1995), 146.

2. African Americans in the United States will probably consider the Beatitudes through their own cultural lens, as we find in Diana L. Hayes, "Through the Eyes of Faith: The Seventh Principle of the *Nguzo Saba* and the Beatitudes of Matthew," in *Taking Down Our Harps: Black Catholics in the United States*, ed. Diana L. Hayes and Cyprian Davis, O.S.B. (Maryknoll, N.Y.: Orbis Books, 1998), 49-67. In Priscilla Pope-Levison and John R. Levison, *Return to Babel: Global Perspectives on the Bible* (Louisville: Westminster John Knox, 1998), Matthew 5:1-12 is viewed from "A Latin American Perspective," by J. Severino Croatto (pp. 117-23), from "An African Perspective," by Hannah W. Kinoti (pp. 125-30), and from "An Asian Perspective" by Helen R. Graham (pp. 131-35). A very popular book on the Beatitudes from the Latin American perspective is Segundo Galilea, *The Beatitudes: To Evangelize as Jesus Did*, trans. Robert R. Barr (Maryknoll, N.Y.: Orbis Books, 1984). Unfortunately Galilea skips back and forth between the Matthean and Lukan versions.

3. Robert N. Bellah, Richard Madsen, William M. Sullivan, Ann Swidler, and Steve M. Tipton, *Habits of the Heart: Individualism and Commitment in American Life* (Berkeley: University of California Press, 1985).

4. See especially Michael H. Crosby, "Biography: Story and My Story," chapter 8 in *The Dysfunctional Church: Addiction and Codependency in the Family of Catholicism* (Notre Dame, Ind.: Ave Maria, 1991), 147-73.

5. Ibid.

6. Bruce J. Malina, *The New Testament World: Insights from Cultural Anthropology* (Atlanta: John Knox, 1981), 26-27.

7. Michael H. Crosby, *Rethinking Celibacy, Reclaiming the Church* (Eugene, Ore: Wipf & Stock, 2003), esp. 133-67.

8. For more on the unfortunate way Roman Catholics have been taught such a selective way of interpreting the notion of "church," see my *House of Disciples: Church, Economics and Justice in Matthew* (Eugene, Ore: Wipf & Stock, 2004 [orig., 1988]), 50-54; and "Matthew's Gospel: The Disciples' Call to Justice," in *The New Testament: Introducing the Way of Discipleship*, ed. Wes Howard-Brook and Sharon H. Ringe (Maryknoll, N.Y.: Orbis Books, 2002), 19-20.

9. Although the Beatitudes represent an adult choice, there are some wonderful examples of people at other levels finding great meaning in them. For instance, Jean Vanier's whole approach at L'Arche among people developmentally challenged is grounded in the Beatitudes.

10. For more on the ways people have discussed "religion" and "spirituality," see Sandra M. Schneiders, "Religion vs. Spirituality: A Contemporary Conundrum," *Spiritus* 3 (2003): 163-85.

11. Walter Wink, *The Bible in Human Transformation: Toward a New Paradigm for Biblical Study* (Philadelphia: Fortress, 1980), 10.

12. For more on this, see my *House of Disciples*, 5-15.

13. Wolfgang Iser, *The Act of Reading: A Theory of Aesthetic Response* (Baltimore and London: Johns Hopkins University Press, 1980); Seymour Chatman, *Story and Discourse: Narrative Structure in Fiction and Film* (Ithaca, N.Y.: Cornell University Press, 1978).

14. Warren Carter, *Households and Discipleship: A Study of Matthew 19-20*, Journal for the Study of the New Testament Supplement Series 103 (Sheffield: JSOT Press, 1994), 32.

15. Sharon Daloz Parks, "Home and Pilgrimage: Companion Metaphors for Personal and Social Transformation," *Soundings* 72 (1989): 299.

16. Ibid., 303.

1. The Relevance of Matthew's Gospel for First World Christians of the Twenty-First Century

1. As will be shown, the "Matthew" who represents the final author of the Gospel as we know it today was not the "Matthew" traditionally known as the tax collector but is representative of all followers of Jesus who are committed to translating Jesus' words and deeds into their lives and world. This puts the stress on the disciple of "whatever" era who makes such a commitment. However, allowing for the traditional understanding of "Matthew" as a "he," this pronoun will be used as the pronoun for the "author" of the First Gospel.

2. The image of "empire" used of the United States came into the popular lexicon at the turn of the third millennium. Niall Ferguson wrote an op-ed piece after the publication of his book *Empire* (New York: Basic Books, 2003), in which he declared: "The greatest empire of modern times has come into existence without the American people even noticing. This is not absence of mind. It is mass myopia. The U.S. may be a 'hyperpower,' the most militarily powerful empire in history. But it is an empire in denial, a colossus with an attention deficiency disorder. That is potentially very dangerous" (*The Wall Street Journal*, June 6, 2003). *Newsweek* had a feature piece by Fareed Zakaria, "The Arrogant Empire," March 24, 2003. The notion first began to be used by neoconservative writers concerned that the United States should accept its "imperial" status and act accordingly throughout the world.

3. While most scholars have interpreted Matthew's community along sectarian lines, Petri Luomanen, appealing to the work of Rodney Stark and William Sims Bainbridge, argues that Matthew's community should be designated a "cult" rather than a "sect" ("The 'Sociology of Sectarianism' in Matthew: Modeling the Genesis of Early Jewish and Christian Communities," in *Faith Play: Diversity and Conflicts in Early Christianity: Essays in Honour of Heikki Räisänen*, ed. I. Dunderberg, C. Tuckett and

Notes to Pages 2-7 197

K. Syreeni (Leiden: Brill, 2002), 107-30. A few others discount the notion of the sectarian nature of Matthew's house churches. See Robert H. Gundry, "A Responsive Evaluation of the Social History of the Matthean Community in Roman Syria," in *Social History of the Matthean Community: Cross-Disciplinary Approaches,* ed. David L. Balch (Minneapolis: Fortress, 1991), 62-63.

4. For more on the subversive notion of "the reign of God," see Paul J. Wadell, "The Subversive Ethics of the Kingdom of God," *The Bible Today* 41 (2003): 11-16.

5. See Wes Howard-Brook, *The Church before Christianity* (Maryknoll, N.Y.: Orbis Books, 2001), 125.

6. John H. Elliott, *A Home for the Homeless: A Sociological Exegesis of I Peter, Its Situation and Strategy* (Philadelphia: Fortress, 1981), 45.

7. Michael H. Crosby, *House of Disciples: Church, Economics, and Justice in Matthew* (Eugene, Ore.: Wipf & Stock, 2004), 11.

8. For more on this, see John H. Elliott, "Jesus Was Not an Egalitarian: A Critique of an Anachronistic and Idealist Theory," *Biblical Theology Bulletin* 32 (2002): 75-91.

9. K. K. McIver has stated that, since 1990, sociology has become the "dominant methodology used in research into the Matthean community" ("Twentieth Century Approaches to the Matthean Community," *Andrews University Seminary Studies* 37 [1999]: 37).

10. Leland J. White, "Grid and Group in Matthew's Community: The Righteousness/Honor Code in the Sermon on the Mount," *Semeia* 35 (1986): 61.

11. G. Stanton, following the work of sociologists Wilson and Burridge, interprets the Matthean community from the perspective of a "sect." See his "The Gospel of Matthew and Judaism," *Bulletin of the John Rylands University Library* 66 (1984): 281-82 and *A Gospel for a New People: Studies in Matthew* (Edinburgh: T & T Clark, 1992), passim, esp. 165. See also Ulrich Luz, *Matthew 1-7: A Commentary,* trans. Wilhelm C. Linss (Minneapolis: Augsburg, 1989), 219; Jack Dean Kingsbury, "Conclusion," in *Social History of the Matthean Community: Cross-Disciplinary Approaches,* ed. David L. Balch (Minneapolis: Fortress, 1991), 265; and A. J. Saldrini, *Matthew's Christian-Jewish Community* (Chicago: University of Chicago Press, 1994), 1-10, 107-23. L. Michael White elaborates on the sectarian nature of Matthew's community in his "Crisis Management and Boundary Maintenance: The Social Location of the Matthean Community," also in *Social History of the Matthean Community,* ed. Balch, 222-26. Following Victor Turner, Warren Carter argues that for the Matthean community a group is identified by permanent or normative liminality. Adapting the model of social stratification in the Roman Empire of Matthew's day, Denis C. Duling argues for Matthew's community as marginal. See his "Matthew and Marginality," in *1993 Society of Biblical Literature Seminar Papers,* ed. E. H. Lovering (Atlanta: Scholars Press, 1993), 642-71.

12. John P. Meier, *Matthew* (Wilmington, Del.: Michael Glazier, 1980), 2.

13. For a thorough approach to Matthean discipleship, see Michael J. Wilkins, *The Concept of Disciple in Matthew's Gospel as Reflected in the Use of the Term Mathetes,* Novum Testamentum Supplement 59 (Leiden/New York/Copenhagen: Brill, 1988).

14. For a more extended discussion of this notion, see my *House,* 43-48. See also Donald Senior, C.P., "Matthew's Gospel as Ethical Guide," *The Bible Today* 36 (1998): 273-74.

15. Donald A. Hagner, "Matthew: Apostate, Reformer, Revolutionary?" *New Testament Studies* 49 (2003): 200.

16. For more on this, see the monumental work by Robert Horton Gundry, *The Use of the Old Testament in St. Matthew's Gospel: With Special Reference to the Messianic Hope* (Leiden: Brill, 1967).

17. For further elaboration on this, see C. M. Tuckett, "The Beatitudes: A Source-Critical Study," *Novum Testamentum* 25 (1983): 193-207.

18. Katherine M. Skiba quoting Iraqi expert Patrick Basham in "Establishing Democracy Will Be Difficult in Iraq, Analyst Argues," *Milwaukee Journal Sentinel*, December 19, 2003.

19. As early as 1925 John Pederson highlighted honor and shame as fundamental values constituting social interaction in ancient Israel. See his *Israel: Its Life and Culture*, trans. A. Moller (London: Oxford, 1926), 213-44.

20. For more on this, see John Peristiany, *Honour and Shame: The Values of Mediterranean Society* (London: Weidenfeld & Nicolson, 1965); Bruce J. Malina, *The New Testament World: Insights from Cultural Anthropology* (Atlanta: John Knox, 1981); Bruce J. Malina and Richard L. Rohrbaugh, *Social-Science Commentary on the Synoptic Gospels* (Minneapolis: Fortress, 1992); Jerome Neyrey, *Honor and Shame in the Gospel of Matthew* (Louisville: Westminster John Knox, 1998). K. C. Hanson, "How Honorable! How Shameful! A Cultural Analysis of Matthew's Makarisms and Reproaches," *Semeia* 68 (1994): 81-111.

21. Julian Pitt-Rivers, "Honor and Social Status," in Peristiany, *Honour and Shame*. For the Beatitudes of Matthew as reflecting peoples' "interior disposition," see H. Benedict Green, C.R., *Matthew, Poet of the Beatitudes,* Journal for the Study of the New Testament Supplement Series 203 (Sheffield: Sheffield Academic Press, 2003), 223.

22. Louise Joy Lawrence, "'For Truly, I Tell You, They Have Received Their Reward' (Matt 6:2): Investigating Honor Precedence and Honor Virtue," *Catholic Biblical Quarterly* 64 (2002): 702.

23. For a more expanded discussion of the notion of beatitudes, especially in Matthew, see my "The Beatitudes: General Perspectives," in *New Perspectives on the Beatitudes,* ed. Francis A. Eigo, O.S.A. (Villanova, Pa.: Villanova University Press, 1995), 1-43.

24. David Hill, *The Gospel of Matthew* (London: Oliphants, 1972), 109.

25. Neil J. McEleney, C.S.P., "The Beatitudes of the Sermon on the Mount/Plain," *Catholic Biblical Quarterly* 43 (1981): 3.

26. Francis Wright Beaure, *The Gospel according to Matthew* (San Francisco: Harper & Row, 1982), 127; *Interpreter's Dictionary of the Bible,* ed. Keith Crim (Nashville: Abingdon, 1972), 1:370; Benedict Viviano, O.P., "Eight Beatitudes from Qumran," *The Bible Today* 31 (1993): 221.

27. Hanson, "How Honorable!" 89.

28. Ibid., 85-87.

29. Matthew does, however, make a link between *skandalon* and *ouai,* which seems to make *skandalon* related to unacceptable behaviors in community and *ouai* a veiled reference to some future divine retribution for those behaviors: "If any of you put a stumbling block before one of these little ones who believe in me, it would be

better for you if a great millstone were fastened around your neck and you were drowned in the depth of the sea. Woe to the world because of stumbling blocks! Occasions for stumbling are bound to come, but woe to the one by whom the stumbling block comes!" (18:6-7).

30. L. Michael White, "Crisis Management," 226.

31. In Matthew, of the few times the word for honor (*timasthai*) appears, it usually is connected with familial settings (15:4, 5; 19:19), with the exception of 15:8. Likewise, the only time a word for shaming appears (again in a familial setting) it is connected to the notion of justice: "Her husband Joseph, being a righteous (*dikaios*) man and unwilling to expose her to public disgrace (*deigmatizein*), planned to dismiss her quietly" (1:19).

If the actual words for honor and shame are seldom found in Matthew, there are plenty of related images that appear frequently. Words related to the notion of honor are "worthy" (*axios,* 10:11, 13 [2x], 37 [2x], 38, 22:8, and *hikanos,* 3:11; 8:8) and "value" (*diapherein,* 6:26; 10:31; 12:12). The word closest to shame is "offending" (*skandalizein,* 5:29, 30; 11:6; 13:21; 15:12; 17:27; 18:6, 8, 9; 24:10; 26:31, 33). One way of determining if the notion of *makarios* is a term of honor will be to determine if *skandalizein* is a term of dishonor in a community.

32. While I have found much value in the reflections of Mark Allan Powell, especially his various works on the Beatitudes, I cannot agree with his insistence that the Beatitudes of Matthew "do not describe the attitudes" of those who are blessed in the community of disciples. See his *God with Us: A Pastoral Theology of Matthew's Gospel* (Minneapolis: Fortress, 1995), 129.

33. Meinrad Limbeck, *Matthäus-Evangelium* (Stuttgart: Katholisches Bibelwerk, 1986), 70.

34. Wolfgang Schenk, *Die Sprache des Matthäus: Die Text-Konstituenten in ihren makro- und mikrostruckturellen Relationen* (Göttingen: Vandenhoeck & Ruprecht, 1987), 352.

35. Leland J. White, "Grid and Group," 80.

36. St. John of the Cross, "The Dark Night," in *The Collected Works of St. John of the Cross,* trans. Kieran Kavanaugh, O.C.D. and Otilio Rodrigues, O.C.D. (Washington, D.C.: ICS Publishers, 1964), 711.

37. United States Conference of Catholic Bishops, "Faithful Citizenship: A Catholic Call to Political Responsibility," http://www.usccb.org/faithfulcitizenship/faithful citizenship03.htm/10/18/03.

38. Synod of Bishops, 1971, "Justice in the World," Introduction, 2, in Joseph Gremillion, *The Gospel of Peace and Justice: Catholic Social Teaching Since Pope John,* (Maryknoll, N.Y.: Orbis Books, 1975), 514.

39. Synod of Bishops, 1971, "Justice in the World," no. 3, in Gremillion, *Gospel of Peace,* 514.

40. Sharon Daloz Parks, "Home and Pilgrimage: Companion Metaphors for Personal and Social Transformation," *Soundings* 72 (1989): 311.

41. Ibid., 312-13.

42. Russell Pregeant, *Christology beyond Dogma: Matthew's Christ in Process Hermeneutics* (Philadelphia: Fortress, 1978), 27.

43. Ibid., 1.

44. Mark Allan Powell, "Direct and Indirect Phraseology in the Gospel of Matthew," in *Society of Biblical Literature 1991 Seminar Papers*, no. 30, ed. Eugene H. Lovering, Jr. (Atlanta: Scholars Press, 1991), 409.

45. Juan Luis Segundo, *The Liberation of Theology* (Maryknoll, N.Y.: Orbis Books, 1976), 9.

46. Eduard Schweizer, *The Good News according to Matthew*, trans. David E. Green (Atlanta: John Knox , 1975), 69-70.

47. H. Benedict Green, C.R., *Matthew, Poet of the Beatitudes*, Journal for the Study of the New Testament Supplement Series 203 (Sheffield: Sheffield Academic Press, 2001), 192.

2. Whose Is the Reign of God?

1. Mark Allan Powell, "Matthew's Beatitudes: Reversals and Rewards of the Kingdom," *Catholic Biblical Quarterly* 56 (1996): 465.

2. In an address to 900,000 people, Pope John Paul I said that God "is a father, but even more mother." However, no mention of this was included in the "official" paper of the Roman Catholic Church, *L'Osservatore Romano,* in its printing of the speech on September 21, 1978. Ideology serves the purposes of those who control the media inside and outside the church.

3. For more on how science is using ever more sophisticated means to probe the heavens, see Dennis Oberbye, "Astronomy's New Grail: The $1 Billion Telescope," Science Times, *New York Times*, December 30, 2003, D1.

4. Kenneth E. Untener, in CNS News Briefs "Bishop says Ecclesiology Catholics Need Found in Future; Not Past," November 14, 2004, http://www.catholicnews.com/data/briefs/cns/20036ll14.htm.

5. Lester C. Thurow, *The Zero-Sum Society* (New York: Penguin Books, 1981).

6. Bruce J. Malina, *The New Testament World: Insights from Cultural Anthropology* (Atlanta: John Knox, 1981), 75-76.

7. Ibid., 80.

8. I have suggested that, given our deeper understanding of the house as the ground for the whole imperial reality of Jesus' time, the notion of "kingdom" should be translated as "kindom." See my *The Prayer that Jesus Taught Us* (Maryknoll, N.Y.: Orbis Books, 2002), 88.

9. Warren Carter, "Resisting and Imitating the Empire: Imperial Paradigms in Two Matthean Parables," *Interpretation* 56 (2002): 272.

10. Jane Schaberg, *The Father, The Son and The Holy Spirit: The Triadic Phrase in Matt. 28:19b* (Chico, Calif.: Scholars Press, 1982). Schaberg says that the text should be read not as a response to but as a stimulus of the latter trinitarian question.

11. Sandra M. Schneiders, *The Revelatory Text: Interpreting the New Testament as Sacred Scripture* (San Francisco: HarperSanFrancisco, 1991), 153.

12. The original chart can be found in my *Prayer that Jesus Taught Us*, 52. I have adapted this chart as a result of my sharing it with groups.

13. James M. Reese, O.S.F.S., "How Matthew Portrays the Communication of Christ's Authority," *Biblical Theology Bulletin* 7 (1977): 140-41.

14. "III. The Social Doctrine of the Church," 2425, *Catechism of the Catholic Church* (New York: Catholic Book Publishing Co., 1994), 582.

15. Edward M. Welch, "The Church Was Right about Capitalism," *America* 189 (December 1, 2003): 17-18.

16. Clarence Page, quoting from the *Time* survey, "How Rich Do You Think You Are? Well, Here's the Truth," *Chicago Tribune*, January 19, 2003.

17. Donald Senior, *Invitation to Matthew* (Garden City, N.Y.: Doubleday Image Books, 1977), 223 (emphasis in original).

18. Michael H. Crosby, *The Dysfunctional Church: Addiction and Codependency in the Family of Catholicism* (Notre Dame, Ind.: Ave Maria, 1991); idem, *Rethinking Celibacy, Reclaiming the Church* (Eugene, Ore.: Wipf & Stock, 2003).

19. Anne Wilson Schaef, *When Society Becomes an Addict* (San Francisco: Harper & Row, 1987), 93.

20. For more on the impact of Wal-Mart on the global economy, see the cover story by Anthony Bianco and Wendy Zellner, "Is Wal-Mart Too Powerful?" *Business Week,* October 6, 2003, 100-109.

21. Pope John Paul II, Homily at Mass at Yankee Stadium, *Origins* 9 (October 25, 1979): 311.

3. Blessed Are the Poor in Spirit

1. Eduard Schweizer, *The Good News according to Matthew* (Atlanta: John Knox, 1975), 88.

2. Hans Kvalbein, "Jesus and the Poor: Two Texts and a Tentative Conclusion," *Themeleios* 12 (1987): 86.

3. Among those promoting the "spiritualized" approach to the first Beatitude are John P. Meier, "Matthew 5:3-12," *Interpretation* 44 (1990): 283; G. D. Kilpatrick, *The Origins of the Gospel according to St. Matthew* (Oxford: Clarendon, 1946), 124-26; Augustine Stock, O.S.B., "The Method and Message of Matthew" (Collegeville, Minn.: Liturgical Press, 1994), 73.

4. Robert H. Gundry, *Matthew: A Commentary on His Handbook for a Mixed Church under Persecution,* 2nd ed. (Grand Rapids: Eerdmans, 1994), 67.

5. For reference to these, see Mark Allan Powell, "Matthew's Beatitudes: Reversals and Rewards of the Kingdom," *Catholic Biblical* Quarterly 56 (1996): 463 n. 13.

6. Benno Przybylski, *Righteousness in Matthew and His World of Thought* (Cambridge: Cambridge University Press, 1980), 112.

7. For more on the notion of the Matthean household code, see my *House of Disciples: Church, Economics and Justice in Matthew* (Eugene, Ore.: Wipf & Stock, 2004 [1988]).

8. For more on the power dynamics contained in this section of Matthew, see my *The Dysfunctional Church: Addiction and Codependency in the Family of Catholicism* (Notre Dame, Ind.: Ave Maria, 1991), 45-48.

9. Mary Ann Hinsdale, I.H.M., "Blessed Are the Persecuted . . . Hungering and Thirsting for Justice: Blessings for Those Breaking Boundaries," in *New Perspectives on the Beatitudes,* ed. Francis A. Eigo, O.S.A. (Villanova, Pa.: Villanova University Press, 1995), 165.

10. Thomas Hoyt, Jr., "The Poor/Rich Theme in the Beatitudes," *Journal of Religious Thought* 37, no. 1 (1980): 40.

11. Nathan E. Williams, "A Second Look at the First Beatitude," *Expository Times* 98 (1987): 209.

12. Mary R. D'Angelo, "'Blessed the One Who Reads and Those Who Hear:' The Beatitudes in Their Biblical Contexts," in *New Perspectives on the Beatitudes,* ed. Eigo, 72.

13. Synod of Bishops, 1971, "Justice in the World," Introduction, in Joseph Gremillion, *The Gospel of Peace and Justice: Catholic Social Teaching Since Pope John* (Maryknoll, N.Y.: Orbis Books, 1975), 514.

14. Synod of Bishops, 1971, "Justice in the World," no. 2, in Gremillion, *Gospel of Peace,* 519.

15. Monika K. Hellwig, "The Blessedness of the Meek, the Merciful, and the Peacemakers," in *New Perspectives on the Beatitudes,* ed. Eigo, 210.

16. I discussed this approach in my book, *The Dysfunctional Church.*

17. Pope Paul VI, "On the Renewal of the Religious Life," *The Pope Speaks* 16 (1971): 115. My interpretation of this text.

4. Blessed Are Those Who Mourn;
They Will Be Comforted

1. Evelyn Mattern, *Blessed Are You: The Beatitudes and Our Survival* (Notre Dame, Ind.: Ave Maria, 1994), 39.

2. Mark Allan Powell, *God with Us: A Pastoral Theology of Matthew's Gospel* (Minneapolis: Fortress, 1995), 125.

3. John Pilch, "Healing in Mark: A Social Science Analysis," *Biblical Theology Bulletin* 15 (1985): 146.

4. See, e.g., Elisabeth Kübler-Ross, *Death and Dying* (Pittsburgh: Institute of Man, 1974); eadem, *On Death and Dying* (New York: Macmillan, 1970).

5. Walter Brueggemann, "A Shape for Old Testament Theology: The Embrace of Pain," *Catholic Biblical Quarterly* 47 (1985): 395-415.

6. Bruce J. Malina, *Christian Origins and Cultural Anthropology: Practical Models for Biblical Interpretation* (Atlanta: John Knox, 1986), 203.

7. Michael H. Crosby, O.F.M.Cap., *Thank God Ahead of Time: The Life and Spirituality of Venerable Solanus Casey,* 2nd ed. (Quincy, Ill.: Franciscan Press, 2000). The official account is found in Michael Crosby, O.F.M.Cap., *Solanus Casey: The Official Account of a Virtuous American Life* (New York: Crossroad, 2000).

8. Originally I wrote these two volumes for the Vatican, building on a third volume of testimonies of people who knew Solanus. The two have been brought together (without the mandatory footnotes) in *Solanus Casey: The Official Account of a Virtuous American Life.*

9. Solanus Casey, O.F.M.Cap., quoted in Michael H. Crosby, O.F.M.Cap., *Thank God Ahead of Time,* 31; *Solanus Casey,* 44.

10. Gerald Walker, O.F.M.Cap., quoted in Crosby, *Thank God Ahead of Time,* 229-30; *Solanus Casey,* 139.

11. Solanus Casey, quoted in Crosby, *Thank God Ahead of Time,* 285-86.

12. Letter of Solanus Casey, in Crosby, *Thank God Ahead of Time,* 106-7; *Solanus Casey,* 79.

13. See, e.g., Malina, *Christian Origins and Cultural Anthropology,* 203. Faithful to his perspective of persecution as the context for Matthew's Gospel, Robert H. Gundry writes: "Mourning refers to the abject condition of persecuted disciples, not to mourning in repentance from sins or in sorrow over the dead" (*Matthew: A Commentary on His Literary and Theological Art* [Grand Rapids, Mich.: Eerdmans, 1982], 68-69).

14. Warren Carter, *Matthew and the Margins: A Sociopolitical and Religious Reading* (Maryknoll, N.Y.: Orbis Books, 2000), 132.

15. Richard Rohr, with John Bookser Feister, *Jesus' Plan for a New World: The Sermon on the Mount* (Cincinnati: St. Anthony Messenger Press, 1996), 133.

16. For more on this, see my *The Prayer that Jesus Taught Us* (Maryknoll, N.Y.: Orbis Books, 2002).

17. David P. Reid, SS.CC., "'A Strategy of Endurance': The Book of Revelation as Commentary on the Beatitudes, Blessed Are the Mourning and the Suffering," in *New Perspectives on the Beatitudes,* ed. Francis A. Eigo (Villanova, Pa.: Villanova University Press, 1995), 96.

18. St. Francis of Assisi, in Thomas of Celano, Second [Life of Francis by Thomas of] Celano, "The Remembrance of the Desire of a Soul," 193, in *Francis of Assisi: Early Documents* II, ed. Regis J. Armstrong, O.F.M.Cap., J. A. Wayne Hellmann, O.F.M.Conv., and William J. Short, O.F.M. (New York/London/Manila: New City, 2000), 371.

19. Rupert Dorn, O.F.M.Cap., "Jubilee Homily," *Messenger: Chapter, 1978,* 8 (Detroit: Province of St. Joseph of the Capuchin Order Archives, 1978), 22.

20. Guy Gugliotta, "Warming May Threaten 37% of Species by 2050," *Washington Post,* January 8, 2004, at http://www.washingtonpost.com/wp-dyn/A63153-2004Jasn7.htm/Feb1004.

5. Blessed Are the Nonviolent;
They Will Inherit the Earth

1. Leo Tolstoy, *What I Believe* (London: Elliot Stock, 1885), 23.

2. Ibid., 12. I am indebted to Mary Ann Hinsdale, I.H.M., for leading me to Tolstoy. See her "Blessed Are the Persecuted . . . Hungering and Thirsting for Justice: Blessings for Those Breaking Boundaries," in *New Perspectives on the Beatitudes,* ed. Francis A. Eigo (Villanova, Pa.: Villanova University Press, 1995), 167-69.

3. For more on the *Acts of Judas Thomas* 9.82-87, see Mary R. D'Angelo, "'Blessed the One Who Reads and Those Who Hear': The Beatitudes in Their Biblical Contexts," in *New Perspectives on the Beatitudes,* ed. Eigo, 68. For a more recent translation of *praüs* as "nonviolence," see H. Benedict Green, C.R., *Matthew, Poet of the Beatitudes,* Journal for the Study of the New Testament Supplement Series 203 (Sheffield: Sheffield Academic Press, 2001), 187-88.

4. Schalom Ben-Chorin, *Bruder Jesus,* 2nd ed. (Munich: Paul List, 1969), 71.

5. G. F. Hauck and S. Schulz, "*Praüs,*" in *Theological Dictionary of the New Testa-*

ment, ed. Gerhard Kittel and Gerhard Friedrich, trans. Geoffrey W. Bromiley (Grand Rapids: Eerdmans, 1981), 6:647-51; Gottfried Vanoni, "Shalom and the Bible," *Theology Digest* 41 (1994): 120; Norbert Lohfink, "The Appeasement of the Messiah: Thoughts on Ps 37 and the Third Beatitude," *Theology Digest* 44 (1997): 234ff.

6. Herman Sasse, "*Gē*," in *Theological Dictionary of the New Testament*, 677-81.

7. Walter Brueggemann, "The Earth Is the Lord's: A Theology of Earth and Land," *Sojourners* 15 (1986): 28.

8. John Kenneth Galbraith, *The Affluent Society* (Boston: Houghton-Mifflin, 1958), 88. Pope John Paul II, General Audience, Sept. 1, 2004. Zenit news.

9. Walter Wink, "Unmasking the Powers: A Biblical View of Roman and American Economics," *Sojourners* 15 (1986): 44.

10. Brueggemann, "Earth Is the Lord's," 29-30.

11. Bruce J. Malina, *The New Testament World: Insights from Cultural Anthropology* (Atlanta, Ga.: John Knox, 1981), 83.

12. Walter Brueggemann, *The Land* (Philadelphia: Fortress, 1982), 174.

13. For more on the nonviolence of Jesus, see L. H. Rivas, "El 'pacifismo' del Sermón de la Montaña (Mt, 39-40 y 44-48; Lc 6, 27-38)," *Revista Biblica* [Buenos Aires] 64 (2002): 5-52.

14. I discovered this in 2002 when a cousin, Dan McGarry, gave me a very large collection of obituaries of our common ancestors that had been saved by his mother, Cecile Murphy McGarry. We all were descendants of Jeremiah Murphy. My great-grandfather, Patrick Crosby of Kilkenney, had married Mary Murphy of Cork. She was Peter's sister.

15. Such findings are regularly reported by The Pew Global Attitudes Project. See its website at: http://www.people-press.org/121901que.htm.

16. My study of the *Federalist Papers* led me to this conclusion in my *Thy Will Be Done: Praying the Our Father as Subversive Activity* (Maryknoll, N.Y.: Orbis Books, 1977), 93-94, 151ff.; 223-24.

17. Walter Bauer, *A Greek-English Lexicon of the New Testament and Other Early Christian Literature*, 4th rev. ed., trans. William F. Arndt and F. Wilbur Gingrich (Chicago: University of Chicago Press; Cambridge: Cambridge University Press, 1952), 705.

18. United States Conference of Catholic Bishops, "When I Call for Help: A Pastoral Response to Domestic Violence Against Women," November 12, 2002, *Origins* 32.24 (2002): 400.

19. St. Francis of Assisi, quoted in "Legend of the Three Companions," 35 (p. 89) and John of Perugia, "The Anonymous of Perugia," 17 (p. 41), in *Francis of Assisi: Early Documents*, II, ed. Regis J. Armstrong, O.F.M.Cap., J. A. Wayne Hellman, O.F.M.Conv., and William J. Short, O.F.M. (New York/London/Manila: New City Press, 2000). See also Bernard of Besse, "Book of Praises of St. Francis, 26," in ibid., III, 46.

20. As of this writing, René Girard's "mimetic desire" theory of the root of violence is very popular in the literature and in the work of popular speakers such as Gil Blailie and Richard Rohr. My approach revolves around the abuse of power.

21. United States Catholic Bishops, "When I Call for Help: Domestic Violence against Women," 10th anniversary ed., 2002, *Origins* (2002). The bishops use the same

basic definition for violence in their 10th anniversary edition that they did of "abuse" in their original (1992) version. Thus it would appear that, in their minds, abuse and violence both can be defined as "any way one uses to control another through fear and intimidation." For the 1992 version, see *Origins* 22.21 (1992): 355.

22. Clarence Page, "How Rich Do You Think You Are? Well, Here's the Truth," *Chicago Tribune,* January 19, 2003.

23. I discussed some of the characteristics of civil religion in my *Thy Will Be Done,* 62ff.

24. Synod of Bishops, 1971, "Justice in the World," no. 3, in Joseph Gremillion, *The Gospel of Peace and Justice: Catholic Social Teaching Since Pope John* (Maryknoll, N.Y.: Orbis Books, 1975), 523-24.

25. Nicholas von Hoffman, "Parochial Funds Pleas Unheeded," *Buffalo Courier Express,* August 14, 1977.

6. Blessed Are Those Who Hunger and Thirst for Justice; They Will Be Satisfied

1. Leland J. White, "Grid and Group in Matthew's Community: The Righteousness/Honor Code in the Sermon on the Mount," *Semeia* 35 (1986): 61, 70, 80.

2. I once argued for a more egalitarian community in Matthew than I now think is the case. See my *House of Disciples: Church, Economics and Justice in Matthew* (Maryknoll, N.Y.: Orbis Books, 1988), 30, 97-110, passim. The fact that I have moved to see "father" less as a paternal function than as a patron has contributed to my slight revision. For more on Matthew's limited egalitarianism, see Dennis C. Duling, "'Egalitarian' Ideology, Leadership, and Factional Conflict within the Matthean Group," *Biblical Theology Bulletin* 27 (1997): 124-37.

3. The connection between justice and perfection will be shown later in the text when we consider 5:20 and 5:48 as the bookends for the six antithetical statements that outline the new way of justice/perfection.

4. Synod of Bishops, 1971, "Justice in the World," Introduction no. 6, in Joseph Gremillion, *The Gospel of Peace and Justice: Catholic Social Teaching Since Pope John* (Maryknoll, N.Y.: Orbis Books, 1975), 514.

5. Jacques Dupont, *Les Beatitudes* (Paris: Gabalda, 1969-73) 3:667.

6. Mary R. D'Angelo, "'Blessed the One Who Reads and Those Who Hear': The Beatitudes in Their Biblical Contexts," in *New Perspectives on the Beatitudes,* ed. Francis A. Eigo (Villanova, Pa.: Villanova University Press, 1995), 64.

7. White, "Grid and Group in Matthew's Community," 79.

8. Donald Senior, "The Gospel of Matthew and the Ministry of Social Justice," *Spirituality Today* 31, no. 1 (1979): 45.

9. Mary Ann Hinsdale, I.H.M., "Blessed Are the Persecuted . . . Hungering and Thirsting for Justice: Blessings for Those Breaking Boundaries," in *New Perspectives on the Beatitudes,* ed. Eigo, 165.

10. Jack Dean Kingsbury, *Matthew as Story* (Philadelphia: Fortress, 1986), 132.

11. Ronald Rolheiser, *The Holy Longing: The Search for a Christian Spirituality* (New York: Doubleday, 1999), 7.

12. Evelyn Mattern, *Blessed Are You: The Beatitudes and Our Survival* (Notre Dame, Ind.: Ave Maria, 1994), 73, 71.

13. John P. Meier, *The Vision of Matthew: Christ, Church and Morality in the First Gospel* (New York: Paulist, 1979), 161.

14. Daniel Harrington, *The Gospel of Matthew*, Sacra Pagina (Collegeville, Minn.: Liturgical Press, 1991), 97.

15. For more on this, see my *The Prayer That Jesus Taught Us* (Maryknoll, N.Y.: Orbis Books, 2002), 12ff.

16. Ibid., passim.

17. Paul Hosetoss, photo with caption: "President Bush joined members of his cabinet in prayer at the beginning of a meeting on Friday afternoon," *New York Times*, August 5, 2001.

18. Arianna Huffington, "Publicly Parading Piety in the Service of Political Expediency," *Los Angeles Times*, August 10, 2001.

19. Anthony Bianco and Wendy Zellner, "Is Wal-Mart Too Powerful?" *Business Week,* October 6, 2003. See also Zenit news service, "Low Wages: The Heavy Price of Cheap Goods: One Reason Why Wal-Mart Can Sell for Less," Zenit, December 20, 2003. Weekly News Analysis, December 20, 2003.

7. Blessed Are the Merciful;
They Will Receive Mercy

1. C. H. Dodd, *The Bible and the Greeks* (London: Hodder & Stoughton, 1935), 56. Another word meaning justice or "right" was *mishpat*. *Mishpat* stressed the doing of good deeds. The two words often were used together as in: "But let justice (*mishpat*) roll down like waters, and righteousness (*tsedāqāh*) like an overflowing stream" (Amos 5:24). For a fuller treatment of the relationship between justice and mercy, see Benno Przyblyski, *Righteousness in Matthew and His World of Thought* (Cambridge: Cambridge University Press, 1980), 99-101.

2. Pope John Paul II, Encyclical Letter "Rich in Mercy," Nov. 30, 1980 (Washington, D.C.: United States Catholic Conference, 1981), 28.

3. Ibid.

4. Eduard Schweizer, *The Good News according to Matthew*, trans. David E. Green (Atlanta: John Knox, 1977), 92.

5. Pope John Paul II, "Rich in Mercy," 3.

6. Marcus J. Borg, *Meeting Jesus Again for the First Time: The Historical Jesus and the Heart of Contemporary Faith* (San Francisco: HarperSanFrancisco, 1994), 58.

7. I expand these ideas in my chapter "Matthew's Gospel: The Disciples' Call to Justice," in *The New Testament: Introducing the Way of Discipleship*, ed. Wes Howard-Brook and Sharon H. Ringe (Maryknoll, N.Y.: Orbis Books, 2002), 25-35.

8. Elaine M. Wainwright, *Shall We Look for Another? A Feminist Rereading of the Matthean Jesus*, Bible and Liberation Series (Maryknoll, N.Y.: Orbis Books, 1998), 92.

9. Günther Bornkamm, "Enderwartung und Kirche im Matthäusevangelim," in *Überlieferung und Auslegung im Matthäusevangelium* (Neukirchen: Neukirchener Verlag, 1961), 30-31.

10. Jack Dean Kingsbury, "The Title 'Son of David' in Matthew's Gospel," *Journal of Biblical Literature* 95 (1976): 601.

11. Jacob Neusner, *From Politics to Piety: The Emergence of Pharisaic Judaism* (Englewood Cliffs, N.J.: Prentice-Hall, 1973), 80.

12. That Jesus probably had his own house is my contention in *House of Disciples: Church, Economics, and Justice in Matthew* (Eugene, Ore.: Wipf & Stock, 2004), 263.

13. Borg, *Meeting Jesus*, 61.

14. Richard Byrne, O.C.S.O., "Living the Contemplative Dimension of Everyday Life" (diss., Duquesne University, 1973), 198.

15. Joseph A. Grassi, "'I Was Hungry and You Gave Me to Eat' (Matt. 25:35ff.): The Divine Identification Ethic in Matthew," *Biblical Theology Bulletin* 11 (1981): 84. See also his "'You Yourselves Give Them to Eat': An Easily Forgotten Command of Jesus," *The Bible Today* 16 (1978): 1704-9.

16. Abraham Heschel, *The Prophets, An Introduction* (New York: Harper & Row, 1962), 11.

17. Marshall Sahlins, "On the Sociology of Primitive Exchange," in *The Relevance of Models for Social Anthropology*, ed. Michael Banton (London: Tavistock, 1963), 151.

18. Crosby, *House of Disciples*, 70-73.

19. Mark Allan Powell, *God with Us: A Pastoral Theology of Matthew's Gospel* (Minneapolis: Fortress, 1995), 131.

20. Sharon H. Ringe, *Jesus, Liberation, and the Biblical Jubilee: Images for Ethics and Christology* (Philadelphia: Fortress, 1985), 76-77.

21. Jerome Murphy-O'Connor, *St. Paul's Corinth: Texts and Archeology* (Wilmington, Del.: Michael Glazier, 1983), 153.

22. "General Instruction of the Roman Missal, 4th ed., March 27, 1975, in *The Sacramentary of the Roman Missal* (New York: Catholic Book, 1985), nos. 7, 22. In the revised, 2003 "General Instruction on the Roman Missal" (Washington, D.C.: United States Catholic Conference, 2003), it is no. 27, found on page 20. This teaching on the manifold forms of the "real presence" extends beyond the Eucharist to the other sacraments as well. See Second Vatican Council, "Constitution on the Sacred Liturgy," no. 7 in Walter M. Abbott, S.J., general editor, *The Documents of Vatican II*, ed. Walter M. Abbott, S.J. (New York: Guild Press, American Press, Association Press, 1966), 140-41.

23. David Hill, "On the Use and Meaning of Hosea VI: 6 in Matthew's Gospel," *New Testament Studies* 24, no. 1 (October 1977): 110.

8. Blessed Are the Poor of Heart;
They Will See God

1. Otto Bauernfeind, "*Haplous*," in *Theological Dictionary of the New Testament*, ed. Gerhard Kittel and Gerhard Friedrich, trans. Geoffrey W. Bromiley (Grand Rapids: Eerdmans, 1982), 1:386. H. J. Cadbury discusses it as "generous" in "The Single Eye," *Harvard Theological Review* 47 (1954): 68-74.

2. Günther Harder, "*Ponēros*," in *Theological Dictionary of the New Testament*, 6:552-55.

3. For an expansion on ideas contained in this section, see Michael L. Barré, "Blessed Are the Pure of Heart: Levels of Meaning in the Sixth Beatitude," *The Bible Today* 22 (1984): 236-42.

4. Richard Byrne, O.C.S.O., "Living the Contemplative Dimension of Everyday Life" (diss., Duquesne University, 1973). I am indebted to the late Richard Byrne for his approach to contemplation, which grounds the rest of this chapter.

5. Ibid.

6. Evelyn Underhill, *Practical Mysticism* (New York: Dutton, 1943), 21-22.

7. Lance Morrow, "'I Spoke . . . as a Brother,' A Pardon from the Pontiff, A Lesson in Forgiveness for a Troubled World," *Time*, January 9, 1984, 33.

8. Louis J. Puhl, S.J., *The Spiritual Exercises of St. Ignatius* (Chicago: Loyola University Press, 1951), passim.

9. Byrne, "Living the Contemplative Dimension," 63, quoting T. S. Eliot, "Ash Wednesday," in *The Wasteland and Other Poems* (New York: A Harvest Book, 1962), 66.

9. Blessed Are the Peacemakers; They Will Be Called Children of God

1. G. Zampaglione, *The Idea of Peace in Antiquity* (Notre Dame, Ind./London: University of Notre Dame Press, 1973), 135.

2. Mark Allan Powell, "Matthew's Beatitudes: Reversals and Rewards of the Kingdom," *Catholic Biblical Quarterly* 58 (1996): 473, see n. 43.

3. H. Benedict Green, C.R., *Matthew, Poet of the Beatitudes,* Journal for the Study of the New Testament Supplement Series 203 (Sheffield: Sheffield Academic Press, 2001), 216.

4. The Eucharist is always involved in freeing people from their sins, liberating them from their enslavements. Thus, in the *community,* people gather in the name of the trinitarian presence with their gifts. The *conscientization* begins with a reflection on the people's reality. The reconciliation service deals with their sins, and the absolution offers empowerment, along with the gathering prayer. God's word always shows how God views each person and promotes a better sharing of the earth's goods in the household. The eucharistic service stands as a sign to all of the equality of each member able to share in the resources of bread and wine. With the Spirit of Jesus in each member, *conversion* from sin can enable people to enter the world calling for its conversion. I am indebted to Dale Olen of Milwaukee for the original idea I have adapted here.

5. William Thompson, *Matthew's Advice to a Divided Community* (Rome: Biblical Institute Press, 1970). Thompson begins his discussion about the division of the Matthean community and Matthew's way of dealing with the tension with the second prophecy of the passion, 17:22. Because it seems to be a *Haustafel,* I think it more appropriate to begin with 17:24 and continue through chapter 18.

6. Ephesians 5:21-6:9 treats only the groups dealing with domestic submission.

For more on the *Haustafeln*, see my *House of Disciples: Church, Economics and Justice in Matthew* (Eugene, Ore.: Wipf & Stock, 2004), passim.

7. Leland J. White, "Grid and Group in Matthew's Community: The Righteousness/Honor Code in the Sermon on the Mount," *Semeia* 35 (1986): 75-76.

8. Ibid., 84.

9. Donald W. Winnecott, *The Maturational Process and the Facilitating Environment: Studies in the Theory of Emotional Development* (New York: International Universities Press, 1965).

10. St. Francis of Assisi, "Approved Rule of 1223," 6, in *Francis of Assisi: Early Documents* I, ed. Regis J. Armstrong, O.F.M.Cap., J. A. Wayne Hellman, O.F.M.Conv., and William J. Short, O.F.M. (New York/London/Manila: New City Press, 2000), 371.

11. Contrary to a popular idea that the "sin" of Sodom and Gomorrah was sexual, it is clear that the basic immorality that made these cities unfaithful was their social injustice (Isa. 1:9-10; Amos 4:1, 11).

12. Jack Dean Kingsbury, *Matthew as Story* (Philadelphia: Fortress, 1986), 133.

13. Warren Carter, *Matthew and the Margins: A Sociopolitical and Religious Reading* (Maryknoll, N.Y.: Orbis Books, 2000), 136.

10. Blessed Are Those Persecuted for Justice' Sake; The Reign of Heaven Is Theirs

1. Douglas R. A. Hare, *The Theme of Jewish Persecution of Christians in the Gospel according to St. Matthew* (Cambridge: Cambridge University Press, 1967), 19-61.

2. W. D. Davies, *The Setting of the Sermon on the Mount* (Cambridge: Cambridge University Press, 1964), passim, esp. 289-90.

3. Hare, *The Theme of Jewish Persecution,* 130-40. See also Robert H. Gundry, *Matthew: A Commentary on His Handbook for a Mixed Church under Persecution,* 2nd ed. (Grand Rapids: Eerdmans, 1994).

4. The opposition to this pastoral letter came especially from the Catholic neoconservatives. See U.S. Bishops' Pastoral Message and Letter, "Economic Justice for All: Catholic Social Teaching and the U.S. Economy," November 13, 1986, *Origins* 16 (1986): 409-55.

5. Jennifer S. Lee, "Exxon Backs Groups that Question Global Warming," *New York Times,* May 28, 2003.

6. Rev. Gerald Zandstra, "Beware When Secular Agendas Are Cloaked in Robes of Religion," Perspective, *Plastics News,* December 1, 2003.

7. Dan Schutte, "Here I Am, Lord," in *Gather* (Chicago: GIA Publications; and Phoenix: North American Liturgy Resources, 1988), 291.

8. Evelyn Underhill, *Mystics in the Church* (New York: Schocken Books, 1971), 32-33.

9. The following reflections are a more general summary of an expanded investigation of the part this call of Isaiah can play in religious life that can be found in my *Can Religious Life Be Prophetic?* (New York: Crossroad, 2004).

10. A wonderful effort to consider the vows as a way of cosmic holiness can be

found in "Tending the Holy," The Leadership Conference of Women Religious, *The Occasional Papers* 32 (2003).

11. Abraham J. Heschel, *The Prophets, An Introduction* (New York: Harper & Row Torchbooks, 1969), 202.

12. Warren Carter, "Matthew 4:18-22 and Matthean Discipleship: An Audience-Oriented Perspective," *Catholic Biblical Quarterly* 59 (1997): 58-59, quoting Dennis C. Duling, "Matthew and Marginality," *Society of Biblical Literature 1993 Seminar Papers*, ed. E. H. Lovering, Jr. (Atlanta: Scholars Press, 1993), 648.

13. Sonya A. Quitslund, "The Nature of the Prophetic Role," *The Bible Today* 92 (November 1977): 1330, 1331.

14. "While the Church is bound to give witness to justice, she recognizes that anyone who ventures to speak to people about justice must first be just in their eyes. Hence we must undertake an examination of the modes of acting and of the possessions and life style found within the Church herself" (Synod of Bishops, 1971, "Justice in the World," no. 3, 40, in Joseph Gremillion, *The Gospel of Peace and Justice: Catholic Social Teaching Since Pope John* [Maryknoll, N.Y.: Orbis Books, 1976], 522).

15. Quitslund, "Nature of the Prophetic Role," 1331.

16. Mark Allan Powell, *God with Us: A Pastoral Theology of Matthew's Gospel* (Minneapolis: Fortress, 1995), 139-40.

17. M. Jack Suggs, *Wisdom, Christology, and Law in Matthew's Gospel* (Cambridge, Mass.: Harvard University Press, 1970), esp. 120ff.

18. Ibid., 122.

19. Ibid., 126.

Scripture Index

General Index

Pilch, John: on leprosy, 61
poor
    and rich: increasing gap between, 31
    in spirit, 39-58; as those doing God's
        will by doing good, 48-54; as those
        who submit to God's will, 44-48
    See also possessions; poverty; rich;
        wealth
possessions: and entering reign of God, 38
poverty
    in Gospel of Matthew, 41-44
    material and social, 40
Powell, Mark Allan
    on beatitudes, 191
    on coherence of Jesus' words and
        actions, 17
    on mourning, 60
    on those whom God rules, 21
power (*exousia*)
    abuse of, xii
    of God, 21
    obsession with, xi
    See also authority
prayer
    Jesus Prayer, 155-56
    and spirituality of justice, 106-7, 112,
        114-15
Pregeant, Russell: on biblical hermeneutics
    and spirituality, 16-17
prophetic call. *See* call
prophetic stance: in communities, 188-91
Przybylski, Benno: on essence of disciple-
    ship, 47
purity of heart: beatitude of, 140-58

Quitslund, Sonya: on being prophets, 189-
    90

reciprocity, 27-28
reconciliation: and mercy, 132-33
Reese, James: on authority of Jesus, 30
Reid, David P.: on second beatitude, 74
reign of God, 28-29
    belonging to persecuted, 176-93
    constituted by healing and restoration,
        126
    entering, 35-36; wealth and, 37-38
    See also kingdom
restoration: constituting reign of God, 126

rich
    and poor: gap between, in ancient
        Near East, 112-13; gap between,
        today, 31; responsibility of rich
        toward, 101-2
    See also poor; possessions; wealth
rich young man, story of, 43, 50-51
    and entering reign of God, 35-36
Ringe, Sharon H.: on forgiveness, 133
Rohr, Richard: on second beatitude, 73
Rolheiser, Ronald: on spirituality, 108
Roman Catholic Church
    patriarchal, celibate structure of, 32
    sex abuse scandal in, 65
    and women, 24, 32

Sahlins, Marshall: on mercy, 132
Schaef, Anne Wilson: on dysfunctional
    systems, 32-33
Schweizer, Eduard
    on authority of Christian community,
        18
    on mercy, 120
    on poor in spirit, 39-40
science: and cosmology, 27
Segundo, Juan Luis: hermeneutic circle of,
    17-18
Senior, Donald
    on hypocrisy, 32
    on righteousness, 105
sin of the world, xi
skandala (stumbling blocks)
    avoiding, 168-69
    to justice, 117-18
    to mourning, 64-66
    and woes, 198n. 29
social structures, 54-55
solitude, 154-55
spirituality
    authentic biblical, 19-20; in our land,
        98-99
    and Beatitudes, xvi-xviii
Suggs, M. Jack: on ending of Beatitudes,
    192-93
Summer Institute of Retreats Interna-
    tional, xiii

technology, x